P9-CQM-270

LINCOLN CHRISTIAN COLLEGE AND SEMINARY

STUDENT MINISTRY FOR THE 21st CENTURY

STUDENT IMPACT

STUDENT MINISTRY FOR THE 21st CENTURY

TRANSFORMING YOUR YOUTH GROUP INTO A VITAL STUDENT MINISTRY

BO BOSHERS

With Kim Anderson

ZondervanPublishingHouse
Grand Rapids, Michigan

A Division of HarperCollins*Publishers*

WILLOW CREEK RESOURCES

Student Ministry for the 21st Century
Copyright © 1997 by The Willow Creek Association

Requests for information should be addressed to:

ZondervanPublishingHouse
Grand Rapids, Michigan 49530

Library of Congress Cataloging-in-Publication Data

Boshers, Bo.
    Student ministry for the 21st century : transforming your youth group into a vital student ministry / Bo Boshers with Kim Anderson.
        p.   cm.
    Includes bibliographical references.
    ISBN: 0-310-20122-5 (hardcover : alk. paper)
    1. Church work with teenagers. I. Anderson, Kim, 1965–   . II. Title.
BV4447.B685   1997
259'.23—dc21   97-4240
                                                                                                          CIP

This edition printed on acid-free paper and meets the American National Standards Institute Z39.48 standard.

All Scripture quotations, unless otherwise indicated, are taken from the *Holy Bible: New International Version*®. NIV®. Copyright © 1973, 1978, 1984 by International Bible Society. Used by permission of Zondervan Publishing House. All rights reserved.

Verses marked NASB are taken from the *New American Standard Bible*, © The Lockman Foundation 1960, 1962, 1963, 1968, 1971, 1972, 1973, 1975, 1977.

Verses marked TLB are taken from *The Living Bible*, © 1971 by Tyndale House Publishers, Wheaton, Ill.

Verses marked KJV are taken from *The King James* version of the Bible.

Verses marked NCV are taken from *The New Contemporary Version* of the Bible.

All rights reserved. No part of this publication may be reproduced, stored in a retrieval system, or transmitted in any form or by any means—electronic, mechanical, photocopy, recording, or any other—except for brief quotations in printed reviews, without the prior permission of the publisher.

Interior design by Sue Vandenberg Koppenol

Printed in the United States of America

97 98 99 00 01 02 03 04 /❖ DH/ 10 9 8 7 6 5 4 3 2 1

To all of you who have been called to student ministry, whether you are a volunteer or full-time, may God bless you in your efforts as you help students find hope in Christ.

—2 Timothy 4:5

92595

Contents

Through my experience over the past four years with Student Impact, the high school ministry of Willow Creek Community Church, I have truly learned what a difference Christ can make in the lives of students and, in turn, the difference those students can make in the lives of their non-Christian friends. Impact was God's tool to change my life, and I believe that the mission, vision, and strategy that have been developed here can help your ministry effectively reach the students in your areas.

Starting in a new school in eighth grade brought me a new best friend. It was Christi Parker's first year, too, and the closer we got the more I realized that my friendship with Christi was different than any other I had experienced before. Our friendship was built on trust and integrity, and I could see that she had something in her life that made her special. I quickly realized the reason she was different from other friends was her relationship with God. I had other friends who went to church on Sundays with their families, but they went because they had to and they never really liked it. Christi, on the other hand, seemed to have so much fun at church that she invited all her friends to come with her.

Christi asked me to go with her on Tuesday nights to a place called Student Impact, but I knew it was church, so I made excuses not to go. Every week of my freshman year, Christi asked me to go to Student Impact with her. No matter how many lies I told and excuses I made up not to go, she kept asking me and challenging me to investigate what I believed.

I hadn't grown up in a religious family at all, but we had just recently begun attending a local church. I went and sat through songs everyone else seemed to know and a message that I felt was completely irrelevant to my life. I believed that there was a God, but these mornings didn't make me want to have anything to do with Him. There was no way I was going to spend a Tuesday night at church, too!

But in March of 1993, Christi came to me with a proposal. She told me that if I came to Student Impact with her that Tuesday, she would never ask me again. Now, after two years of her asking me every week, this sounded like a small price to pay for her never to bother me about church again! So I agreed. On March 3, 1993, I climbed into a car with a whole bunch of Christi's friends and went to Student Impact.

What I found there amazed me. I saw hundreds of high school kids just like me, but who wanted to be at church. I met leaders who said they'd heard a lot about me from Christi and had been praying for me for a long time—it made me feel that people really cared about me. I walked into a gym and participated in competition like those I had seen on TV and had more fun than I had ever thought possible at a church. Sitting down in the auditorium, I heard what God was really about and how He wanted to be a part of my life. That night Bo shared the gospel and I accepted Jesus Christ into my life as my Lord and Savior. I began an incredible adventure that I'm still on today.

After that night, with a little shepherding from a leader, I began coming regularly to Student Impact. I also began to come to Student Insight, the worship service, where I learned to love God. I joined a small group where I was fed and molded by people who cared about me and were a part of my life. The girls in my small group became my best friends, and they still are today.

I began to understand how fulfilling it was to give back to the ministry through tithing and participating in STRIVE, the annual fund-raiser. When I was ready, I was baptized in the lake in front of our church with my small group surrounding me. As my faith grew, I learned what it meant to care about my lost friends and how I could use evangelism to reach them. I realized what Christi went through to keep asking me to come to Impact with her, and I began to use Impact as a tool to help me reach my non-Christian friends. Never will I forget the way it felt to have a friend for whom I had been praying accept Christ into her life, or the way I felt the day I walked into the water beside her at her baptism.

When I was a junior, I participated in a student missions trip to the Dominican Republic with Student Impact. It was there that I realized that God is bigger than Impact as I witnessed life change coming about through sports ministries and vacation Bible schools. As a senior, I stepped up and began learning what it takes to be a small group leader, and when I was ready I got the opportunity to lead a group of freshman girls. It was exciting to make a difference in a younger student's life the way my leaders made a difference in mine.

God used Impact to show me He could make a difference in my life and that I could, in turn, make a difference for Him in others. Students need Christ! I know that God wants to use you to change the lives of students for Him. I urge you to take a close look at the values in this book; I hope they will encourage and motivate you as you help to turn irreligious high school students into fully devoted followers of Christ. Forever I will be amazed at the power God has to use high school student to change their friends' lives. Especially when I look at my own.

Brandy Ogata
High school senior

ACKNOWLEDGMENTS

As I finish the last page of this book, I feel overwhelmed with gratitude to God for His grace and love. He has blessed me beyond belief! His calling on my life into full-time ministry has been and continues to be a privilege. A part of that privilege is to be on staff at an awesome church like Willow Creek Community Church. I love my church and am glad to be part of such a thriving body.

This book is not just about student ministry; it's about my life and the valuable lessons I have learned from many, many people over the past sixteen years. God has brought some special people into my life for whom I am very grateful.

I want to thank Pastor Richard Lowe for believing in me and giving me an opportunity to lead in my early years at Calvary Bible in California.

I also want to thank all my friends at Sonburst student ministries—what a special and fruitful time we shared!

The Student Impact staff believes and lives out the values in this book. What an amazing team God has assembled! I'm thankful for each of you. I'm also thankful for the dedicated volunteers who serve so faithfully and with such joy.

I want to thank my friend Dan Webster for being a mentor and a role model of an authentic, godly leader. Your example has marked my life.

I've been incredibly fortunate to "do life" with Troy Murphy, the Timothy in my life for the past twelve years. Your fingerprints are all over this book.

Mark Hoffman's faithful support, unending energy, and intense desire to make a difference in students' lives has been an inspiration to me. Don't ever stop dreaming!

Thanks to Bill Hybels for his vision and leadership that has changed my life.

The Zondervan team, particularly Dave Lambert, have worked hard to make resources available for student ministers. I'm grateful for their desire and pray that our work together makes a difference in people's lives.

A very special thanks to my gifted friend, Kim Anderson, for without her gifts this book would not have been possible. You made this a delightful experience and gave me the assurance that God wanted this book completed. I pray we can do it again sometime.

Thanks, too, to my three kids: Brandon, Tiffany, and Trevor. Your prayers and support were so helpful during this project. You mean more to me than words can say. I love you!

And finally, I'm so thankful for my best friend, my beautiful wife, Gloria. I love you so much. Thank you for your encouragement and complete support over these past sixteen years. You are truly a gift from God.

Reevaluate Your Purpose

Leading with Authenticity

A few years ago, Gatorade ran an advertising campaign featuring its most famous spokesman: Michael Jordan. In the ad, Michael played pick-up basketball in a park with kids from the neighborhood. You could see the adoration in their eyes. It was obvious that many of them wished that someday they, too, could play basketball like Mike. The ad's theme song, "Be Like Mike," played repeatedly on Chicago radio stations.

In fact, people around the world want to "be like Mike." He is one of the best professional athletes on the planet, and he makes thirty-five million dollars a year in endorsements. His fame brings him special perks, and millions of people adore him.

Imagine if Michael Jordan visited your student ministry. What a day that would be! The auditorium would be packed with students anxious just to see him. But while meeting Michael Jordan would certainly be a thrill, the One our students really need to meet and be like is Jesus Christ. That's where we come in as student ministers. We can be like Jesus.

I believe if our students truly saw Jesus in us, we would hear more students saying, "I want to be like you. What makes you different?" That's why being called to student ministry is so exciting! We cannot model the ability of Michael Jordan, but we can model someone who is far more attractive and can save lives for eternity: Jesus Christ.

We all need to be asking ourselves regularly: Are my students able to see Jesus Christ in the way I live my life and lead the ministry? Am *I* living a life worth emulating? If they don't see the love of Christ in our lives, it's time to make some serious changes. Student ministry is really all about modeling Christlikeness. As leaders, we must "walk our talk" and allow our students to see Christ in our daily lives. They are watching our every move.

If you picked up this book, I'm sure you want to learn how to be an effective leader in student ministry. For the past seven years, I have led one of the largest student ministries in the country, and I have learned some great lessons. The values and principles I am going to share with you can really make a difference in your ministry. But before we jump into strategies, this chapter focuses on you, the youth leader, and what it will take for you to develop and maintain an authentic walk with God. First Timothy 4:16 poses the challenge to "pay close attention to yourself" (NASB). You need to slow down and take a close look at your personal life, because if you don't, all the strategies in the world will prove meaningless. By staying spiritually authentic, you will be better equipped to lead your students to "be like Christ." After all, being like Christ is what student ministry is all about.

Some leaders believe that to be effective they need advanced college degrees and years of training. Sure, education is beneficial, but there are many educated, ineffective leaders out there. Others think effectiveness comes from developing a dynamic personality. Dynamic and charismatic leaders may be compelling for a time, but in order to influence students for Christ, we must be effective in communicating what matters most.

What is it that matters most?

In the movie *City Slickers,* three New York men head West for a cattle drive, hoping to find that "one thing" that satisfies. Upon arriving at the ranch, a gruff, leathery cowboy named Curly (Jack Palance) greets them. Out on the trail, Mitch (Billy Crystal) seeks the advice of Curly about the meaning of life. Curly responds by holding up his index finger and replying, "It's all about one thing. Just one thing." Mitch is left wondering about what this one thing could be.

Effective student ministry is all about sticking to "one thing"—an authentic connection with God. Without this, you will fail miserably. Your goal to stay spiritually authentic and to be like Christ will require hard work and tremendous discipline. But it is worth all the effort, because your students will not achieve a higher level of spiritual commitment than is reflected in your life. Theologian John Stott wrote that "the Scripture comes alive to the congregation [in our case, student ministry] only if it has come alive to the preacher first."[1] You will mislead your students if you communicate a "do as I say, not as I do" attitude.

How can you keep after that "one thing"? What can you do to ensure that you will finish the race God has called you to run? In the rest of this chapter, we will concentrate on four key areas that will help you stay REAL with Christ:

> **Believe what you live so you can live what you believe!**

- Recognize your fatal flaws;
- Experience God daily;
- Adjust your gauges; and
- Learn discipline.

RECOGNIZE YOUR FATAL FLAWS

Student ministry can indeed be hazardous to your spiritual health. Leaders face incredible pressures: limited finances, expectations from the senior pastor, conflicts with students' parents, and shepherding other leaders, to name a few. The demands of ministry sometimes feel like a black hole.

Is it any wonder that so many student leaders crash and burn? Take a moment and think of the leaders you know who have fallen. Whenever I ask groups of leaders around the country if they know a leader who has fallen, almost every hand goes up. Why do so few leaders last over the long haul? I believe part of the problem is that we don't recognize our fatal flaws.

Fatal flaws are those private, hidden places we know the Enemy is working on, trying to tempt us to take small steps away from innocence and into sin. People don't *fall* into sin; they *walk away* from innocence and the Lord step by step. When a person makes volitional decisions to turn away, the real battle begins. Ephesians 6:11–12 (NASB) says:

> Put on the full armor of God, that you may be able to stand firm against the schemes of the devil. For our struggle is not against flesh and blood, but against the rulers, against the powers, against the world-forces of this darkness, against the spiritual forces of wickedness in the heavenly places.

You are in a spiritual battle and waging war against the Enemy daily. He would love nothing more than to take you down and prevent you from making a difference in the lives of students. One of the ways he tries to do that is by attacking your fatal flaws. He knows your weaknesses and will do anything to make you vulnerable.

I have found two ways to face my fatal flaws and equip myself for the battle. I pray they will be helpful to you.

Identify Your Flaws

To better understand how the Enemy can and will attack you, the first step is to identify your fatal flaws. I am indebted to a good friend and mentor, Dan Webster, for showing me the importance of this truth. We all have at least one fatal flaw, but sometimes we're ashamed or afraid to admit it. Some examples of fatal flaws are greed, pride, anger, lying, lust, and jealousy. At the end of this chapter, you will find a listing of biblical characters who struggled with various fatal flaws. Take some time this week to study these passages. I'm confident you will relate to a few of them. If not, keep looking!

Determining your fatal flaws requires that you be brutally honest with yourself. Think about the area or areas of your life the Enemy could attack. Spend some time quietly reflecting on those areas. If you have a difficult time identifying your fatal flaw, pull a few close friends together and ask them to help you identify your weak areas. By taking this first step and recognizing your fatal flaws, you can then begin building protections around yourself to decrease the likelihood that you will crash.

Seek Accountability

When you see leaders stumble, do you ever think, "Oh, that would never happen to me" or "I'll never struggle with that"? If you do, you have taken the first step in being deceived. As leaders, many of us sometimes mistakenly feel we are immune to sin. Others enforce these feelings; they assume that because we are leaders, we have it all together. In fact, leaders are as close to sin as the last step we have taken away from innocence. Most student leaders urge their students to build accountability into their lives, but the sad fact is, many of us have neglected accountability in our own lives.

Sometimes leaders use the lack of accountability as an excuse. If a leader has stepped away from the Lord, I'll ask him or her, "What happened?" Often, the response is, "If only I had accountability in my life, this would not have happened!" There is no doubt that accountability can be a safeguard to help us control our fatal flaws. But accountability requires "I" ability.

"I" ability is the desire for accountability in order to be like Christ. It is the admission that "I" need help in certain areas of my life. Once I recognize that I need help, I need to be honest with myself, for it is only then that accountability will help. Without sincere desire, accountability is futile. If I say I want accountability in my life, yet look a friend in the eye and answer his questions untruthfully, I do not have "I" ability. Accountability without "I" ability is useless.

How does accountability work, practically speaking? First, choose a trusted friend with whom you have already built a safe relationship. You need to feel comfortable saying, "I messed up here" or "I need help here." Honesty, transparency, and truth-telling are crucial components of accountability. Proverbs 27:17 offers this accountability benefit: "As iron sharpens iron, so one man sharpens another." Accountability can be a powerful tool to help refine each other's character.

Second, select one or two areas in your life that address your fatal flaws and then ask a friend to check with you regularly on the specifics. For example, suppose you are struggling with lying and stretching the truth. Your friend should ask you tough questions like, "Have you lied today?" or "When was the last time you lied?" Be direct in what you want your friend to ask you as well as honest with your answers.

I lead and mange a full-time staff of eight. Each of them has shared with me privately one of their fatal flaws. After talking with them about "I" ability, I regularly encourage them to grow and take steps in controlling their fatal flaws.

A few years ago I worked with a young intern who was trying to incorporate "I" ability into his life. He shared with me his fatal flaw—a struggle with purity related to his attraction to a particular high school girl on the team he led. As you can imagine, this posed a real challenge. Our interns and adult leaders are not allowed to date high school students. I sat down with this intern in my office and we talked about the struggle he was facing. He explained that nothing had happened, but that he realized the attraction was increasing. I asked him what we should do.

"I really want to be a godly man and to stay on track spiritually," he said. "I need accountability in my life."

We developed a series of steps that could help. I suggested the need to tell the female coleader on his team. He looked embarrassed. I asked, "Is it more important to you to avoid telling your coleader or to be a godly man?" We brought his coleader into the meeting and together we helped him draw boundaries. I held him accountable by observing him and regularly asking him, "How are you doing with . . . ?"

This intern discovered the power of "I" ability. Struggling with a weakness in his life, he came to me early and asked for help with an area in his life that could have disqualified him from what God had called him to do. I'm thankful he was willing to expose his weakness for the sake of integrity. He now leads a large student ministry in another part of the country. Accountability with "I" ability was effective in keeping him spiritually authentic.

Accountability does not indicate weakness; it helps to keep us strong. In his book *In the Name of Jesus*, Henri Nouwen said, "I am convinced that priests and ministers, especially those who relate to many anguishing people, need a truly safe place for themselves. They need a place where they can share their deep pain and struggles with people who do not need them, but who can guide them ever deeper into the mystery of God's love."[2] Sometimes in leadership, we feel alone. We need to make it a priority to fight those feelings of aloneness by finding a friend who will keep us accountable.

> Accountability does not indicate weakness; it helps to keep us strong.

God has called you to "run in such a way as to get the prize" (1 Cor. 9:24). One of the ways you can help ensure you will finish the race is by facing your fatal flaws honestly. By recognizing your fatal flaws and seeking accountability with "I" ability you will be better prepared to withstand any missiles the Enemy fires your way.

EXPERIENCE GOD DAILY

A few years ago, I was deeply affected by the book *Experiencing God: Knowing and Doing the Will of God* by Henry T. Blackaby and Claude V. King. We also taught from this book at Student Insight, our weekly program for Christian students. The premise of the book is that we can know God as we experience Him in and around our lives, and that God created us for a love relationship with Himself. The second area in which we can stay authentic in our leadership is to experience God daily.

The authors explain how we can know and experience God:

> Knowing God does not come through a program, a study, or a method. Knowing God comes through a relationship with a Person. This is an intimate love relationship with God. Through this relationship, God reveals Himself, His purposes, and His ways; and He invites you to join Him where He is already at work. When you obey, God accomplishes through you something only He can do. Then you come to *know God* in a more intimate way by *experiencing God* at work through you.[3]

God wants you to know and experience Him first before you start wondering what you can do for Him. He wants you to experience a love relationship with Him that is real and personal and to "love the Lord your God with all your heart and with all your soul and with all your mind and with all your strength" (Mark 12:30). Your effectiveness in student ministry hinges on how this verse is played out in your life.

Do you really love God? Blackaby and King state that if you really love God, then you can trust Him to do great things in you. If you trust Him, then you will desire to obey Him and realize that His commands are for your good. If you obey Him, then you will be able to experience Him. If you experience Him, you will know Him. If you know Him, you can do nothing but love Him. It is a cycle that begins and ends with loving God.

This whole cycle really came alive for me last year. I enjoy meeting with student leaders, and during our annual Student Impact Leadership Conference (SILC) I try to talk with as many attendees as possible. At a recent conference, I made appointments with various leaders, but unfortunately, overcommitted myself. I told one group of leaders from Florida to meet at 9:15 P.M. in my office and asked another student pastor from Australia to join us. Well, the Florida group showed up at my office, and we left early. The next day, the Australian student pastor came up to me and said, "Bo, I must have missed you. I was at your office at 9:15." Right then I realized I had forgotten all about this man! I should have said, "I'm sorry," but instead I stretched the truth and answered, "Oh, I must have just missed you. I looked for you." Actually, I blatantly lied to this man's face!

Later that day, the Holy Spirit was working me over and pointing out my sin.

I felt the Lord asking me, "Bo, do you love Me?"

"Of course, Lord!"

"If you love me, then trust Me."

"Okay, Lord."

"And if you trust Me, then obey Me."

"Sure, Lord, anything You say!"

"Find this man and apologize for lying to him."

It wasn't easy, but I wanted to be obedient to what God wanted me to do. So I approached this pastor and told him I had lied to him and had really forgotten all about him. I asked for his forgiveness. He looked at me and said, "No problem. I just wanted to talk to you about integrity friendship." We both smiled, and he added, "You just taught me." At that moment, I saw God not only working in my life, but also how God can work in another person's life when I follow and experience God.

Each morning I remind myself that God is at work. I need to be quiet enough and look hard enough to see where He's working and join Him there. Years ago, Jesus asked His disciples the same question He asks us today: "Do you love Me? If you love Me, trust Me. If you trust Me, obey Me. If you obey Me, you'll experience Me." It's so true! And when you experience Him, you'll love Him even more.

Take a moment and think about where you are in this cycle. Right now, if you are struggling to trust God completely, think about the reason why. What is in your life that God can't handle? There is nothing! God is love, and He wants the best for you. Chances are you need to let God reveal Himself to you and be reminded, "This is how we know what love is: Jesus Christ laid down his life for us" (1 John 3:16).

Because He loves you, He chooses to involve you in carrying out His kingdom purposes in the world. He *wants* and *needs* you to become involved in what He is doing around the world.

Unfortunately, we are sometimes unwilling to wait for God to reveal His assignments for us. We are a "doing" people. We always want to be doing something. Often you will hear the phrase, "Don't just stand there; do something!" The idea of doing God's will sounds fairly exciting. But sometimes individuals and churches are so busy doing things they think will help God accomplish His purpose that He can't get their attention long enough to use them as servants to accomplish what He wants. We often wear ourselves out and accomplish very little of value to the kingdom.

As it says in the book *Experiencing God*, "I think God is crying out and shouting to us, 'Don't just do something; stand there!

Enter into a love relationship with Me. Get to know Me. Adjust your life to Me. Let Me love you and reveal Myself to you as I work through you.' A time will come when the doing will be called for, but we cannot skip the relationship. The relationship with God must come first."[4]

In the busyness of ministry, we must never forget that experiencing God daily is the foundation for authentic leadership. When that foundation is laid, we can then be leaders who make a difference for Christ.

ADJUST YOUR GAUGES

Today was the day that our family decided to get a Christmas tree. My wife and three children piled in the van and we were off to the Christmas tree lot. On the way, I noticed a stranded car on the side of the road. I pulled over to see if I could help the driver in any way. The poor young man had simply run out of gas! As I drove him to the nearest gas station, I had to ask the question: "How long did you drive on empty?" He answered, "Obviously, too long!"

This driver had forgotten to look at his gauges. I'm sure he kept trying to convince himself he could make it to the next station. If you have ever run out of gas, you've probably thought the same thing! Obviously, the gas gauge serves a very important purpose in a car.

Like cars, we need to check the gauges in our personal lives. Adjusting these gauges is the third key to staying balanced and leading authentically. We want to finish the race well. To do that, we need to pace ourselves and take frequent breaks to look at our gauges. I have discovered that when I neglect to monitor the gauges in my life, I don't give God, my family, or my students my very best.

During a church staff meeting a few years ago, Bill Hybels, my senior pastor, taught me some life-changing ministry survival skills. In order to stay balanced, he challenged me to regularly check three gauges in my life:

1. The spiritual gauge: How are my spiritual disciplines like time in the Word, prayer, and fasting? Am I consistent? Am I growing in my walk with God?
2. The physical gauge: Am I taking care of my body by exercising and eating healthy food? Do I make time in my schedule for workouts? Am I honoring God with my body?

3. The emotional gauge: Am I being honest with my emotions? Am I doing things that fill me up? Do I make time for recreation and relaxation?

I learned that these three gauges can be depleted independently without my even realizing it is happening. For me, the emotional gauge is the toughest one to read. I love ministry, and in the midst of my zeal I often fail to discern the effect it has on me emotionally. Bill taught me about "Intensive Ministry Activities," or IMAs. These are activities that drain student ministry leaders over time, such as message preparation and delivery, counseling, funerals, confrontations, strategic meetings, staff tensions, or pressing decisions. I'm sure you could add a few to the list!

The problem with IMAs is that they cause massive drains on emotional energy. Physically and spiritually you may feel fine, but your emotional tank has red-lined. Unfortunately, the emotional tank cannot be replenished quickly. It's like a car battery that has gone dead. Sure, you can jump start it and hope to make it home, but to effectively fix the problem, you need a slow charge. Time is the best charger. This principle is so true in ministry. If you don't take the time to charge up your emotional tank, you will leave yourself weak and vulnerable to making poor decisions or using quick fixes.

Bill also taught me specific ways to read my emotional gauge. First, I need to read it honestly to accurately assess its present level. This requires some quiet introspection and time to reflect. Second, I need to keep learning which IMAs cause the massive drains on my emotional gauge. Once I am able to identify the activities that sap my emotional energy, I can then better prepare myself by "filling my tank" before they happen. Third, I must learn how to replenish my emotional tank and how long it will take. This will vary for everyone. Some people are replenished by reading a book or taking a walk. Others may relax in a hot tub and enjoy a time of solitude. For me, I get filled up by spending a day off with no agenda. I am a fairly structured and driven person and always have a goal in mind. To spend a day relaxing, without a plan, gets me charged up. And, fourth, I cannot fall into the trap of thinking I am an exception to the rule. If I do, I am setting myself up for disaster.

Student ministry can beat leaders up. I know. It is challenging, demanding, and at times it can be lonely. There seems to be a misconception in Christian service that says, "I'm going to bite my upper lip and keep my head up, even if I am hurting. I'll keep on marching like a good soldier." Some of us get "shot" and start bleeding emotionally, but we feel like we can't stop and say something is wrong. There's too much ministry to do! However, if the wounds are not attended to, we will eventually die emotionally or spiritually. This is why checking our gauges is so important.

Checking your spiritual, physical, and emotional gauges will give you a quick read on how you are doing. Staying balanced and healthy is crucial to a leader's effectiveness in student ministry. We owe it to our families, our students, but, most important, to God.

LEARN DISCIPLINE

How does a person move from desire to experience? Everyone wants to be in good shape, but not many want to exercise. Everybody wants a great marriage, but few are willing to work hard at being a great spouse. Lots of people enjoy a nice garden, but not many like pulling the weeds. We can desire all these things, but what about experiencing them? Discipline is the means to move us from desire to experience. It is the fourth key area in staying real with Christ.

> Disciplines allow us to place ourselves before God so that He can transform us.... By themselves the spiritual disciplines can do nothing; they can only get us to the place where something can be done.
>
> Richard Foster, *Celebration of Discipline* (San Francisco: Harper & Row, 1988), 7.

Spiritual fruit is born through spiritual people. Strategies and programs are important, but what really matters is your walk with God and how many of your students love the Lord. Spiritual disciplines take time and effort. Henri Nouwen has this to say about discipline:

> The word *discipleship* and the word *discipline* are the same word—that has always fascinated me. Once you have made the choice to say, "Yes, I want to follow Jesus," the question is, "What disciplines will help me remain faithful to that choice?" If we want to be disciples of Jesus, we have to live a disciplined life.
>
> By *discipline*, I do not mean control. If I know the discipline of psychology or of economics, I have a certain control over a body of knowledge. If I discipline my children, I want to have a little control over them.

But in the spiritual life, the word discipline means "the effort to create some space in which God can act." Discipline means to prevent everything in your life from being filled up. Discipline means that somewhere you're not occupied, and certainly not preoccupied. In the spiritual life, discipline means to create that space in which something can happen that you hadn't planned or counted on.[5]

We need to carve out time daily to make sure everything in our life is not filled up with meetings, phone calls, activities, counseling, studying, planning.... You get the idea. Student ministry demands much of our time and energy. If we neglect incorporating spiritual disciplines in our life, we will leave no room for something to happen that we hadn't planned or counted on. We need to create room for God to speak to us and act in and through our lives. I know this is easier said than done.

Some of the spiritual disciplines such as quietness, prayer, fasting, service, solitude, and study of God's Word will take you from simply desiring to walk with God to actually experiencing His presence in your life. There can be no shortcuts in your walk with Christ.

How can leaders practice spiritual disciplines? Many excellent books on the topic of spiritual disciplines are available that offer different methodologies and ideas. If we really desire to be like Christ, we should look at the spiritually disciplined life He modeled for us and the kinds of activities in which He participated. Dallas Willard states:

> If we have faith in Christ, we must believe that He knew how to live. We can, through faith and grace, become like Christ by practicing the types of activities He engaged in, by arranging our whole lives around the activities He Himself practiced in order to remain constantly at home in the fellowship of His Father.[6]

When we read the gospels, we find that Jesus practiced many spiritual disciplines, such as prayer, meditation, fasting, service, submission, and solitude. Which spiritual discipline do you need to implement or strengthen in your life? For me, the struggle is with the discipline of solitude. Sitting for an extended amount of time is challenging enough, let alone doing so silently! My friend Dan Webster really models this discipline in his life. When I was under his leadership a few years ago, he encouraged and sharpened me in this discipline. He gave me this verse in a frame: "And he continued to seek God . . . and as long as he sought the Lord, God prospered him" (2 Chron. 26:5 NASB). I still have this verse sitting on my desk; it serves as a visual reminder to practice the discipline of quietness. Dan now counsels others to be authentic leaders, and he continues to be an example to me.

Spiritual disciplines are important so our hearts become more like Christ's. As Bill Hybels contends:

> Every true Christian wants to live like Jesus lived—to love the unlovely, to serve with grace, to resist temptation, to uphold conviction, to exhibit power. But we can only live that way if we devote ourselves to the same disciplines He practiced. If Jesus pursued these disciplines to maintain spiritual authenticity, how much more must we.[7]

CHOOSING AUTHENTICITY

Being an authentic leader begins with you and the daily choices you make. How real are you? You may be a person who has fatal flaws that no one knows about or you may be a person who regularly red-lines your gauges. Or you may not be consistent with your spiritual disciplines or make it a priority to experience God daily. Eventually, it will all catch up with you. As Josh McDowell often says, "You can con a con, fool a fool, but you can't kid a kid." You will not be able to fool the people you are leading. This may be a good time to slow down and ask yourself, "How am I doing? Which of the four areas of REAL do I need to address?"

If you choose to be an authentic, godly leader, you will be modeling Christlikeness to your students. In time, they too will desire to be like Christ because of your example. Your commitment to authenticity is a precious gift you can offer your students, and one that is far more important than any program or retreat. Be encouraged knowing that "God who began the good work within you will keep right on helping you grow in his grace until his task within you is finally finished on that day when Jesus Christ returns" (Phil. 1:6 TLB). What a privilege and responsibility we have to practice authenticity!

The following quote summarizes the heart of this chapter. Spend some time reflecting on it before you begin reading the next chapter, and honestly answer its last question:

The question is not: How many people take you seriously? How much are you going to accomplish? Can you show some results? But: Are you in love with Jesus?[8]

REWIND

What Did You Learn?

Leading with authenticity is no easy task. It requires that your words and actions be consistent so that your students see Christ in how you live your life. You can be REAL if you focus on four key areas:

	WAYS TO STAY REAL	**STEPS TO TAKE**
R	Recognize your fatal flaws	• Identify fatal flaws • Seek accountability with "I" ability
E	Experience God daily	Participate in the cycle: Love—Trust—Obey—Experience—Know—Love
A	Adjust your gauges	Monitor your: • spiritual • physical • emotional gauges
L	Learn discipline	• Practice spiritual disciplines • Move from desire to experience

Pause

What Action Will You Take?

1. Ask yourself:
   - What is your potential fatal flaw(s)?
   - What are you doing to control your fatal flaw(s)? Do you desire "I" ability?
   - Do you truly know God and are you experiencing Him daily?
   - Have you read your gauges recently?
   - Which spiritual discipline needs sharpening in your life?

2. Take some time to study the fatal flaws these biblical characters faced:
   - Rich young ruler—Mark 10:17–27
   - Herod—Acts 12:21–25
   - David—2 Samuel 11:1–4
   - Martha—Luke 10:38
   - Pilate—Luke 23:20–25
   - Nebuchadnezzar—Daniel 4:29–37
   - Ananias and Sapphira—Acts 5
   - Judas—Matthew 26:14–16
   - Demas—2 Timothy 4:10
   - Simon the Sorcerer—Acts 8:19
   - Samson—Judges 16

Fast Forward

What's Next?

You've checked your personal life with Christ. Now, how effective is your leadership?

FOLLOWING THE LEADER

Think back to when you were small. Perhaps you remember playing a silly group game called "Follow the Leader." The way it worked was that each person got a turn to be the leader and dictate what the rest of the group had to do. This game was an early introduction into the art of leadership!

I always enjoyed playing this game. I could hardly wait until it was my turn to lead the group! When it finally was my turn, I liked to lead the group to places they hadn't been yet. I also devised innovative things for the group to do, like climbing over obstacles in uniquely challenging ways. And I liked it when someone else would lead in new and clever ways; it was exciting to follow such a leader.

In a way, high school students are still playing this game today. They are desperately searching for a leader—someone to follow and show them the way. They want to be led.

Those of us to whom God has given the gift of leadership need to be regularly reminded to steward this gift carefully. This chapter will focus on leadership and how you can best become a leader worth following.

ARE YOU A LEADER?

How can you tell if you are a leader? Are some people born leaders while others develop this skill? Can leadership ability be decided by reading a book, praying, or taking a test? I heard a saying that goes, "You will know if you have the gift of leadership by looking behind to see who is following." Is this a true statement? Does this mean that great leaders are measured by the number of people following them?

What if you are a point person in your ministry and you feel you are not a strong leader? Should you step down? Or what if you are in a church situation where your pastor is not a gifted leader? Are you just stuck? These are great questions. I am not sure I can answer all of them, but I can tell you about my experiences in leadership and how I have seen God work in my life and in others.

How would you evaluate yourself as a leader? Have you ever questioned your leadership skills? Perhaps the test on the next page will help you assess your role as a leader. Go ahead and answer the questions and spend some time reflecting on your answers.

What did you discover about yourself? Do you think you are a leader? Or do you find yourself fitting the description given in the first column—more driven than led?

God has a plan for the leaders in His church. He has entrusted the spiritual gift of leadership to some and has given them the responsibility to lead groups of people. Let's take a few moments to look more closely at the spiritual gift of leadership.

THE SPIRITUAL GIFT OF LEADERSHIP

Spiritual gifts are special abilities given by the Holy Spirit to every believer for use within the body of Christ. They allow us to make a unique contribution. The gift of spiritual leadership can be defined as *the divine enablement to attract, lead, and motivate people to accomplish the work of ministry.* In Romans 12:6–8, the mention of the gift of leadership is accompanied by the charge to lead "diligently."

God, in His infinite wisdom, knew there had to be men and women who could motivate and lead teams of people to turn a vision into reality. The gift of leadership is very important to the church. Unfortunately, I meet youth leaders who have the gift of leadership but, for whatever reasons, are not free to use it in their churches. How this must break the heart of God! I believe one of the primary problems youth ministries are facing is the lack of strong leadership. The gift of leadership must be identified, harnessed, and used properly so that the body of Christ can minister as He intended.

One of the gifts I have been blessed to receive from God is the gift of leadership. Over the years, I have had the privilege of being led by some strong men and women with the gift of leadership, and I have benefited from their examples. They have really

∎ What Type of Youth Leader Are You? ∎

Check below which of the two statements most accurately
describes you as you lead at your church:

Statement 1:	**Statement 2:**
◇ I spend a majority of my time planning various activities for the students.	◇ I spend a majority of my time planning how I can minister to the students. (Matt. 15:32)
◇ I often feel like I am "putting in my time" at my job.	◇ I am often overwhelmed by the compassion I feel for high school students. (Matt. 9:36)
◇ I often find it easier to do all the work myself.	◇ I delegate most of the work to the right people, and I serve them as they minister. (Luke 9:1–2)
◇ It is important to me that my students and leaders like me.	◇ It is important to me that reproof and correction are given when needed, even if I won't be liked. (John 2:13–16)
◇ I do not have a clear vision of where God is taking my ministry.	◇ I regularly communicate to the students and leaders the vision God has given me for my ministry. (Mark 1:17)
◇ I seem to be driven by my calendar.	◇ I have an overall plan, born out of my ministry vision, that drives my calendar. (Psalm 127:2)
◇ I often have to make decisions in "crisis mode," without adequate prayer or quietness.	◇ I lead from quietness. (Mark 14:32–42)
◇ Many of our ministry acvities target both believers and nonbelievers, trying to meet everyone's need at once.	◇ Every activity of my ministry is designed to hit a specific target or accomplish a specific purpose. (1 Cor. 9:26)
◇ I spread myself very thin in my relationships, in an effort to care for as many people as possible.	◇ I invest much of myself in discipline of a few key people. (2 Tim. 2:2)

helped and encouraged me to develop my leadership gift. In the remainder of this chapter, I'd like to share some of these lessons about leadership with you.

LEAD, FOLLOW, OR GET OUT OF THE WAY

Some of you might think the above title is a bit harsh, but I believe there is a lot of truth in this simple saying. This phrase is often used in athletics, but why not in ministry? In ministry, we need to decide if we are going to lead, follow, or simply get out of the way until we are ready to be a part of God's work. We must make the choice.

An interesting article in a recent *The Wall Street Journal* addressed the issue of management and leadership. It stated that people don't

> The difference between management and leadership can be summed up like this: managers make sure that people are doing their daily routines; leaders determine whether those routines are worth doing at all.

want to be managed; they want to be led! There are many kinds of leaders: world leaders, educational leaders, political leaders, religious leaders, scout leaders, community leaders, labor leaders, and business leaders. Student ministries need leaders!

The difference between management and leadership can be summed up like this: managers make sure that people are doing their daily routines; leaders determine whether those routines are worth doing at all. Managers are primarily concerned about a person's performance; leaders spend their time figuring out the directional issues facing the organization. Leaders ask questions like:

- Where are we going?
- What is our mission?
- What is it that we are really trying to do?
- How can we structure our organization and attract people?

How about you? Do you find yourself more often in the management camp, caught up in the day-to-day routines of ministry? If so, I challenge you to consider moving over to the leadership camp. If God has given you the gift of leadership, lead! To encourage you to take this step, I want to focus on three leadership essentials I have learned over the years: vision, focus, and confidence.

LEADERSHIP ESSENTIAL #1: VISION

Be Clear and Concise

We've learned so far that God has chosen certain people to serve the body of Christ with the gift of leadership. To this group of people He has bestowed a precious gift: the ability to develop and cast a clear and concise vision. It is a necessity for kingdom-building.

Author George Barna defines vision as

> a clear mental image of a preferable future imparted by God to His chosen servants and . . . based upon an accurate understanding of God, self, and circumstances. . . . Vision for ministry is a reflection of what God wants to accomplish through you to build His Kingdom.[1]

All true leaders have a vision that includes their values, convictions, thoughts, emotions, and dreams. When leaders are seized by a clear and concise vision, they can't stop talking about it. They are determined to make their vision become reality. It becomes their burning passion and life's mission. Barna states, "Vision is not dreaming the impossible dream, but dreaming the most possible dream."[2]

Several years ago, Shearson/Lehman Brothers featured an advertisement that defined vision and its potential impact. The ad read, "Vision is having an acute sense of the possible. It is seeing what others don't see. And when those with similar vision are drawn together, something extraordinary occurs."

Be Compelling

Extraordinary things can happen when people cast a compelling vision. Martin Luther King Jr. was a visionary who knew how to attract, organize, inspire, and lead people. When he spoke, people listened to what he had to say. No one will ever forget the passion in which he gave his "I Have a Dream" speech. He cast a compelling vision that changed the course of history.

John F. Kennedy also knew the power of vision. He cast a vision in 1960 of placing a man on the moon by 1970. Many people concentrated their time and effort to make this vision come to life. People responded and resonated with Kennedy's vision because it united the country to achieve a common goal.

Walt Disney's vision for Disneyland formed well before the ground was broken. Here's what he envisioned:

The idea for Disneyland is a simple one. It will be a place for people to find happiness and knowledge. It will be a place for parents and children to spend pleasant times. Disneyland will be something of a fair, an exhibition, a playground, a community center, a museum of living facts, and a showplace of beauty and magic. It will be filled with the accomplishments, the joys, and hopes of the world we live in. And it will remind us and show us to make those wonders part of our lives.[3]

Bill Hybels is also a compelling vision-caster. His vision to reach the unchurched started a worldwide movement and has given thousands of Christian leaders new hope for building the church. You will read more about how it all started in later chapters.

What made these four leaders so effective in their arenas of influence? Each of them clearly defined his vision in concise terms and a compelling manner. People saw the visions of Martin Luther King Jr., John F. Kennedy, Walt Disney, and Bill Hybels, and were compelled to help bring those visions to life.

Jesus was the master vision-caster. He not only used His leadership skills to attract people, but He cast His vision of redeeming the world and establishing the church. His disciples caught this vision, and because of this, each of our lives have been forever changed.

Four years ago, Bill Hybels presented me and three members of my staff team with the opportunity to go on a sailing trip in the Caribbean aboard a thirty-five-foot sailboat. None of us had ever sailed much, and we were excited to try something new.

Tom, the captain of our sailboat, was an experienced and skilled sailor. He knew what it would take for us to reach our destination, and he gave each of us assignments to do around the boat. Tom knew how to lead a crew effectively. He had carefully planned out the trip and knew exactly where we were going.

> Selecting and articulating the right vision, this powerful idea is the toughest task and the truest test of great leadership.
>
> Burt Nanus, *Visionary Leadership*, 1992:16, 28–29.

Tom pointed to a beautiful island in the distance, explaining that we would head there first. When I asked Tom how long it would take to get there, he said three or four hours. I couldn't believe it! I thought, *Wow! That's a long time to go such a short distance! This sure is a lot of work!*

What Tom did next reminded me about the power of vision. Before we even started, he took some time to cast the vision for our trip. He began telling us about the island: how it was one of the most famous snorkeling spots in the world, and how its rarely-visited beaches stretched for miles. By the time he had finished painting the vision for the island, I was ready to do the work to get there. I was willing to be patient and enjoy the ride knowing what was ahead of me. Tom's vision-casting also unified us a team; we each had a task to do so that we each could enjoy getting to the island.

I think that sometimes we get so anxious to reach our destinations in student ministry that we forget to enjoy the process. Yet the process is just as important as the product or end result. It is so important for us as leaders to point out the "islands" to our students, to tell them where we are headed as a ministry and what it will be like once we get there. Our students want to sail with us. They just need some vision-casting from their leader. We will talk more about creating and communicating a vision statement for your ministry in chapter 7.

LEADERSHIP ESSENTIAL #2: FOCUS

Focus is a great word when it comes to leadership. Have you ever sat in a movie theater where the film being shown was out of focus? Until the lens is finally adjusted and clarity restored, it is a frustrating experience. In much the same way, we need to constantly adjust the lenses of our student ministry to focus on what we are all about.

I was a head football coach for many years before entering full-time student ministry. One of the words I often used with my players was "focus-up." My players knew, whenever I yelled this phrase from the sidelines, that they needed to refocus on the fundamentals out on the field.

We need to focus-up on four keys areas in our leadership:

1. Team performance
2. "A" priorities
3. Excellence
4. Christlike character

Team Performance

It is imperative that a leader honestly and consistently evaluate his or her team of people on a regular basis. Evaluations provide opportunity to look at goals and assess progress. Whether a person is doing "A" work or "C" work, he or she deserves to know three things:

1. What is being done right
2. What is being done incorrectly
3. What specifically needs improvement

I value the leaders and staff God has assembled in Student Impact. At least three times a year, I sit down with each staff person and review the past four months. I ask the staff person how he or she felt about meeting his or her ministry goals and what we should celebrate. We also discuss areas of needed improvement. These times are extremely beneficial to both me and the leaders. It gives me an accurate view of the big ministry picture and keeps me informed. My leaders benefit because they are challenged and stretched to grow personally and professionally.

Not only is it helpful to sit down and evaluate your team, but it is also important to catch them "in the act," doing the job well or doing it poorly. I try to be a good finder. I like to walk around during ministry events and observe leaders doing ministry. It is so much fun to catch a leader in the act and to affirm him or her by saying: "What I just saw you do with that student showed strong leadership and Christ-like qualities. I just want you to know I'm proud of you. Keep up the good work!" We must be good finders and encourage those we are leading.

> The key to developing people is to catch them doing something right.
>
> Ken Blanchard and Spencer Johnson,
> *The One Minute Manager*
> (New York: Berkley Books, 1982), 44.

Affirming what people are doing well is important, but so is correcting leaders. Jesus was masterful at correcting the members of His team. I have found that the best times of correction have occurred at the moment the action is happening. Recently, I observed a leader's teamroom meeting. In a few minutes, it was obvious to me that this leader had not given much thought to preparing for his teamroom. Afterwards, I approached this leader and asked, "I noticed that you didn't seem to be too prepared. Are you okay?" I first wanted to show care and concern to this leader and make sure that nothing was wrong. When he said he was fine, just unprepared, I was then able to sharpen this leader by asking: "What could you have done better? What exactly was the problem?" This leader was challenged to be better prepared for the next meeting.

The disciplined leader cares about his or her people and wants to see each of them reach their full God-given potential. Your team is a precious gift and needs to be treated as such. You should always look for ways to encourage and affirm the people you lead and also discern the times when correction is needed. There will be times when, unfortunately, you will need to let some people go.

"A" Priorities

Some youth leaders get so consumed by the daily grind that they rarely do the needed work of forward, and proactive thinking. Without strategic planning, a youth leader can become a responder and begin to live in crisis mode. He or she becomes like a firefighter, putting out fire after fire. Instead of putting out fires, effective leaders ask the question, "Why are these fires even happening? What are the causes?"

One of the biggest challenges for me is to stay focused: to die on the hills that are worth dying on and to walk away from those that aren't. It can be difficult to deal with other people's expectations. Find me ten people and I will give you ten different ways to do ministry: "The music is too loud"; "We should only play Christian music"; "We meet too much"; "We don't meet enough." We must listen to God for His expectations. We need to stay in touch with God and with what He wants.

Dave Richa,
Community Christian Church, Naperville, IL,
former Student Impact Campus Director

Disciplined leaders have to get out in front of their people instead of getting trapped fighting fires. They need to listen to God's voice in order to discern which fights to fight. They have to ask these kind of questions:

• Where do we want to be five years from now?
• What will it take for us to get there?

- What must we start doing today if we want to wind up being in the right place tomorrow?
- What new steps are we going to have to take?
- What needs to change?
- What kind of resources will be required in order for us to fulfill our mission?

One of the ways I help my staff focus-up and discern priorities is through a weekly schedule. Once a week, we meet to pray and talk over what needs to be done during the week to reach our goals and, ultimately, our vision and mission. After the meeting, each staff member returns to his or her office to individually set "A" and "B" priorities for the

> **Efficiency is doing the thing right, but effectiveness is doing the right thing.**
>
> Peter Drucker, quoted by Max DePree in *Leadership Is an Art* (New York: Doubleday, 1989), 16.

week. The following week they each report back to me the status of their priorities: which of them were accomplished and which were not. They have told me this helps them to focus on the right things and they appreciate the accountability.

Excellence

Disneyland is a place filled with excellence. It is a value that runs deep throughout the Magic Kingdom, from the performances to the vendors to the grounds. They strive for excellence 365 days a year! It permeates everything they do.

Disneyland may claim to be the Magic Kingdom, but we serve in *the* kingdom. God is so worthy of our best! Why don't we, as youth leaders, have the same drive for excellence as do the vendors at Disneyland?

Excellence is hard work. I like the following definition of excellence I heard at our church's leadership conference: *excellence is doing the best with what you have.* This is what God has asked us to do.

When I travel, I can tell almost immediately if youth pastors have incorporated this value of excellence. Often I hear leaders complaining that, if only they had bigger facilities or more equipment or a larger budget, *then* great things would automatically happen. But excellence starts well before issues of facility, equipment, and budget ever come up in meetings; excellence starts with attitude. That attitude is one that says, "Regardless of what we have, we are going to do everything with excellence."

I remember visiting a small ministry in California as they were getting ready for Sunday school. I could tell right away that they valued excellence. They had thought through how to set up the chairs, cleaned up the room, created sharp hand-outs, and used a small video camera to show a video on the wall. They were doing the best with what they had, and the students who came that morning were excited to be there.

Excellence is doing the best with what you have.

I challenge you to pause for a moment and to be thankful for what God has given you. Ask yourself: Am I doing the best with what I have? Excellence matters. We serve the King, and He deserves the best.

One of the most dramatic track events to watch is the high jump, in which athletes try to jump over the bar at the highest point possible. Each time an athlete clears the bar, the bar is raised higher.

In Student Impact, we like to use the saying, "The bar needs to be raised," to indicate areas in which we need to improve. There are times we need to raise the bar of excellence and keep it high. When we are planning events, we ask each other, "Where's the bar in this event? Where do we need to raise it?"

Leaders can reinforce the value of excellence in many ways. In Student Impact, one of the ways we measure excellence is by videotaping our programs and evaluating them. We go over details because details matter. We ask, "Did this work? What can we improve? What could have been done to improve with what we have?" By evaluating our programs, we can see the areas that need adjustments in order to achieve excellence. This evaluation process gives value to what we do and allows the process to be fun.

Not every ministry can or will want to use video for reviewing a program, but every ministry can embody excellence through attention to detail. Have you thought through how you will set up your room? Do you work to make it clean and inviting? Are you well prepared for each program or event? Can your students see the value of excellence in your ministry?

Excellence does not come overnight; it is a process. It requires a team effort committed to the value of doing things with excellence. And while excellence will be measured differently in student ministries around the country, all of us can commit to "do the best with what we have."

Christlike Character

To be Christlike in your leadership, you must constantly wrestle with questions like:

What would Jesus do in this situation?
- Would He laugh, cry, encourage, or rebuke?
- Would He show patience or say "enough is enough"?
- Would He tell the people to get to work or to rest a while?
- Would He steer straight or change course?
- Would He consolidate or venture out?

We all desire to be disciplined kingdom leaders. We must continually ask these kind of hard questions to ourselves in order to gauge how we are doing in our walk with Christ. When we yield ourselves daily to the control of the Holy Spirit, He is able to show us the areas in our life in which we need to become more like Christ. When we hit snags or bumps along the way, we can search the Scriptures to come up with the right answers.

I know that everyone on my staff team desires to demonstrate Christlike character. I also know that it helps to focus in on this objective. I once led a meeting where I asked the leaders in the room to list as many Christlike character traits they could think of. I listed all of these traits on a flip chart. I took a pen and gave it to Lynette, one of the leaders in the room, and asked her to circle the traits she had recently seen in Dave's life. After Lynette was finished, the rest of leaders also circled any traits they had observed in Dave's life. It was a growing experience for Dave to see which character traits were circled and which were not. He felt encouraged by the Christlike characteristics others saw in his life, and he was also stretched in some areas to become more like Christ.

Each leader got a chance to be in the "hot seat" and was reminded that we must live lives worth emulating. It was a great experience as each person was challenged to grow in Christlike qualities and become more like Christ in all we do.

In other meetings we select one individual at a time and attempt to sharpen his or her Christlike character. I remember one particular time when it was my turn. The staff was given an opportunity to evaluate me and my performance as the ministry director. I was challenged in several ways: First I was told to be more patient. They felt I had a tendency to be goal-oriented and unwilling to be patient in the process. They were right! Second, a staff member told me I needed to celebrate God's goodness to the ministry more often. Right again! I run at a pretty fast pace at times and I do forget to slow down and reflect on all God is doing. I was also encouraged during this time as I was told ways the others saw Christ reflected in my life.

Another way I have challenged the staff in their Christlike character is by having them write each fruit of the Spirit on a index card with a phrase like, "I saw Christ in you this week when you showed love to. . . ." or "I saw Christ in you when you were patient with . . . ." They then used these cards to encourage one another and affirm one another's Christlike character.

How is the Spirit bearing fruit in your life? Do people see any or all of the evidences listed in Galatians 5 when they watch how you live? Before we dare challenge others to grow, we must take a hard look at our own character and strive to be more like Christ.

LEADERSHIP ESSENTIAL #3: CONFIDENCE

As a high school football coach, I learned very quickly that I had to be bold and confident in order to build a winning team. One area that required confidence was in selection. I knew that I had to determine which players should play and where. Sometimes this was difficult, but a selection process was necessary and unavoidable.

I also had to be confident in my direction of the team. The team had to know what our defense and offense plans would be so we could focus on winning football games. They needed clear, concise direction.

The third area in which I had to show confidence was in my teaching and coaching on the field. I often monitored what I and the other coaches were telling the players to do and watched to see how the players responded to our teaching. If we were teaching the right things to do, most often we would win.

The urgency of what we do in student ministry is so much more important than scoring points on a football field. We're talking about eternity! This realization has motivated me to take what I learned about confidence through coaching football and apply it to student ministry. In ministry, too, we need confidence in selection, direction, and teaching. Let's look at each of these areas as it relates to student ministry.

Selection

So often in ministry we are so desperate to fill positions that we'll take just about anybody who has a pulse and can breathe! As a result, people get placed where there are holes instead of where God has gifted them. People with the gift of evangelism love to evangelize and those with the gift of teaching love to teach. Using your top spiritual gift should breathe life into you and be a source of joy.

I talk with youth leaders around the country who are frustrated because they are missing leaders or do not have the right people selected. I ask them, "If you had to make adjustments on your team, what would you do or who would you adjust?" I usually hear a story about having a leader who shouldn't be in a leadership role and the difficulty involved in telling that leader he or she doesn't fit. This is a frustrating situation for everyone involved.

Positioning people to serve outside their area of giftedness leads to discouragement and defeat. You, as the ministry leader, need to be bold in making the proper selection. If you have someone who is not a leader leading or someone teaching who does not have the gift of teaching, make the necessary changes. Having an ineffectual leader is extremely frustrating for those who sit under such leadership. As the point person, you must constantly examine to see if the right people are serving in the right places. When the right person is positioned in the right place, it is exciting to see God work as the Holy Spirit is able to use this person in powerful ways. (Chapter 10 develops some specific guidelines for selecting and building a leadership team.)

Be patient in the selection process; don't compromise and place people hastily. In the long run, you will see the fruit of selecting people with the gift mix needed to serve in the various areas of your ministries.

Direction

Have you ever tried to reach a destination without directions? It can be frustrating, if not impossible. With clear directions, though, you can reach your destination. Clear direction is crucial in ministry, too.

Direction means staying focused on your mission. In student ministry, we hear many voices that try to tell us what to do—voices of parents, pastors, congregation, and even students. As youth leaders, we must be clear on the direction we are going and communicate it with boldness.

I meet weekly with the campus directors (those who lead campus teams) who are in a position of strong leadership in our ministry. During one of our meetings, I felt they had begun to lose their direction and their focus seemed unclear. I knew they needed a reminder of what we were all about as a ministry and the direction we were headed. I saw an opportunity to do this at the lake on our church's campus. We walked outside and I took a rock and threw it in the lake. I asked them, "What did you see?" People answered that the rock had disappeared; that they saw ripples in the water; that there was a splash. I then told each of them to throw a rock into the lake at the same time. "Now what did you see?" I questioned. They replied: Bigger ripples and a bigger splash.

I then used this simple illustration to discuss the spiritual ripples that need to be happening in our ministry and how we can help make them happen with God's strength. We sat down outside and I continued to talk about what our ministry is all about, our God-given vision, and where we were headed. I reminded the leaders that we need to do student ministry together in order to make spiritual ripples. With this direction, they became clearer about what they could contribute to turn Student Impact's vision into reality.

Teaching

Students today want and need to hear the truth. They want authenticity. They want to know you care, that you will accept them for who they are and help them along in their spiritual journeys. God's Word is our truth source in all teaching. There is power in the Word of God.

The world sends our students so many mixed messages. It is difficult for many of them to discern right from wrong because they are pulled in all kinds of directions. It is our responsibility as student ministers to teach our students about God's unconditional love and His saving grace. We have the answer they are looking for! Please don't ever forget the tremendous privilege we have to tell each student how much he or she matters to God! God's Word needs to be shared with boldness and in a relevant way so that students can begin to apply truth to their daily lives.

We face tremendous pressures in student ministry in building relationships with all kinds of students. I think youth leaders lack boldness at times because they want to be liked by everyone in their group. I have seen some strong communicators get up front and do an excellent job telling great stories and making students laugh, but there was no boldness in their teaching about Christ. Students walk away from this kind of teaching saying, "That guy was really funny!" But if you asked these students, "What did you learn about God?" I'm afraid they'd say, "Not much."

We must teach the Word of God with boldness and challenge students to become more like Jesus. We cannot give in to the temptation to merely entertain students while we teach. Our students need to hear that the Word of God is practical and relevant to their daily lives. Students want to follow. Teach in such a way that they are able to follow and become more like Christ.

THE CALL TO LEADERSHIP

You are probably reading this book because God has placed on your heart a desire to make a difference in the lives of our youth today. That is a worthy call and one that should not be taken lightly. Student ministry needs leaders like you.

Earlier in this chapter, I made the statement, "Lead, follow, or get out of the way." In order to make that type of statement to others, which at times is necessary, *we* need to be leaders: men and women who are living a life worth following and helping people along the way. As we lead lives worth following, people will indeed begin to follow us. We can then help people draw closer to Christ and challenge them to cross the line of faith.

If you have the gift of spiritual leadership, something inside you will stir with a strong desire to stand up and start leading! If you have the gift of spiritual leadership, you have been *chosen* to lead—and you need to do it! This time it's not just a game of "Follow the Leader"—this time it's all about life. It's about students who want to follow you and need to know where you are taking them.

It's up to us as leaders to establish the vision and help our students see the "island." We need to focus on the right things. As we boldly lead these students, it's up to us to encourage them to be like Christ.

Ezekiel 22:30 says, "I searched for a man among them who should ... stand in the gap before Me for the land, that I should not destroy it; but I found no one" (NASB). God is looking for men and women to stand in the gap for Him. You can be the one. If He has placed a passion for student ministry on your heart, I encourage you to commit to being a leader worth following. If you will lead with this kind of focus and enthusiasm, God will honor your efforts and you will see tremendous changes in your student ministry.

REWIND

What Did You Learn?

The effective youth leader needs to develop and implement three leadership essentials: vision, focus, and confidence.

LEADERSHIP ESSENTIALS	REMEMBER TO ...	GOD'S TRUTH
Vision	• Make it clear and concise • Make it compelling	"Where there is no vision, the people perish." *Proverbs 29:18*
Focus	• Evaluate team performance • Establish "A" Priorities • Strive for excellence • Demonstrate Christlike character	"Do your best to present yourself to God as one approved, a workman who does not need to be ashamed and who correctly handles the word of truth." *2 Timothy 2:15*
Confidence	• Select carefully • Direct with confidence • Teach with authority	"For God did not give us a spirit of timidity, but a spirit of power, of love and of self-discipline." *2 Timothy 1:7*

PAUSE

What Action Will You Take?

- Are you leading with vision?
- Are you a focused leader?
- Are you confident in your leadership?

What's Next?

*You've evaluated your ability to lead.
Who is leading with you?*

SURROUNDING YOURSELF WITH SUPPORT

In 1992, British runner Derek Redmond was dreaming of winning a gold medal in the 400 meters at the Barcelona Summer Olympics. He had trained hard for months to prepare himself for this event.

He took his position on the track for his semifinal heat. I'm sure his mind was focused on that finish line. When the starter gun went off, Derek sprang from the blocks. He was in top form.

As he raced down the backstretch, he heard a pop. The hamstring muscle in his right leg had failed him. The excruciating pain sent him to his knees. Imagine the disappointment he felt! As Derek rolled on the ground in agony, runner after runner passed him.

Derek was determined, though, to finish the race. Slowly, he got back on his feet to begin the long, painful limp to the finish line. The fans began cheering him on.

One fan was especially moved by the scene before him. He dashed from the stands and onto the track to help the injured runner. This fan was Derek's dad, Jim. Jim Redmond steadied his son and together they walked the final eighty meters. Together they crossed the finish line. Derek had found the support he needed to finish the race.

You, too, have decided to run a race. It's called student ministry. You have prepared and trained hard to run this race. You may be in the starting blocks, waiting for the gun to signal the start of the race. Or maybe you have sprinted out of the blocks and are running full speed ahead, hoping for stamina to finish the race. You may even be on the third lap and pacing yourself for the finish line. Wherever you are in the race, God's Word tells us to

". . . run with perseverance the race marked out for us" (Heb. 12:1b). There will be times when we get weary and want to quit, but God wants us to persevere.

I believe we can persevere to a certain point on our own through discipline, authenticity, prayer, time in God's Word, and personal growth. But I also believe we need people around us who are willing and available to help us run the race God has called us to run. There will be times when we will need someone to pick us up, just as Derek Redmond needed his dad. Other times, we will just want someone to run alongside us. In Scripture, God encourages us to not run the race alone; we need other people who will run the race with us and encourage, protect, and support us.

Who is running the race with you? Are there people who will come to your side in a time of need or simply cheer you on in your ministry? I hope you have already identified some running partners. This chapter will focus on five different groups of people who can help you run the race of student ministry and win.

PRAYER TEAM SUPPORT

I'll never forget a gift I received from a student leader in southern California. This mature, godly young woman gave me a gift of prayer: the commitment to pray for me, my family, and the ministry every day for an entire year. She followed up by regularly adding new prayer requests to her list. Her gift marked my life and my ministry.

That experience showed me the value and power of prayer in a new way. I decided from then on that I would search for a few men and women each ministry season who would commit to pray for me and the ministry. Building a prayer team has become a meaningful, vital part of my ministry. The prayers of these men and women have no doubt covered and protected me over the years. Without this prayer cover, I know I would be more susceptible to the attacks of the Enemy. Their desire to support the ministry through prayer is invaluable to me.

I do not spend a lot of time with these people individually, and the members of the team change every year, but I do send them letters and keep them informed of what is happening in the ministry, as well as share prayer requests. I know that each team member is committed and passionate about prayer. I value each one of them and am so grateful for the important role they play in student ministry.

I hope you too will consider building a prayer team. God has gifted some people in your church to be prayer warriors. They are the faithful ones who walk closely with God and believe in the power of prayer. There are some people who have a heart for high school students but, because of time commitment, age, or season of life, cannot commit to regularly serving in your ministry. You need to find these people and offer to them an opportunity to serve the body of Christ through the ministry of prayer. In this way they can faithfully offer requests and praises to God and undergird your ministry.

> Mastering the art of prayer, like any other art, will take time, and the amount of time we allocate to it will be the true measure of our conception of its importance. We always contrive to find time for that which we deem most important.
>
> J. Oswald Sanders, *Spiritual Leadership* (Chicago: Moody Bible Institute, 1989), 104.

If you lead a staff, encourage your staff members to build their own support prayer teams, too. A few years ago, Troy, our programming director, brought a friend to our summer camp. I asked him what role his friend was serving in, and Troy said, "Bo, he's here to pray all week." I was excited to see that Troy, too, understood the importance of prayer support.

A few years ago, we started a parents prayer team called PIPS (Parents in Prayer for Students). Every month, a group of parents representing the various campus teams would meet for prayer on a Tuesday night. Prior to the meeting, each campus team would write down specific prayer requests as well as praises for answered prayer. These parents then took the requests and spent time in prayer for the ministry.

It was especially powerful when the parent prayer group would meet on target nights (a night when the gospel is shared). Just knowing that they were meeting and praying in a room under the auditorium during our program gave me supernatural confidence to share the gospel with boldness. I knew they were praying for God's truth to be communicated clearly and with power and that the Enemy was being rebuked. It was prayer cover that God honored time and time again as many students made decisions to trust Christ on those nights.

Look for people who are passionate about prayer. Be careful of people who say, "I'll pray for you and your ministry," but don't really mean it. I think this phrase gets tossed around too casually, just like "Have a good day." On a number of occasions, I have caught myself saying this to people and then not following up with prayer. You need people on your prayer team who will regularly, authentically pray for you and the needs of your ministry.

ELDER SUPPORT

Student ministers have told me, "My elders don't understand me or student ministry and they don't support what I do." I like to respond by asking, "Well, have you ever talked with your elders about student ministry and informed them about what it is you are doing?" Surprisingly, many of these ministers shake their head no. It's time we realized that elders are not the enemies; rather they form another group of people who can lend support to your ministry.

It is your responsibility to paint the ministry vision to your elders and tell them stories about your ministry to high school students. If you are a pastor-supported church instead of an elder-driven church, then do the same with the pastor. Often elders are several generations away from students and not as current on adolescent trends.

Sometimes elders aren't supportive because they do not have the right information. I would encourage you to try to identify one elder you connect with and to whom you feel comfortable talking. To begin building a relationship with this elder, you may want to take him or her out to lunch and share stories about how God is changing students' lives. You could even bring a student with you to tell his or her story!

I try to keep the eight elders of my church regularly informed on what is happening ministry-wide and letting them know the direction we are headed. I have identified one person, Dick, as my primary liaison who has a passion for high school ministry, in part because his daughter's life was changed through this ministry. He also realizes that the students in the ministry today will be key leaders in the church ten years from now.

Dick has shown me tremendous support and been a great source of encouragement. Last summer, our ministry suffered the tragic deaths of a leader and a student in a car accident. Dick attended both of those funerals. Just having him there provided me with strength and comfort during a difficult and emotional time.

He has also encouraged me with phone calls that always seem to come at exactly the right time. One such call came after a long day of meetings and I was feeling discouraged. Unknown to me, a woman had written a letter to the elders expressing her gratitude for the ministry of Student Impact and how it had affected her daughter in several positive ways. Dick called me and said, "Bo, you are making a huge difference. Don't ever forget that." His call boosted my spirits on a day when they were low.

The elders at my church are an important part of my support team. I need Dick and the rest of the elders to know me and my heart so that they can support the ministry and understand why I do what I do. When they know me, trust can develop. Dick said, "When I know a leader's heart, see that his or her gifts are perfectly suited for a certain position, and observe humility in his or her life, I can back off because I trust this leader and I know the product will be right." I'm thankful the elders know me and trust me and understand the "whys" of the ministry.

I have also experienced what it feels like to not have the support of the elders. When I lived in California, I was excited to start a student ministry that would be seeker-sensitive. I began planning and moving ahead, but, unwisely, without first building elder support. It was a confusing time for the elders and they did not understand what I was trying to do. Once I met with the elders and shared my vision with them, they began to understand and see my heart for student ministry. They also were able to better understand me and who I am. It's so easy to be misunderstood without this support.

Elders don't have to understand popular music or how to best reach students, but they *do* need to be kept informed about the right information. They *do* need to understand our hearts for ministry. They *do* need to understand that students are becoming fully devoted followers of Christ. They *do* need to understand the struggles we face in student ministry.

Dick works in the construction field as a site manager. In many ways, he says, his role there is similar to his role as an elder. He said, "In both arenas, I am a facilitator helping gifted people do their job effectively. It's a team effort. I've never built anything alone in construction or in ministry. In ministry, you cannot be the person God wants you to be all alone. We're in the trenches together."

This statement is so true! We cannot do ministry alone. I am privileged to be supported by such a wise and godly man as well as the rest of the elder board at my church. When the battles come and conflicts arise, my back is covered because the elders know me and trust me. Have you taken steps to build trust with your elders? If not, I would strongly encourage you to do so. Your elders can become a vital part of your support team.

PASTOR SUPPORT

Times have certainly changed since your pastor was a high school student. Back then, his biggest struggles may have been finding a date for the prom or getting the keys to the family station wagon on Saturday night. Today, high school students are bombarded daily by the media, their peers, and society with messages urging them to conform to the culture around them. As with the elders, it is your responsibility to keep the pastor informed about the pressures students are facing today and to paint a vision to reach students with the love of Jesus Christ.

Too often, communication between pastor and youth minister breaks down. Instead of the pastor's hearing about God's activity in the lives of high school students, he hears about what went wrong: the hall light that was broken at the outreach; the Sunday school rooms that were messed up; or that the deacons found gum on the carpet in the auditorium. Instead, make it a top priority to tell your pastor inspiring, positive stories about what is happening in the lives of your students so he can see that high school ministry is its own mission field.

I feel extremely fortunate to have Bill Hybels as my senior pastor. We share a common passion in high school ministry. Over twenty years ago, Bill led a dynamic high school ministry called Son City. As it continued to grow and life after life was changed by God's grace, students wanted a place to bring their parents so that they, too, could be changed by God's amazing grace. Bill followed God's leadings to start a church for these unchurched adults, and Willow Creek Community Church was formed.

Because of Bill's background in high school ministry, he understands what I am trying to do and, most of the time, the reasons why. But he is no longer in student ministry. I need to communicate with him and keep him current on student ministry with today's youth. I do not meet on a regular basis with Bill, but I do try my best to keep him informed in various ways. A while ago, I asked Bill, "What is the most effective way to keep you informed about the ministry in light of our schedules?" He told me that written information would be the best way and that he would read whatever I sent him and respond. And that's exactly how it's worked. Anytime I have sent something to Bill, he has always responded to me and given me the leadership direction and encouragement I need. When I do meet with him face-to-face, I share stories of life change with him and how God is working in the ministry.

What is the best way to build a relationship with your pastor? Everyone's situation is different. Find what works for you and stick to it.

The Bible says that we are to submit to our leaders. Hebrews 13:17 says:

> Obey your leaders and submit to their authority. They keep watch over you as men who must give an account. Obey them so that their work will be a joy, not a burden, for that would be of no advantage to you.

God has placed the pastor in your church to shepherd and teach the flock. As student ministers, we must support him and do what we can to be team players. We must stop blaming him for the lack of growth if our ministry is stagnant or questioning his every decision. God designed the church to live in true community. Our role is to do our part in building and preserving that unity by respecting those in leadership.

PARENT SUPPORT

"Why is the program on a school night?"

"Why is my son in a small group and who is his leader?"

"Why did you plan camp during our family vacation?"

"Why do my daughter's emotions keep changing each hour?"

"Why did my son end up in the emergency room from your competition?"

Why, why, why. Parents seem to have a natural tendency to ask a lot of questions that start with the word *why*. If you have not noticed this phenomenon, just wait! Your phone will soon begin to ring with parents who have lists of questions for you. You'd better be prepared! Parents need to know the "whys" of what you are doing.

I try to keep parents as informed as possible about what is happening in the ministry and to notify them about upcoming events. I send a monthly newsletter to all the parents of our students that has a calendar of key dates as well as information on the ministry of Student Impact. I try to do my part in answering the "whys" through this newsletter. But I have learned that I need help from other parents.

Building a network of parents is an invaluable part of my ministry support team. A team of parents who believe in me and what I am doing can help answer some of those "why" questions. This group can talk parent-to-parent to those with questions and defuse any confusion or concerns. This allows me to focus on ministering to students. I am certainly available to any parent who wishes to talk to me, but my parent support team is capable of handling many of the issues that arise. They put out many of the little fires without my direct involvement.

In choosing parents for my support team, I look for people with whom I resonate and who I know will support me. Every ministry season is different. Some years, I have tremendous parent support; other years are weaker. A few years ago, God blessed me with two tremendous parent leaders.

Karen and Jim became involved in Student Impact through their two sons, Chris and Terry. A friend from Chris's high school had invited Chris to try Student Impact, and he began regularly attending, often bringing his younger brother, Terry. Over time, Karen and Jim noticed changes in their boys' attitudes. Some nights, when Jim walked up to their bedrooms, he found both Chris and Terry reading their Bibles. This had never happened before! Eventually, Karen and Jim began attending Willow Creek and are key core members today. A few years ago, they stepped forward to launch a parents' ministry as their way of contributing to the high school ministry.

One of the first things Karen, Jim, and I discussed involved boundaries and expectations: What were they expecting from me and what could I expect from them? What exactly was their playing field? We decided that the parents' ministry would not function as "youth sponsors," but as a supportive role. Jim has told me that "one of the hardest things to convey to parents who want to jump in and be a part of the decision-making is that we're not here to make decisions or determine which way the ministry should go. We're here to support the leadership." This distinction is so important!

Parents on the support team can certainly voice their opinions, but if they feel the music is too loud or not the kind they like, they need to realize it's not their role to question or change it. Too often, student pastors give in to the pressure placed by parents, and they become responders instead of proactive thinkers. In a healthy ministry, parents can be part of the team without running the team.

Finding the right parents and setting appropriate parameters are the keys to building an effective parent support team. It's imperative to find parents who understand the definition of a support role and are comfortable with its parameters. Once the right team has formed, you'll be amazed at how they can help your ministry. I'm so thankful for my team of parents and the numerous ways they serve. For example, at our summer camp and winter retreat our parents' team assists with many details, from assisting students checking in to making sure they're in their rooms by the set curfew to organizing the meals. During the ministry year, they help on Tuesday nights with administration; direct the flow of students between competition, teamroom, and program; and are available to answer any questions from visitors or other parents.

In the past, the parents' team has also assisted me in planning a Parents' Night at Student Impact. This is a night where parents can observe and participate with their son or daughter in the different components of the night: competition, teamroom, and the program. Parents are invited to see what we do. It's an evening that builds a bridge with the parents of our students and gives them a glimpse of student ministry.

We are always looking for more effective ways to get our parents involved. Some of the parents currently involved have continued serving even though their children have graduated from high school. You may discover some parents in that situation. Make it a priority to build relationships with a few parents who can support your efforts in student ministry and, together, help reach high school students for Christ.

LEADER SUPPORT

It's difficult—virtually impossible—to lead a ministry without leader support. Perhaps you have experienced a lack of leader support and discovered the massive drain it takes on your energy level. You can only gain leadership support by having a life filled with integrity and worth following. Leaders need to see your shepherd's heart and know that you want to help them along the way.

Supportive leaders have your best interest in mind and an "I won't take you down" mind-set. They live out Philippians 2:2, rising to the challenge to be "like-minded, having the same love, being one in spirit and purpose." Supportive leaders are on the same page regarding your ministry vision, mission, and strategy.

I was introduced to Student Impact through a friend who attended Willow Creek. He was involved in Student Impact as a volunteer and encouraged me to check it out while I was in town. When I saw all of the kids, the program, and the activities that the students were involved in, I got excited and wanted to take the idea home with me. I gathered all of the information I could about this new way to do student ministry.

I was very fortunate, because I had just started working at a church where our senior pastor was young, open-minded, and had been in youth ministry himself for over fourteen years. The church I had been in previously was of a traditional mind-set and viewed being creative and open to change as a threat rather than an opportunity to reach young people for Christ. I was excited to have the opportunity to build a youth ministry rather than creating another youth group similar to the one I had been involved in at my previous church.

As I returned home from Willow Creek, one of the first things I did was surround myself with people who had a heart for youth ministry and were willing to do whatever it took to reach the youth in our community. I began planting the vision and the dreams of what God had given us to do into these people's hearts and minds. As time passed on, the excitement grew, and we began to recruit volunteers to help us start our own Impact-style ministry. A lot of time, effort, and prayer was put into preparing for the new ministry we were about to jump into. Once we had our workers and volunteers in place, we planned our kickoff date. We promoted and pushed this idea with our students and within our community until we were ready to go. Our first night was a great success. There were students everywhere, the program and competition went smoothly, and we were excited about the way God had blessed us.

Garland Robertson, Impact Ministries of South Florida,
Flamingo Road Baptist Church, Fort Lauderdale, FL

We all need people in our life with whom we can process our ministry frustrations, but it saddens me when I hear other leaders bad-mouth their leader without any intention of acting on it. The Bible is very clear about the way we are to handle conflict and discord. Matthew 18 tells us we are to go to the person who has grieved our spirit and work it out with him or her in private. If that fails, we are to bring in a neutral third party to help us work through the conflict. If even that fails, then the elders must get involved.

Conflict can be handled appropriately only in a safe environment. I regularly tell my leaders that they can write me a note and put "SOS" on the envelope. I will respond within twenty-four hours. I also encourage any leader who has a problem with my leadership or something I have done to apply Matthew 18 and come to me first. I want that leader to feel safe enough to say to me, "Bo, I disagree with you on this issue and here is the reason why." Sometimes it is okay to agree to disagree.

Recently, I made some adjustments in our small group structure, values, and strategic plan. I knew that when we shared the "whys" it would take time for our students and leaders to get on board. One small group leader couldn't agree to some of the adjustments. He told his campus director (who leads a campus team) that he had listened to the reasoning, but wanted to do things his own way. He could not and would not comply with the changes.

It seemed we had hit a wall with this leader. I sat down with both the small group leader and the campus director and asked the small group leader, "What don't you understand? What is the issue?" Our conversation went well. I made it clear what the nonnegotiables were and everything seemed fine.

Everything was not fine. I got reports back a few weeks later that this leader was still not supporting the changes. I sat down with him again and was more direct with my concern and questioning. I could tell he was not resonating with me and what I was saying. It came to the point where I had to say, "Lead, follow, or get out of the way." I asked him to take a break and pull out of ministry for awhile. I knew I had to draw a line.

We went through some chaos with the students in this leader's small group. He had been a great leader. Several weeks later, I saw this leader at church. I asked him how he was doing and told him we missed his leadership in the ministry.

Last summer, he came to camp. He approached me and said, "Bo, I see it now. I didn't quite understand it then. I was stubborn." We laughed and shook hands and committed to building the kingdom together.

In ministry, situations like these will happen. Sometimes they do not end as happily as this one did. Sometimes leaders will not come back. It is important however, to establish what is nonnegotiable and what is flexible. Listening and discernment are key to leading leaders and building a student ministry.

RUNNING THE RACE TOGETHER

If you have ever run before, you know how much more enjoyable it is to have a running partner. When you come to the finish line together, there is a sense of team. Building a support team is so important. Students benefit from seeing you "running" in harmony with other leaders from your church.

We use some phrases in Student Impact that capture the ideas in this chapter: "One hand up" (when you need help); "one hand back" (when you look for someone you can help); and "hands in the middle" (when we work as a team). Our ministry strives for this; we are a team of people who need to support one other. We are the body of Christ and each of us is uniquely gifted to help build the kingdom. I think it is exciting when students see us functioning as a God-honoring team. When they see that we are together, they desire to be a part of that.

I encourage you to do whatever is necessary to get your prayer team, elders, pastor, parents, and leaders on the same page. If needed, make the tough calls. It pleases the heart of God when we work as one.

The race is on to win high school students for Jesus Christ. The Enemy is doing all he can to injure us and prevent us from running the race. We must realize that the real battle is not with our elders, pastor, parents, or leaders; we are in a spiritual battle. Satan does not want us to be a team, and crafts destructive ways to pull us apart. We can't let the Enemy deceive us any longer!

I know you want to run the race. First Corinthians 9:24–27 offers this challenge:

> Do you not know that in a race all the runners run, but only one gets the prize? Run in such a way as to get the prize. Everyone who competes in the games goes into strict training. They do it to get a crown that will not last; but we do it to get a crown that will last forever.

Derek Redmond was pursuing an earthly crown that tarnishes and rots away. We are pursuing a crown that will last for all of eternity: sharing God's free gift of salvation with high school students and helping them become fully devoted followers of Him. It's an incredible privilege! We have been chosen to run the race. Let's commit to doing so with support teams in place.

Rewind

What Did You Learn?

We can run the ministry race more effectively if we build support teams: prayer, elders, pastor, parents, and leaders.

SUPPORT TEAM	STEPS TO TAKE
Prayer	• Recognize the need for prayer support • Look for prayer warriors
Elders	• Realize they are not the enemies • Keep elders informed • Identify one elder liaison
Pastor	• Keep pastor current on contemporary youth culture • Communicate, communicate, communicate
Parents	• Find parents who resonate with your vision • Determine playing field and expectations
Leaders	• Locate leaders living out Philippians 2:2 • Practice Matthew 18 for conflict resolution

PAUSE

What Action Will You Take?

Your pastor or elder board are probably already established, but it's up to you to choose people to be on your prayer, parent, and leader support teams. Think for a moment about the people in your life. Who can you ask for help in running the race? What names come to mind? Write them down here:

PRAYER	PARENT	LEADER

FAST FORWARD

What's Next?

You've evaluated your purpose as a leader. Do you know your ministry's purpose?

MINISTER WITH PURPOSE

2

Maintaining a Youth Group vs. Building a Student Ministry

If you could build the most awesome roller coaster ride around the world, how would you do it?" I had just posed this question to the high school students I was leading in southern California. All the resources needed, like land and money, would be provided. I was curious to hear how they would respond.

"Oh, I'd build it right over Disneyland where everyone could see it!" yelled Coleman.

"Let's make it reach high up in space and then come down and go underwater," added Alex.

"I'd make sure it was so high and radical that only the bravest would dare go on it!" said Mary Jo.

One by one the students continued to respond, and the answers became more and more outrageous. I waited anxiously to hear how Troy would answer. This was his first visit to the group. I was his football coach at the time and had built a relationship with him on and off the field.

"I'd make it drop two hundred feet backward with six one-hundred-and-eighty-degree turns," commented Troy.

The group was catching on! I was trying to teach the students the value of vision and thinking "outside the box." What I didn't realize then was that this illustration, however far-fetched, affected Troy's life in an amazing way. He had grown up in another local church, but had become disillusioned with church and Christianity. God allowed me to instill in Troy the power of vision and what that could mean in his personal life. Here's how Troy tells the rest of the story:

> A friend invited me to attend Bo's new student ministry.
> He was one of the football coaches at my school, and I thought

he was pretty cool. At the first meeting, Bo stood up front and asked us to imagine building the biggest roller coaster ride. At first, I thought, "This is crazy! Why waste your time dreaming?" After a while, though, I started participating and really getting into the discussion.

I'll never forget what happened next. Bo opened his Bible and, with passion in his voice, told us how God was looking for young men and women to stand in the gap for Him. Bo also assured us that God had promised to provide all that we needed to build something more exciting than any roller coaster ride. We could build the greatest student ministry in southern California by providing a place where lives could change and students would be excited to invite friends. Bo told us that all of us could be used by God to become difference-makers for the kingdom. He looked at each one of us and asked: "Do you want to be a part?"

Something clicked inside of me! There was purpose behind all that Bo was saying. I learned that I had a purpose as a Christian! That purpose was to grow in Christ and share Him with others. This was a new concept to me, even though I had been a Christian for many years.

By God's grace, I haven't lost the vision. The ride is still being assembled, now at Willow Creek Community Church. I never thought I'd play a part in the assembly. It really has been quite an adventure!

Troy and the rest of the students realized their role in the group was to become more than just attenders. They began to understand their *purpose* as Christians. The power of vision started to became real in each of these students' lives. They began to take seriously the opportunity to help build the ministry and serve the Lord with their gifts. I saw their faith grow as God began to use them to build the kingdom. I saw many of those students from that original group called to full-time ministry. Troy was one of those students, and we have been partners in reaching high school students for Christ ever since. On a recent trip to California I was invited to attend a new church that was meeting in a house. As I looked around the room, I was amazed to see many of the same faces that were in that room years ago when we dreamed of building a roller coaster. These same men and women are now building a church and are committed to making a difference.

Too often we, as youth leaders, set limitations on our students and do not give them the freedom to dream big dreams. We forget to remind our students that God wants them to become differ-ence-makers, and that there is no limit to what He can do through each of them. Their youth does not exclude them from being God's ambassadors. First Timothy 4:12 states, "Don't let anyone look down on you because you are young, but set an example for the believers in speech, in life, in love, in faith and in purity." Students *can* and *want* to make a difference with their lives. We must make sure to provide our students with training and opportunities so that they *will* become difference-makers.

In this chapter, I want to remind you that God has called you to be a youth leader, not a baby-sitter. Your job is not to keep your students safe, comfortable, or in a box so that you can manage them. You need to lead your students because, if you don't, you will end up *maintaining* a youth group instead of *building* a student ministry. I want to pose the same question to you that I asked that group of high school students fifteen years ago: "Do you want to be a part of building a student ministry?"

EVALUATE YOUR GROUP

What exactly are the differences between maintaining a youth group and building a student ministry? Aren't we really talking about the same thing? Not at all! Maintaining a group and building a ministry are on opposite ends of the continuum.

Take a moment to think about the group of students you are currently leading. Have you ever cast a vision to your group and told them where you are taking them? Would your students even know what vision is all about? The test on the following page will assist you in evaluating the group you are leading and give you a chance to assess your students.

What did you discover? Were you confused, encouraged, or disappointed? I have shared this evaluation with youth leaders around the country and I usually hear one of those three responses. Some leaders are confused because they lead students described in both columns one and two and are not sure how to adjust to meet the needs of each group. Other leaders are encour-aged because they can see they're headed in the right direction, but have hit sticking points in growth and leadership. Some are disappointed when they realize they checked mostly boxes in col-umn one. Whatever your initial response, I hope this evaluation has helped you to honestly evaluate and assess where your stu-dents are. It is only after answering these kinds of questions that

■ What Kind of Group Do You Lead? ■

Check below which of the two statements is most
true of the students you lead at your church:

Statement 1:	**Statement 2:**
◇ My group is made up primarily of students who spectate when it comes to God's work.	◇ My students participate in serving God actively. (Matt. 9:27)
◇ My students get very exctied about different activities we do as a group that are fun and entertaining.	◇ My students get fired up about seeing ministry happen to their friends. (Hebrews 10:24)
◇ My students are introverted and rarely invite non-Christian friends—they don't have many non-Christian friends.	◇ My students have compassion for their friends and have friendships with non-Christians. (Matt. 9:36)
◇ I feel often like my students come because they have to or because they are forced to attend.	◇ My students attend because they want to be there. (Matt. 9:23)
◇ My students complain a lot about our group.	◇ My students are involved in making necessary changes to make our group better. (Hebrews 10:25)
◇ Most of the time I feel all alone in running my group.	◇ My students take ownership, and I feel that they sense that the ministry is partly theirs. (Luke 16:10)
◇ My students attend whenever it's convenient for them.	◇ My students are there—they are committed. (John 15)
◇ My students are not available to participate because they do not see the group as a priority.	◇ My students are available and responsive to me. (Matt. 6:24)
◇ My students sit bored at the teaching of God's Word.	◇ My students are teachable. (Deut. 31:12)
◇ My students see no ultimate purpose beyond fellowship for our group.	◇ My students have a vision for reaching the lost on their campus. (Matt. 19:26)
◇ My students like their Christian friends but are not challenging to each other.	◇ My students intentionally disciple other students. (2 Tim. 2:2)

you will be able to take the necessary steps to move from maintaining a youth group toward building a vibrant student ministry.

MAINTAINING A YOUTH GROUP

Of course, many effective ministries may use the term "youth group." But in this chapter, I'm going to use that term to describe a particular kind of group I have observed time and again. When I refer to a youth group, I mean a group that fits the following description.

First, *a youth group is activity-driven.* These maintenance-style youth groups revolve around activities. The calendar is the prevailing force as students hop from one activity or event to the next without ever knowing what direction the leader is taking them.

Think about your last activity. Why did you do it? Did it fulfill any of your ministry's objectives? Was it a fun event planned simply to fill the calendar or was there a well-thought out purpose behind it? I'm not saying that activities cannot be fun. But if that is the sole reason for gathering, it's time you took a harder look at what you are doing and why.

Second, *a youth group sticks with tradition and forgets to ask the question why.* I enjoy lifting weights; it has become a lifestyle for me. Years ago, when I had just started, I would observe others in the gym to see how they lifted. I remember watching one very large guy do the "lat" machine. He took the seat off the machine, sat on the floor, grabbed the bar a certain way, and began working on his back. When it was my turn to use this machine, I sat on the floor the exact same way and grabbed the bar just like this guy had done. This continued on for weeks.

One day, I lifted with a friend. He watched me do the "lat" machine and asked, "Bo, why do you do the machine like that?" I answered, "Well, I saw the big boy doing it like that." My friend laughed at me and said, "The reason he sits on the floor is because he is too big to fit on the seat! His thighs would hit the bar."

If only I had asked the question why, instead of following a routine without thinking about it. I have observed that youth groups, too, often fail to ask or answer this question. They seem content to let traditions carry on for tradition's sake. They say, "We've always done Sunday school this way. It's tradition!" and keep doing what they know is not working because they are afraid to ask why. It's time to ask why you are doing ministry the way you are. As a ministry leader, you need to know where you are headed and why and how you plan to get there.

Third, *a youth group lacks vision and direction.* If you don't know where God is leading you with your ministry, how can you expect your students to follow? If you lack vision, your students will have no idea where the ministry is going. Too many youth groups are activity-driven with little thought given to the purpose of most activities. Vision brings purpose to those activities and give students direction for the future.

I meet and talk with many youth pastors who are so wrapped up in planning activities that they're burned out and ready to throw in the towel. This shouldn't happen! We need to allow God an opportunity to give us His vision for our ministry and ask Him for direction. This will fill us up and give us purpose, not burn us out.

Fourth, *a youth group tends to focus inward, which can lead to stagnation and minimum growth.* A youth group can become a comfortable bunch of people to hang out with, but nothing more. Students become casual in their spiritual life because they are presented with few opportunities to get out of their comfort zone and stretch their faith. Everyone in the group calls himself a Christian, so the group members stick together on campus, rarely feeling compassion for the lost. The clique is secure—why chance ruining the dynamics by inviting a non-Christian into the group? The group never grows because compassion for the lost never grows.

One of our leaders left last year to attend a seminary in California. He interviewed at several churches for an internship in student ministry. During one of the church interviews, he asked about outreach programs in their current student ministry. The man interviewing him said, "We don't deal with seekers. You'll be working with fourth-generation Christian kids, and that's who we want you to work with." This church had no vision to reach the non-Christian students in their community! It was stuck in a youth group mentality.

BUILDING A STUDENT MINISTRY

I have seen so many youth groups fall into the patterns I just described that I don't even use the term "youth group" to describe what we do in Student Impact. Instead, we consciously identify our task as building a *student ministry.* I'd like to list several characteristics of a student ministry. This is, by no means, an exhaustive list.

First, *a student ministry is purpose-driven.* Every event, activity, and meeting has a clear purpose. Activities are not added simply to fill the calendar, but rather to lead the students according to the ministry's God-given vision and plan. Students know that every activity has purpose, and leaders are not afraid to ask themselves "Why are we doing this?" and "Is it working?"

Car rallies are popular campus team events in our ministry. Last month, one of our teams held a car rally. The leaders had determined that the team needed to come together and have some fun, but with the definite purpose in mind to challenge the students in evangelism. Core students were encouraged to bring a non-Christian friend as a way to introduce that friend to Student Impact. Students broke down into teams and were challenged to decipher ten clues hidden all around town. Afterward, the whole team met at a restaurant for pizza and fellowship. One of the leaders gave a brief testimony and then explained what Student Impact is all about, inviting the new students to come to Impact (our Tuesday night program targeted to non-Christians) the following week.

I smiled as this leader recounted the success of his team's car rally. Students had walked away with more than just finding crazy clues around town; many of them had had intentional conversations about spiritual things with the friends they had brought.

Perhaps the most significant of all values communicated through the Willow Creek/Student Impact model is that of intentional ministry. Developing a more successful youth ministry is not necessarily achieved by solving the "What do I do?" (programming) or "How do I do it?" (methodology) questions typically asked by youth workers across the board. Rather, as Willow Creek/Student Impact has demonstrated, it is more important to answer the question of purpose, namely, "Why should I do it?" (intentional ministry). Programs and methodology must flow out of the answer to this most significant question, and naturally then be determined individually in the context of the setting in which the youth worker finds himself.

Mark DeYmaz, Fellowship Student Ministries,
Fellowship Bible Church, Little Rock, AR

At our recent leadership conference, I talked with a few student pastors about being purposeful and asking the question why. Steve told me he used to simply maintain a youth group. "But asking the question why," he said, "eliminated pointless activities, freeing me to do things that I had previously ignored."

"You know," a student pastor named Rick said, "A lot of people hate the question why. I have had to learn how to deal with people who choose not to even ask it. Asking why helps us in every aspect of ministry."

Joe told me that he recently began asking the question why in order to become more purpose-driven. "Too often, I used to respond to kids and give them what they wanted instead of what they needed," Joe said. "Since I have started asking why, I have weeded out a lot of useless activities and have been able to become very focused in what I am aiming for."

Gary told me that asking why has given him more confidence to lead. He stated, "It has enabled me to become more confident in the Lord's plan for me."

Asking why seems like such a simple question—but it is one we cannot afford to neglect to ask or answer.

Second, *a student ministry's leaders communicate the vision.* I make it a priority to communicate our ministry's vision, mission, and strategy to our core students at least four times a year. I feel so deeply about all God has entrusted to our ministry that I'm fired up to share it with them! It is my responsibility as their leader to tell them *where* we are headed as a ministry (vision), *why* we do what we do (mission), and *how* we are going to accomplish it (strategy). Chapters 7 and 8 will further explain vision, mission, and strategy.

Our students enjoy hearing the vision communicated clearly. When the vision is cast, students turn from spectators into players. They understand their role and see the ministry's larger purpose. They can then charge out of the grandstands onto the playing field, ready to get into the game and play their part. They feel ownership and realize that their participation is needed to turn the vision into reality.

Gretchen was one such student who charged out of the grandstands and onto the playing field. When she understood the ministry vision, Gretchen could hardly wait to become a player. Here's how she responded and owned the ministry vision:

After hearing the vision, I developed such a compassion for my friends and an excitement about the opportunity to introduce them to Christianity. I would invite as many friends as I could fit in my van—usually about seven or eight—to Impact on Tuesday nights. If they told me they had practice until 6:00 P.M. and wouldn't have time to go home, eat, and change, I would pick them up at the high school after practice and bring them home for dinner or make them a sandwich to eat in the car. I would usually spend from the time I got home from school until the time I left for church making phone calls, praying, making meals, and driving.

Gretchen was a student waiting to be led. Once she caught the vision, she became a key player. She has graduated from college and is now back serving as an intern. Communicating vision is one way to inspire and motivate all the Gretchens in your ministry.

Third, *a student ministry is compassionate for the lost and excited about evangelism.* After students' hearts have been changed by God's grace and they have learned how to walk with God, it is crucial that they learn the importance of evangelism and how to reach their non-Christian friends. This is often where youth groups get stuck. The focus needs to become outward, not inward. Jesus Christ commanded us in Matthew 28:19 to "go and make disciples." In student ministry, we must foster a sincere desire and hunger in students to see God work in their individual lives so that they can make a difference in their friends' lives.

Eric had a friend in his gym class last year named Chris whom he had invited to Impact several times. Finally, Chris said he would go. Eric was so excited. He told me what happened the day Chris went to Impact:

> I called Chris after school that day and he wasn't home. I panicked! I started praying real hard. God had shown me that Chris needed to go that night. I called him every two minutes, but he still wasn't home. My dad was in the car, ready to drive me to Impact, when I decided to try Chris one more time. I dialed the phone and Chris picked it up! I told him we were coming right over to pick him up. It was a great night for him to learn more about God, and on June 11 he committed his life to Christ.

We teach our core students about the value of evangelism, and it's exciting when they can experience stories like Eric's. Every

February, we take our core students on a small group retreat called Blast. During the weekend, we cast a vision and encourage everyone to participate in it. The vision is for every student at Blast to begin thinking about one to three non-Christian friends. We challenge our students to write these names down and over the next two weeks to pray for their friends and invite them to the upcoming target night, where the gospel is boldly shared.

Our Christian students see that their non-Christian friends are facing a hopeless eternity. The stakes are high, and our Christian students take this challenge very seriously. It gives them a chance to rally together around a shared vision and a common goal: to see their non-Christian friends come to know Jesus Christ. Our students understand the important role they play to make the vision come to life and are excited to do their part.

> A student ministry carefully considers the kind of environment a student needs in order to feel valued, accepted, and heard.

Fourth, *a student ministry values prayer and worship.* The value placed on prayer and true worship is a key indication of where a ministry stands. So often, youth groups seem afraid to worship and would rather stick with playing games or giving shoulder rubs. In a student ministry, students learn how to really worship the Lord and focus on Him. They learn how to worship and pray individually and corporately. Some of our students say worship on Sunday nights is the highlight of their week!

An adult leader in our ministry who grew up in Student Impact once noted, "I think high school is a great time to really teach kids about worship. We're young enough to be crazy about God as we praise Him, yet old enough to be reverent about it!"

Fifth, *a student ministry meets students' needs for acceptance and accountability.* A student ministry carefully considers the kind of environment a student needs in order to feel valued, accepted, and heard. There are not many places to which a high school student can turn these days to feel affirmed and unconditionally loved. Incorporating small groups can play a big part in meeting these needs.

Jeff, a senior, told me that for years he had looked for friends he could trust completely. So often, when Jeff would confide in a friend he thought he could trust, this friend would go behind his back and tell others. "When I got involved in a small group, I finally found great friends I can tell anything and not worry that they will go and tell everyone else," Jeff exclaimed. Small groups provide students with opportunities to trust and be trusted.

Accountability and "I" ability are also part of small groups, so that a student can be challenged to keep his or her faith strong. At Crystal Lake South High School, girls from one small group sharpen each other in the hallways at school. Every time they see each other, they ask, "Are you going my way?" The response is always, "No, I'm going God's way." It has helped each girl to be reminded of her walk with God and the example she is setting to those around her.

We will focus on small groups in chapter 11 by looking at essential core values and how to structure small groups for any size student ministry.

UNDERSTANDING THE DIFFERENCE

I hope it has become clear to you that a maintenance-style youth group cannot effectively meet the changing needs of today's students. Our youth are crying out for answers and direction in order to cope with many of life's challenges. Students desperately want their lives to have purpose and meaning. If your youth group is merely a comfortable place to hang out, after a while boredom will set in and the students will begin to ask the "why" questions: "Why am I here?" "Why doesn't anyone understand me?" "Why should I learn about Jesus?" "Why should I listen to you?" If you are not able to answer their questions and tell them of their incredible value in the eyes of God and of His plan and purpose for their lives, they will begin to search elsewhere in order to fill their empty souls. Look at what happens *every single day* in the United States:

1,000 unwed teenage girls become mothers
1,106 teenage girls get abortions
4,219 teenagers contract sexually transmitted diseases
500 adolescents begin using drugs
1,000 adolescents experiment with alcohol
6 teens commit suicide
2,200 teens drop out of high school
3,610 teens are assaulted; 80 are raped
135,000 adolescents bring guns or other weapons to school[1]

These statistics are sobering. Youth today are facing a crisis unlike any other time in history. Our society continues to deteriorate, and a whole generation is hanging in the balance. Social analysts have already labeled this generation as drifters filled with apathy and unwilling to commit to much. And yet so much of their apathy is simply a cover for their deeper pain and longing for direction and purpose.

At our student leadership conference, we show a multimedia presentation called "Ball of Confusion." It is a graphic, yet moving depiction of the society and culture in which our students are growing up today. Leaders are touched when they see with new eyes the many pressures our youth are facing. Our hearts need to stay tender and filled with compassion just as Jesus "had compassion on them [the crowds], because they were harassed and helpless, like sheep without a shepherd" (Matt. 9:36).

Do you need to slow down in order to feel compassion for the students you lead? As a youth leader called by God, you have the incredible privilege and unique opportunity to communicate the love of Jesus Christ to a struggling generation! Do you realize what an awesome responsibility you have to boldly proclaim saving grace and give your students a purpose in life? Surveys show that more than two-thirds of all adults who have accepted Christ made their decision to do so before the age of eighteen.[2] The "harvest is plentiful" and the time is now.

MAKING A DIFFERENCE

Too many youth groups have a "been there, done that" attitude in which members are spectators, rather than participants. The students in these groups feel no ownership or responsibility, which makes it easy for them to complain and blame others for everything. They have forgotten what it means to be alive to Christ. They have forgotten that God has called them to be difference-makers. They have lost compassion for their non-Christian friends and forgotten that they have the hope their friends are looking for. They have forgotten who they are and whose they are. They have forgotten that the God of the universe is crazy about them. God loves them and wants to use them to build, if you will, a roller coaster for the kingdom.

I interned with Student Impact from '89 to '90. During my involvement, I became excited about the "seeker" approach to student ministry. When my internship ended, I was eager to implement this approach in an average youth group. The following are principles I've learned in the last five years about the transitions from a maintenance-style youth group to a student ministry:

1. *Timing is everything.* In the course of one week, I moved from a traditional youth group to a "seeker" approach. This resulted in a group of unconvinced church students apathetically bringing their unconvinced non-churched friends. It also created a feeling of resentment among the church students. They felt like they didn't matter and that I was only using them to reach their friends.

2. *Reach out to your churched students.* Help them to see that they matter to God; that God is relevant in their everyday lives; and that the Bible is the map to life. For the first time, we created an outreach program targeting our church students on Sunday mornings.

3. *Build your leadership base.* Share your vision of the ministry with your leaders. Show them how vital they are in making it happen.

4. *Create ministry opportunities for students.* This allows students to become the church. The following are some of the opportunities we have created for students in our church:
   - a monthly nursing home ministry
   - work with a local rescue mission
   - food ministry for needy families

5. *Create a sense of community.* Host monthly small group events to instill a sense of family and to remind students that they matter.

6. *Go public.* Read Matthew 28:20. Lost people matter to God. God tells us to reach them. How do we do it?

Mike Huber, The Alternative Greentree Ministries,
English Creek, NJ, former Student Impact intern

Why have so many students forgotten these truths? This book will help answer some of these questions, but your students may already have the answers you are looking for. All you have to do is ask them! After your next meeting, handpick five of your sharpest students and invite them to stick around for a few extra minutes. Ask them to be honest and open with you and to speak the truth. Ask them some direct questions like:

- Why do you come here?
- Are you bored with our group?
- Are you becoming more like Christ?
- Are my messages hitting the mark?
- Why don't you bring your non-churched friends?
- What would you change today?
- What's stopping you from telling your friends about Christ?
- What do we need to improve or change so that your non-Christian friends will want to come to our group?

Believe me, they will talk! Student love to express their opinions and to feel that their ideas count. It may be tough for you to hear what they have to say, but both you and the students will benefit. When you allow your students to offer suggestions, their level of ownership for the ministry will increase. They will begin to take some personal responsibility for the ministry and start turning their eyes outward instead of inward. They will feel valued and heard, and you will start to see truth. Students will want to be led, and it is up to the leaders to start leading.

I trust the Holy Spirit has reminded you of the tremendous impact you can make in the lives of students by showing them that their lives are purposeful, by casting a vision for your ministry, by training them in evangelism and reaching the lost, by teaching them the value of worship and prayer, and by developing meaningful small groups. It is no small task. We have the opportunity to lead a student ministry that guides students into a deeper relationship with Jesus Christ. What a privilege!

REWIND

What Did You Learn?

It is not enough simply to maintain a youth group. Instead, we are called to build student ministries.

MAINTAINING A YOUTH GROUP	BUILDING A STUDENT MINISTRY
• Activity-driven	• Purpose-driven
• Unclear vision	• Clear vision
• Inward focus/content with "clique"	• Outward focus/compassion for the lost
• Minimum growth	• Consistent growth
• Songs and games	• Worship and prayer
• Keep the traditions	• Ask "Why?" and "Is it working?"
• Busy in the world	• Focused on kingdom work

PAUSE

What Action Will You Take?

Take a moment to reflect on the differences between maintaining a youth group and building a student ministry. How would you define your group? Grab a piece of paper and ask yourself these important questions:

- Am I maintaining a youth group or building a student ministry?
- What are the defining characteristics of the group I am leading?
- What steps can I take to begin (or continue) building a student ministry?
- When was the last time God captured my heart with a vision for student ministry and filled me with compassion?
- Is my vision fresh in my mind and soul, or has it been lost in the pressures and tasks of doing ministry?
- What is God telling me to do with the information I've learned?

FAST FORWARD

What's Next?

You're committed to building a student ministry. How well do you know the students to whom you will minister?

UNDERSTANDING
ADOLESCENT DEVELOPMENT

Although times have changed drastically since we were teenagers, I trust we can still remember, resonate, and empathize with the feelings experienced in adolescence. Most people would agree that adolescence is a strange, confusing time of life; a transitional season in which one is neither child nor adult.

So much is changing during these years that many teenagers wonder when life will be "normal." A teenage girl was quoted as saying, "When will it end—so we can just have a body that looks the same from one week to another?"[1] To be sure, the physical changes a teenager experiences are complex. There are also other dimensions of a teenager's development that we as student ministers need to understand. We must study and learn about how students are developing not only physically but intellectually, emotionally, socially, and spiritually as well.

Psychologists and developmental professionals have observed consistent patterns of behavior in these five areas of adolescent change. Adolescent psychologist Steve Gerali has shared with me his expertise regarding these dimensions of adolescent development. Some of the material in this chapter comes from a seminar he taught at our student leadership conference last year.

The following descriptions are by no means exhaustive. I would encourage you to further study adolescent development and become a student of your students. You will then be better equipped to understand and care for them in order to effectively meet their needs.

PHYSICAL DEVELOPMENT

"Help! My body is freaking out!"

My fourteen-year-old son Brandon is in a band called *The Unbendable Coathangers*. He recently wrote a song called "Teenager." Here are a few lines from the song:

> *I've got a cracking voice and I've got acne;*
> *I got all these problems and girls running at me;*
> *I have to look the best, there can't be a single thing wrong;*
> *I try to catch the bus, but it's long gone;*
> *I'm becoming a teenager, it's pretty hard to do.*

As I read the lyrics to this song, I had to laugh. It reminded me of all the changes I went through as a teenager. It captures some of what becoming a teenager is all about.

I remember one day in my ninth-grade English class in particular. The teacher called on me to read out loud. I started to read, and before I even finished a paragraph my voice had cracked five times. I didn't know if I was singing opera or what! I could hardly wait to finish reading.

The adolescent years are a time of tremendous physical changes. Puberty puts the body in rapid overdrive. Hormones kick in, causing massive growth spurts and the start of the sex drive.

These vast internal physical changes also manifest themselves externally: size, weight, body proportions, coordination, sex organs, voice, and strength all begin to change. The rate at which these changes occur varies from student to student, but generally girls mature faster than boys. A student's weight will fluctuate, and girls are especially self-conscious of this change. Guys and girls are also somewhat clumsy and awkward because of these rapid growth spurts.

Another external change common to teenagers is acne. This occurs when the skin's sebaceous glands are active and produce oils at a rate faster than the skin's pores are able to open. The ducts of these glands become plugged and infected, resulting in acne. Acne is a problem for many students, and it can affect their self-esteem in a number of negative ways.

How does the physical development of teenagers affect the way you lead and organize your ministry?

Ministry Applications to Think About

When programming or planning activities, be sure not to ostracize students by forcing them to participate in competition or putting them up front on stage against their wishes. Be sensitive. Many students are extremely self-conscious about their bodies and do not want to participate in things that will draw attention to themselves or embarrass them in front of their peers.

Also, students need biblical teaching and clear direction on the topic of sexuality. Their young bodies are racing with hormones, and many students are uncertain and confused about the new feelings and desires that accompany them. It is our role to teach them the difference between lust and a God-given sex drive and the proper context for sex.

INTELLECTUAL DEVELOPMENT

"That's not a blackboard—it's green!"

Psychologist Jean Piaget described the intellectual development of children ages seven through eleven as the *concrete operations stage*. Children in this stage can organize facts but are unable to conceptualize complicated ideas. At about the age of twelve, however, they move into the early stages of abstract thinking and what is called the *formal operations stage*. They begin to understand abstract concepts such as "God is love," and are able to contrast the ideal with the real. The ability to reason also develops. It seems the desire to argue closely parallels the onset of reasoning! I am sure you have observed this phenomenon with your students or your own children!

For example, if you are writing something on the blackboard, a student may decide to start an argument: "That's not a blackboard—it's green." To appease him or her, you agree that, yes, it is indeed a green board. This student may sit back and gloat in victory and eagerly await the next chance to further develop this new ability to reason.

Around age eighteen, students become idealistic thinkers. They start to reason in terms of black and white; gray is considered a compromise. Many of the political uprisings throughout history have started on college campuses because of "black or white" idealistic thinking.

Some students stop attending church during this time because they feel the church is filled with too many hypocrites. Often this kind of issue may best be handled from an intellectual angle, rather than a spiritual one. You can use logic to help idealists see that not all of life is black and white.

Many of your leaders are in this stage of intellectual development; be cognizant of this. They may have unrealistic expectations from the students they are leading and may become discouraged or disillusioned.

Believe me, these intellectual developments will drive you crazy at times, but the transition from concrete thinker to abstract thinker to idealistic thinker is of utmost importance. We need to give our students and leaders permission to perform their mental gymnastics in order to mature intellectually into adulthood.

God has entrusted you with a valuable gift—the minds of high school students. Students are making critical life decisions during this time. It is your responsibility to understand the process a student is going through intellectually and tailor your actions and programs accordingly.

Ministry Applications to Think About

What does adolescent intellectual development mean for you and your ministry? Be aware of the intellectual dimension as it relates to programming and teaching. Sometimes student ministers forget where students are at and teach over their heads. Other times, they mix the high schoolers with either junior high students or college students. If this occurs, you may be teaching your students about God, but you will probably have intellectually alienated one section of your audience. One solution to this challenge is to teach through small groups. Another way to teach effectively is to aim for a single purpose. For example, try to have each student walk away with one biblical truth a week.

EMOTIONAL DEVELOPMENT

The Life of Brian

6:00 A.M.—Brian's alarm goes off and he hits snooze—it's too early to get up and face the day. Brian is crabby.

6:26—Brian finally decides to get up and jump in the shower. His two sisters have already used up all the hot water, so he ends up taking an ice-cold shower. Brian is mad.

6:50—Brian's mom has prepared scrambled eggs, bacon, toast, and fresh orange juice. Brian is happy.

7:10—Brian gets on the school bus and Suzy sits next to him. Brian is ecstatic.

7:30—In math class, Brian gets back his final exam. He got a D. Brian is bummed.

8:35—During biology lab, Brian dissects a frog. Brian is excited.

9:45—Brian decides to skip his Spanish class and gets caught in the hall. His detention is tomorrow after school. Brian is upset.

Have *you* experienced such a wide range of emotions in recent mornings? It was probably tiring to just look at the variety of emotions Brian faced! Yet such mood swings are not uncommon for teenagers. Mood swings are closely related to the physical and social changes teenagers face during adolescence. Also, their preoccupation with their developing identity can cause emotional turmoil.

It is important to remember that, for teenagers, mood swings are completely normal. William Rowley writes:

> For the most part, adolescents lack experience. When things are down, when their decisions go awry, when circumstances aren't what they expected, they lack the experience to know that their situation is temporary. When they break up with a romantic interest, for example, they aren't at all sure that there will ever be another. They have too little experience, so they have nothing to moderate their emotional responses.[2]

Some adolescents encounter serious problems in their emotional development. Depression has become more common for people across the nation. The American Psychiatric Association states that in any six-month period of time, 9.4 million Americans experience a form of depression.[3] It is estimated that ten percent of all children in this country suffer from some form of depression before they reach the age of twelve.[4] And between three and five percent of the adolescent population is diagnosed with clinical depression every year.[5]

If one of your students fails an algebra exam and says, "Oh, I'm so depressed," it is most likely just a response to an unfortunate situation. Adolescent depression, though, is more complex than feeling discouraged about a single grade. As student ministers, it is imperative that we learn to spot the warning signs of depression and get help for those students immediately. Here are some common clues that a student may be experiencing depression:

- Persistent feelings of hopelessness or worthlessness
- Noticeable change in sleeping patterns

- An inability to concentrate
- A major change in appetite with weight loss or weight gain
- Withdrawal from friends and family
- Complaining about headaches and stomachaches
- Decreasing grades and an unwillingness to work in school
- Loss of energy, fatigue
- Lack of interest in regular activities (sports, church, music, etc.)
- Pessimism about the future
- Overwhelming feelings of sadness and grief
- Feelings of inappropriate guilt
- Preoccupation with death or suicide[6]

These warning signs should not be taken lightly. Experts state that most suicides are preceded by a period of depression. Recent teen suicide statistics reveal the crisis we are facing: between 1980 and 1993, the suicide rate rose 120 percent for ten- to fourteen-year-olds and almost 30 percent for fifteen- to nineteen-year-olds. The executive director of the American Association of Suicidology, Lanny Berman, believes the increase is because "there are more depressed kids."[7] A recent Gallup survey found that 85 percent of the teen respondents believe that "thinking about suicide is endemic in their culture."[8] In fact, another survey of sixteen thousand high school students' found that one in twelve students said he or she had attempted suicide the previous year.[9] The rise in teen suicide has indeed created a crisis in our country.

The emotional development of a student can be a difficult time. But during the mood swings and changing feelings, students can rely on God, who never changes. Hebrews 13:8 says, "Jesus Christ is the same yesterday and today and forever." As student ministers, we must surround our students with the truth of God's Word and help them build a strong, stable foundation.

Ministry Applications to Think About

How can you assist your students in their emotional development?

First, as a student minister, it is your responsibility to create ways your teen students can share their feelings and be unconditionally accepted. Many teenagers feel emotionally unstable as they make the transition from thinking and acting like a child to facing the pressure of being a mature adult. They are looking for a safe place.

Second, be sure your leaders are emotionally mature themselves before you place them in a leadership role with students. They should not be looking to students to meet their emotional needs. Leaders need to keep their issues separate from the students they are leading.

SOCIAL DEVELOPMENT
"Hey, everyone else is doing it!"

Teenagers face many changes socially. The social development of adolescence, identity development, is the fifth of eight life stages postulated by psychologist Erik Erikson. During this period, teenagers wrestle with questions like, "Who am I?" "Do I look okay?" "Am I valuable?" "Do people like me?" and "Who do I want to be?" Teenagers are very egocentric as these kinds of self-focused questions dominate their minds. What they wear, how they act around their peers, and what they say are major concerns in a teenager's world.

This self-focus allows teenagers to develop their own identity apart from their parents. Now teenagers begin to shift their social orientation from parents to groups of peers. They start to develop meaningful peer relationships and don't even want to be seen in public with their parents! Many parents feel rejected and abandoned during this phase and wonder if they have done something wrong. Parents need to realize that these relational changes are a normal and healthy transition as their teenagers move toward autonomy and maturity.

The road toward autonomy and maturity, though, can be a long and bumpy one for some teenagers as they discover the importance of fitting in. Being liked becomes a top priority, and many teenagers will do just about anything to feel accepted. Behaviors once viewed as unacceptable, such as drinking, smoking, drugs, and premarital sex, often begin during adolescence as a result of intense peer pressure. Many teenagers feel that "everyone else is doing it; why shouldn't I?"

And doing it they are. Take a look at some of the things today's students are doing:

- Of the 20.7 million students in seventh to twelfth grade nationwide, 68 percent have drunk alcohol at least once, and 51 percent (10.6 million) have had at least one drink within the past year. Of those who drink, eight million drink weekly. By the time they reach their senior year in high school, nine out of ten teens will have experimented with alcohol, and 39 percent will get drunk at least once every two weeks.[10]

- In its "Morbidity and Mortality Weekly Report," the Centers for Disease Control reported that 600,000 teenagers began to smoke from 1985 to 1989, a 5.5 percent increase in that age group. Approximately 3,000 teenagers begin smoking every day.[11] Last August, President Clinton announced a plan of attack to decrease teen smoking by cracking down on advertising, vending machine sales, and over-the-counter sales to persons under eighteen. These regulations may be successful, but one adolescent psychiatrist stated that "if the peer group smokes, they are much more likely to smoke. . . . It's probably the most predictive of whether they smoke or not." [12]

- Six out of ten teenagers will have used illicit drugs at least once before finishing high school. In 1990, 33 percent of America's high school seniors reported using illicit drugs during the last year. [13]

- A 1990 nationwide survey by the Centers for Disease Control reported that by ninth grade, 40 percent of those surveyed had already engaged in sex. At tenth grade, it's 48 percent. By eleventh grade, it's 57 percent. And by the time senior year rolls around, 72 percent of teens have had sex.[14]

- One in four teenage girls gets pregnant by age eighteen. Half become pregnant by age twenty-one. Eighty-five percent of teen pregnancies are unplanned; half end in births, a third in abortion, and the rest in miscarriage.[15]

- About 2.5 million people under the age of twenty are infected with some form of a sexually transmitted disease, including AIDS.[16]

These statistics are sobering; they reveal the confusing, pressure-filled culture in which our students are living. Pick up any newspaper and you will most likely read about the consequences some students pay as a result of giving in to peer pressure. Just this week, three teenagers from my neighborhood lost their lives in a horrific car accident. The driver's blood-alcohol level was nearly twice the legal limit when the car he was driving slammed into a tree a few blocks from my home.

There are, indeed, a number of ways in which teenagers succumb to negative peer pressure. Sometimes, though, God uses peer pressure to draw students to Himself and the truths of His Word.

A few years ago, a sophomore guy in our ministry was facing tremendous peer pressure. He was a star basketball player at his high school and well-liked by his peers. The hot topic in the locker room usually focused on girls and who had done what with whom. The guys on his team started to pressure him to have sex with his girlfriend of four months. Here's how this student tells the rest of the story:

> I was feeling such pressure from the guys, and I wanted so badly to fit in. During this time, my parents were encouraging me to attend Student Impact. I finally decided to try it, and the first series I went to was called "Love, Sex, and Dating." The messages hit me like a ton of bricks, and I listened to every word.
>
> In the midst of this series, my girlfriend gave me a card containing six condoms for my birthday. Her gift indicated she was ready to have sex with me. Her parents were going out of town that weekend and she suggested I lie to my parents and spend the weekend with her. I was struggling with the pressure from my peers and now from her. I kept putting sex off, though, and finding all kinds of excuses.
>
> I was invited to Blast, the weekend winter retreat, and it was there that I became a Christian. The Lord began to change my heart. Two weeks after Blast, I broke up with this girl and began to get into the Word and grow in my faith. Everything didn't get easier, but God was now a part of my life.

I'm thankful this young man was able to resist sexual temptation and not cave in to the pressure around him. God intervened at just the right time!

Ministry Applications to Think About

How will you and your ministry enable students to socially develop in a positive manner?

First, know your students' needs as they move through various stages of social maturity. At times, some may have a need for large group interaction while others crave the attention of a small group.

Second, as teenagers become more independent, the size of their social group becomes smaller. They form same-sex friendships with two or three others. This is one reason the ministry of small groups is so effective.

Third, because peer pressure is so intense during adolescence, students sometimes make unwise choices. Be aware of signs of drug and alcohol abuse and get help immediately if necessary.

SPIRITUAL DEVELOPMENT

"I don't want to go to church today!"

Teenagers, in a quest for their own identity, also begin to search for a personal faith. They are no longer content to believe what parents and ministry leaders have taught them to this point; they want to understand what they believe and why. Their ability to reason is further developed as teenagers challenge accepted beliefs in order to internalize their own.

Too often, student ministers become alarmed when their students begin to question or doubt the existence of God. They think, "Oh, no! What's wrong with my teaching? Am I doing something that causes them to run from God?" This time of soul-searching is critical in a teenager's spiritual development. We don't want students simply "rubber stamping" everything we or their parents say, leaving our ministries unchanged and unchallenged.

Student ministers also become alarmed when the number of upperclass students begins to dwindle. I believe one of the reasons that upperclassmen disappear is that too many student ministries are trying to serve both the junior high and high school students during the same meeting or program. I have seen such immaturity in these mixed groups. The needs of these two groups of students are vast! The older students tend to be pulled down spiritually instead of built up.

My friend Tim encountered this very problem as a student pastor at a church in Las Vegas. When he came on staff, the twenty-five-year-old traditional church was in the process of transitioning to a seeker-sensitive model. Tim began by building a core and organizing small groups, with the junior high and high school students combined into one group. After a few months, he observed that the junior high group was growing, but the high school group was shrinking. He realized that by mixing two different target groups, he was not effectively reaching half the group. After Tim separated the two groups, he noticed steady growth and more focused ministry taking place.

Keep the junior high ministry separate from the high school ministry. That way you will be able to address students' needs appropriately and in a way that will truly minister to them.

Our actions and responses to the spiritual dimension of a student's growth require much grace, sensitivity, and patience. Each student will make the transition through this stage in different ways and at a different pace. The outcome, we trust, will be worth the wait as students begin to really own their faith for the first time in their lives.

Ministry Applications to Think About

How can you effectively address your students' spiritual development?

First, don't be offended if a student challenges everything you say. He or she is in the process of internalizing faith and values and needs to understand the "whys."

Second, if you have new Christians who come from unchurched families, realize that they may not wrestle as intensely as Christian students from Christian families in personalizing their faith.

THINKING HOLISTICALLY

It's amazing to witness God's master plan as the five developmental stages of adolescence work together in producing young adults: boys become young men and girls become young women. This synergy of development causes changes in one area, which, in turn, causes changes in another area.

As student ministers, we need to think about the needs of our students on a holistic level. Often, we get so caught up in trying to meet spiritual needs that we forget to notice the inter-connectedness of the other areas of development. Failure to recognize this may be a deterrent to ultimately meeting the spiritual needs of our students. We can more effectively meet the needs of students if we know and understand the whole adolescent development process. God is the cornerstone, the one constant during the rapid changes of adolescence. He is the hope students can hold onto during this confusing period of their lives.

Rewind

What Did You Learn?

The stages of adolescent development in five key areas—physical, intellectual, emotional, social, and spiritual—have implications for student ministry.

AREA OF DEVELOPMENT	IMPLICATION FOR MINISTRY
Physical	• Be sensitive to self-conscious students • Provide clear, biblical teaching on sexuality
Intellectual	• Keep junior high and high school ministries separate • Aim for a single purpose in teaching
Emotional	• Provide a safe place for sharing emotions • Choose emotionally mature leaders
Social	• Balance large group and small group interaction • Capitalize on small groups to foster healthy intimacy • Be aware of signs of substance abuse
Spiritual	• Accept questioning as a part of internalizing values

Pause

What Action Will You Take?

1. Given the five dimensions of adolescent development, brainstorm some realistic ideas to meet the needs that derive from those five areas. For example, how does your ministry meet the intellectual needs of students?

2. Does your teaching line up with students' developmental needs and abilities? If not, what needs to change?

Fast Forward

What's Next?

You understand the stages of adolescent development. How well have you identified the different audiences among the adolescents you reach?

Taking Aim at Your Target

The Marine Corps understands targets. During boot camp, new recruits are trained to hit targets with pinpoint accuracy. I had a friend in the Marines who told me they would spend hour after hour in the range shooting barrels and trying to hit bull's-eyes. Each soldier had to hit the targets consistently and precisely in order to be prepared for any potential combat.

This discipline of knowing and hitting your targets applies to student ministry as well. Sometimes student ministers start shooting their rifles before they have practiced hitting their targets at the range. Once a group has formed, the shots fly out, but rarely do those shots hit the bull's-eye of reaching students for Christ. We need to know what we are aiming at and the people we are trying to "hit." I have always liked the saying, "If you aim at nothing, you'll hit it every time." How true! As student ministers we must know our targets, because the stakes are eternal.

I think all of us could use some target practice. Sometimes it is so easy to get wrapped up in "doing ministry" that we fail to stop and evaluate if we are indeed hitting the needs of our various audiences. With a greater understanding of a teen's developmental stages, we can now target three groups of people: seekers, believers, and leaders. Let's begin by looking at the seeker target.

TARGETING SEEKERS

A seeker is someone who is interested in spiritual things and in investigating the claims of Christianity. The needs of a seeker are very different from a believer, yet the seeker target is often overlooked in student ministry. So much thought and effort goes into ministering to the already convinced that those who most need to hear about the love of God are neglected. We all want to see high school students come to know Christ. We simply cannot try to target both seekers and believers at the same meeting. It is confusing to the teacher and the students.

Think back to the time you were a seeker. What was it like? Perhaps you became a Christian at a young age. I became a Christian when I was twenty-five years old. For years, I had looked to fill the void in my life. I had tried everything: the party scene, relationships, sports. . . . Some of these things filled the void for a short time, but it wasn't long until I was left feeling empty once again. God used a variety of people to change my life, particularly one of my football coaches, who kept pointing me to spiritual truth. He knew me and really understood my world and my needs. Through the love of that coach and other Christians, I received Christ.

I think I would have been picked as the most unlikely person to become a Christian. It amazes me that someone stepped out of his comfort zone, saw right through my hurt, and took a chance to share the truth I so desperately needed to hear. My conversion was so real. I had never bowed down to anything in my life, but for the first time I realized there was a God worthy to bow down to.

I longed for my friends to experience faith in Christ too. I wanted to bring them to a place where they could be touched by God's grace, but I could not find a church that was seeker-sensitive and able to relate to their spiritual level. I did the best I could to witness to them, but I needed help. I didn't have the answers to their questions. I felt all alone in my evangelism efforts.

Help came when I learned about a church in South Barrington, Illinois, with a vision to reach unchurched people by targeting services specifically for them. You will read in the next chapter how that vision changed my life. Willow Creek Community Church's seeker services had started a movement that hundreds of churches around the world are beginning to follow.

When was the last time you brought a seeker to your church service? I hope it was not too long ago. Do you remember what was racing through your mind? Maybe you were praying that the message was not on the topic of giving, or that it wouldn't go too long. Perhaps you were concerned that the right people would sing or that no one would embarrass your friend by calling on him or her. Most likely, you wished that someone would talk about something that would touch your friend's life.

We all want our friends to know Christ. Students are no different. We need to help them reach their friends for Christ. At Student Impact we see the importance of understanding the seeker target and providing an environment where our core Christian students can bring their friends to investigate Christianity.

Who are these seekers and what are their needs? Do you understand their world?

Let's see how well you know the seekers' world. Get your pencil out and answer the following questions as best you can:

- Name the top two TV shows that your high school students watch each week.
- Name three places students in your area hang out on weekends.
- Name three magazines students read.
- Name three popular secular bands.

If we are to help our Christian students in their evangelism efforts, we need to know the seeker's world. Too often, we forget what a seeker thinks and needs. The needs of a seeker and believer are very different. In order to do everything we can to meet seekers where they are spiritually, we must evaluate: What are they thinking? What are their needs?

First, *seekers need to feel accepted*. The world tells students that, in order to feel accepted, they should conform to those around them and compromise their standards. Seekers need a safe place where they are shown unconditional love and are accepted no matter what. We must accept the fact that a seeker's life is different; their behaviors often reflect the darkness in which they are living. They may smoke or use bad language, but it is because they do not know the truth. We need to open our arms to them, regardless of what they bring to our church environment. So often, we miss this and that is why seekers don't come back to church. They need to feel welcomed. Jesus always looked at the inner person, not the outward appearance.

It is in this safe place that seekers can learn and ask questions about God in order to investigate the claims of Christianity. They want someone to respect the spiritual journey they are on and not feel pressure to make any decisions until they are ready.

Second, *seekers need to be understood.* Rebellion is so common among teenagers because they feel no one understands them. Why bother following the rules? No one seems to care. We can show seekers that we understand them, and, more important, that God understands them. We can also show them that we understand that life is tough and, at times, seemingly unfair, but God cares for each of their burdens.

Third, *seekers need purpose in their lives.* The world's lures of money, power, and success do not bring lasting peace and happiness; there is still a void that seekers try to fill. We can teach seekers how to fill that void with God's love—a love that will last and bring meaning to their lives.

And fourth, *seekers need to be loved.* With the steady demise of the family unit, many adolescents do not receive the kind of love and attention they need at home, so they look elsewhere. Some look to gangs to feel worthwhile and accepted. The National Institute of Justice reported that the police are aware of five thousand gangs with two hundred fifty thousand members in America's seventy-nine largest cities.[1] Others look to sex, hoping to find love along the way. Research shows that teens will often use sex as a "means to express and satisfy emotional and interpersonal needs that have little or nothing to do with sex. Sex becomes a coping mechanism to deal with the absence of love and affection at home."[2] Often the kind of love students find leads to destruction and heartache.

As the influence of the family and even the church continues to deteriorate, so does the sense of security, self-esteem, and value in the lives of many students. Many of them really are looking for love in all the wrong places. The good news is that we can show students a different kind of love and one that loves unconditionally regardless of performance: the love of Jesus Christ.

MEETING THE NEEDS OF SEEKERS

How does your ministry meet the four needs of seekers mentioned above? Do you have any kind of plan or strategy in place that focuses solely on the unique needs of seekers? If not, don't feel bad. Perhaps this is a new concept to you or one on which you are just beginning to focus.

At Student Impact, we want every student who walks through the doors to feel accepted. Some who come have mohawks and tattoos, while others look as if they just shopped at the Gap. No matter what these students look like, each is accepted into a team with other students from his or her high school. New students are introduced to other team members and get an overview of the night. It's like a party just for them.

To help seekers feel understood, we work hard to stay current on their world so we can begin breaking down any barriers they may have built up against the church. Imagine a seeking student's surprise when we refer to current movie titles, songs, or world events during our message or program. He or she is probably sitting there thinking, "Wow, this guy is current on what's happening! He knows a little bit about my world." I am not saying we should ever sacrifice biblical integrity, but we do need to be relevant and show seekers that we care about them and understand the challenges they are facing in today's culture.

We also want to be relevant to where seekers are at in order to help keep the integrity our core students have built with their unchurched friends. Our core students trust us; they know we will do what we can to make God's Word come alive to their friends in a way that reflects excellence and relevance.

I have observed other student ministries offering outreaches for seekers. Yet when I look at the topic of the night and observe the program, often it does not hit the seeker target at all; it is targeted to the believer. We will talk more about programming in the final section of the book.

Our task is to find ways to reach the unsaved with the gospel of Jesus Christ and show them how purpose-filled their lives can be. Jeremiah 29:11 promises, "'For I know the plans I have for you,' declares the LORD, 'plans to prosper you and not to harm you, plans to give you hope and a future.'" God has a purpose for each student's life and desires to give each of them hope and direction for the future. It's our challenge to point our students to God and help them find their purpose in life.

We need to do whatever it takes (without compromising our biblical standards or watering down the Gospel) to touch this confused generation.

Paul recorded some of his strategy for reaching the unsaved in 1 Corinthians 9:20–23:

To the Jews I became like a Jew, to win the Jews. To those under the law I became like one under the law (though I myself am not under the law), so as to win those under the law. To those not having the law I became like one not having the law (though I am not free from God's law but am under Christ's law), so as to win those not having the law. To the weak I became weak, to win the weak. I have become all things to all men so that by all possible means I might save some. I do all this for the sake of the gospel, that I may share in its blessings.

Like Paul, we are called to be God's ambassadors and to share Christ with the seekers around us. It's an enormous challenge, but richly rewarding. How well are you hitting your seeker target?

TARGETING BELIEVERS

Julie became a Christian when she was six years old. She was raised in a strong Christian home and her parents serve faithfully in a church. Julie has been attending Sunday school for many years now and is familiar with most Bible stories. She tries to read her Bible on a regular basis, but her life is busy as she is involved in several activities at school and works hard to maintain a B average. Julie says she wants to grow in her walk with God, but how?

Do you have any Julies in your ministry? They are good students who want to grow, but seem to be stuck spiritually. What exactly do believers need in order to further their walk with God?

First, *believers need to be fed from God's Word regularly*. The world throws our students many confusing messages filled with deceit and false hopes. Christian students need to hear God's absolute truth in order to make wise choices and become fully devoted followers of Christ. Psalm 119:105 says, "Your word is a lamp to my feet and a light for my path." How our students desperately need a light for their paths!

Second, *believers need community with other Christians*. Christian students taking a stand for Christ on their campuses can feel all alone. They need a place where they can find support and encouragement from their peers to press on. Hebrews 10:24–25 says:

And let us consider how we may spur one another on toward love and good deeds. Let us not give up meeting together, as some are in the habit of doing, but let us encourage one another—and all the more as you see the Day approaching.

Third, *believers need to become active participants in the church and discover their spiritual gifts.* At some point, believers should understand their unique role in helping to build the kingdom of God by discovering their spiritual gift and putting it into action. We are told in Romans 12:6 that "we have different gifts, according to the grace given us...." Christian students can make significant contributions in the life of the church and serve with enthusiasm and effectiveness.

And fourth, *believers need a place where they can celebrate communion and worship God on a regular basis.* Christian students can easily stray from their walk with God, and the Enemy does his best to confuse their priorities and values. They need a place to recalibrate and reset their eyes on Christ. Christians can do this through meaningful worship and celebrating the sacrament of communion on a regular basis.

Lindsay, a junior, is not unusual among Christian students. She needs a consistent opportunity to, as she states, "focus on God and reflect on the week and see what God has done." She says, "I like to think of how good He has been to me and to get back on track, especially if I've had a tough week." Christians need to be reminded of all that Christ has done for them by regularly focusing on Him.

Our ministry calendar and schedule has some bearing on who our target audience is and how often we aim at that audience. Given the frenetic pace of life for many high school students these days, finding time for families to be together on weeknights can be difficult. We have elected not to contribute to this problem by adding another ministry event on weeknights. Sticking to a one night per week (for us, it's Sundays) schedule means we have to pick and choose whom we are going to target on that night.

The flagship of our high school ministry is our Sunday morning class. Although many seekers attend, it is primarily targeted at believers. That leaves us with

Sunday nights for virtually every other purpose we have in ministry.

In early- to mid-fall, we focus on seeker-driven events. For three or four weeks straight, we arrange off campus events to which our core students can invite seeking friends.

In mid-fall, we launch into small groups, our primary vehicle for shepherding. The idea is that maybe we can get some students to funnel into small groups from the seeker events. Every fourth Sunday, we have a "celebration night" where everyone (especially those in small groups) gather to celebrate what God is doing among us.

On celebration nights we spend more extended time in worship, testimony, corporate prayer, and celebrating the Lord's Table, or baptism, if needed. Some special events designed more for core building or fellowship fall on celebration night weekends as well—for example, our fall retreat.

After spring break, the use of our Sunday nights becomes more erratic. We usually do some seeker-driven events, including a canoe trip to which no believers can go without one non-Christian guest.

In the summer, we use Sunday nights for more of a loose, fellowship hang time for students who are generally more involved in our ministry. We usually meet off campus outdoors, and it makes for a great night to invite friends who are interested in getting a first impression of our ministry in a relational setting.

Colin Kerr, Christian Fellowship Church,
Evansville, IN, former Student Impact intern

MEETING THE NEEDS OF BELIEVERS

How does your ministry meet the four needs of believers mentioned above? Are you building a biblically functioning community of believers?

I love to read about and imagine what it must have been like to be part of the early church in the book of Acts. That model of biblical community is still such a powerful example for us today. Acts 2:42–44 paints an incredible picture of God's design for community:

> They devoted themselves to the apostles' teaching and to the fellowship, to the breaking of bread and to prayer. Everyone was filled with awe, and many wonders and miraculous signs were done by the apostles. All the believers were together and had everything in common.

Did you catch that last phrase, "all the believers were together"? The verse does not say "all the believers and seekers were together." God knew that believers needed a special time to meet together for Bible teaching, community, and worship.

We pray each week that God would anoint the teaching at our believer program (Student Insight) and use it to help students draw closer to Him. Students need and want to hear bold teaching; they desire clear direction for their lives and a road map to help them find their way. We can also teach our believers about spiritual gifts and the unique ways God has designed each one of them to serve in His church.

Believers need biblical teaching, but they also crave community. Mike comes to our believer program to get renewed. "When school gets to me or my family drives me crazy, I can come and see my Christian friends and get encouragement," he says. "It helps me to refocus and get ready for the next week." Students need to experience community; for many it provides the necessary support for which they are looking. One student told me, "The people here are my family."

One of the main methods we use to meet the believer's need for community is through the ministry of small groups, which we will talk about in greater detail in chapter 11. In small groups, Christian students meet regularly with other believers from their high school for accountability, encouragement, and Bible study. They cheer each other on as they strive to become more like Christ.

As students grow in their Christlikeness, their love for worship increases. Some students have approached me after our believer's programs to tell me that worship was too short; they wanted to sing longer. It's amazing to see the ways worship changes believers' lives, including mine, and gives us new perspectives into kingdom living.

> I can worship on my own, but when we come together as brothers and sisters in Christ, it's incredible.
>
> Aimee, junior in high school

The last couple of verses in Acts 2 motivate me as I think about targeting believers and growing them up in Christ. I'm reminded again about the tremendous impact a community of believers can make in the lives of unchurched people. Read this passage and marvel anew at God's magnificent plan:

> Selling their possessions and goods, they gave to anyone as he had need. Every day they continued to meet together in the temple courts. They broke bread in their homes and ate together with glad and sincere hearts, praising God and enjoying the favor of all the people. And the Lord added to their number daily those who were being saved (Acts 2:45–47).

I pray that student ministries around the world would witness the miracle of the early church in their midst.

TARGETING LEADERS

In Student Impact, we have a leadership core of 150 people. Many of our leaders are college students or recent college graduates; some are high school upperclassmen. We also have a number of adults who work full-time in the marketplace. All of our leaders are committed to helping high school students walk with God and follow Him. They are excited to use the gifts God has given them, and they desire to make a difference that will last for all of eternity. What are some of the needs of leaders?

First, *leaders need to feel informed.* Keeping leaders informed is beneficial for several reasons: it communicates value and allows leaders to see that their particular role is important; it demonstrates that you trust the leaders and are confident they will act on the information they receive; and it helps the leaders to be prepared for the future.

Second, *leaders need to know what's expected of them and how to hit that target.* I have seen and heard of many gifted volunteers with servant hearts who start off excited to be a part of high school ministry. Unfortunately, over time, they become frustrated and begin to wonder, "Am I doing the right things? What are my ministry objectives? How do I know if I have reached them?" If no one answers their questions, many of them throw in the towel, discouraged and disappointed.

Third, *leaders need to feel valued and cared for.* When leaders keep giving to others and selflessly serving, there has to be someone pouring back into them and encouraging them to keep going. Leaders do not want to feel used; instead, they want to feel valued and treasured. They need to know their time and efforts are making a difference.

And fourth, *leaders need and desire to use their gifts.* Leaders understand the spiritual gift or gifts God has entrusted to them and they want to put it into action. They do not want to be spectators; they are ready to get out on the field and play.

MEETING THE NEEDS OF LEADERS

How does your ministry meet the four needs of leaders? We have discovered some ways to meet the needs of our leaders, and each year we try to improve to better meet their needs.

As Student Impact continues to grow, it is a challenge to find ways to keep our leaders informed and "on the same page." Yet, we know that if we all want to move in the same direction, the flow of information must be consistent and timely. Information is disseminated to our leaders through different channels depending on the area or department in which they serve. For example, the leaders involved in organizing our weekly competition receive information from the competition director. It is this director's responsibility to keep his or her team current on upcoming ministry events and future planning.

We try to keep our leaders informed about what is expected of them and how they can meet those expectations. One of the ways we do this is through written ministry descriptions that detail how success is defined as well as outline specific ministry roles and time commitments.

Each leader receives training in his or her specific area of service and to the degree necessary for the leader's level of commitment. Leaders with light commitment levels receive training in an ongoing, on-the-job fashion. Leaders with heavier commitment levels are trained in weekly meetings, specialized meetings held during the year, and one-on-one coaching with a staff person. Training answers the "whys" of what is happening in the ministry and helps to clarify the ministry's vision and core values. These different methods allow leaders to grow personally and in their ministry skills.

The depth and type of care given to our leaders ministry-wide depends on their commitment level within the ministry. Those with a lighter commitment level usually receive care through the relationships on their service team. Those who lead a small group of students receive care from their campus director (see chapter 12), usually in a ratio of five leaders to one campus director.

Since the campus director carries the heaviest load of responsibility, he or she is given specialized care at a weekly leadership meeting called BTL (Between the Lines). These groups of five male or female campus directors are led by a division director (a paid staff position). They study materials designed to help each person grow spiritually as well as focus on ministry goals. When leaders feel equipped and cared for, their ministry satisfaction is high and they enjoy serving.

Our leaders love the opportunity to use their gifts. Pam, for example, works full-time as a dental hygienist and has served faithfully for over seven years as a campus director and also as a small group leader. She has significantly marked the lives of dozens of high school girls and modeled to these young girls what it means to be a godly woman. She has passed on the baton of faith to numerous girls who in turn have passed it on to their friends. Some have even moved into leadership and now impact those they lead. Pam has indeed left a legacy in our ministry.

"I serve because of my passion for high school students and I believe my gift mix, encouragement and shepherding, can best be utilized with high school students," says Pam. "I'm amazed that God can actually use me, a broken, little mess, by taking my gifts and using them to challenge and change other people."

HITTING THE MARK

Last fall, a friend took me deer hunting for the first time. I was amazed at how a hunter has to prepare to attract a deer. The hunting store I visited sold pictures of deer that showed exactly where on the deer to aim. I discovered that selecting the right bow and arrow is important, along with choosing the optimal location to spot a deer. Some hunters even use an apple scent or deer urine to attract the deer.

I couldn't believe all the time and effort I expended to try to get a deer. I sat perched up in my stand for several hours, but had no luck. It was just as well. On the night before I went hunting, my seven-year old son, Trevor, had said to me, "Dad, please don't kill anything. Just bring one home."

"Just bring one home." This is what we strive to do in student ministry. We focus intently on our target so that we can bring them home to Jesus, just as the prodigal son returned to his father. Ephesians 6:16 encourages us to "take up the shield of faith, with which you can extinguish all the flaming arrows of the evil one." The Enemy does fire flaming arrows at our students; he is out to kill and destroy. Our goal is to spare students from getting hit by the Enemy and to bring them home.

As we think about the audience we are trying to attract, we need to think through some of the same things I had to as I prepared to hunt: What are we doing to attract students? Where do our targets hang out? Have we studied our targets enough to know where and how to reach them?

Effective ministry requires that we know whom it is we are trying to reach and the kinds of needs being expressed. When we know and understand our targets, we can then hit the mark.

Ministering to seekers, believers, and leaders is hard work. Don't take the easy way out and mix these groups all together, hoping to meet some of their needs. Not only will students and leaders get frustrated, but you, too, will grow discouraged in trying to do it all at once. Take the time to know your targets. God will honor your efforts.

Rewind

What Did You Learn?

We must consistently do target practice if we are to hit the needs of three different groups of people: seekers, believers, and leaders.

TARGETS	NEEDS	MEETING THE NEEDS
Seekers	• acceptance • understanding • purpose in life • love	• Plan ways of welcoming seekers in your ministry • Stay current on seekers' world • Be relevant and biblically sound about God's purpose for life • Model God's unconditional love
Believers	• nourishment from God's Word • Christian fellowship • participation in church life • place to celebrate communion and worship God	• Provide strong biblical teaching • Foster community by offering small groups • Participate in authentic worship
Leaders	• information • clear expectations • value and care • to use spiritual gifts	• Keep communication lines open • Write out ministry descriptions • Care for leaders regularly • Place leaders in positions that best utilize their spiritual gifts

Pause

What Action Will You Take?

Think about your ministry and the groups of people you are trying to serve. Write down their names in this chart according to where they best fit:

SEEKERS	BELIEVERS	LEADERS

Fast Forward

What's Next?

*You've done your barrel work and know your targets.
Where are you going to lead them?*

FORMING A VISION AND MISSION

Picture the scene: Two fishermen, Simon Peter and his brother Andrew, are sitting peacefully in their boat on the shores of the Sea of Galilee. Perhaps they are talking about the weather or what they ate for breakfast or maybe about their upcoming weekend plans. As they cast a net into the water, a man named Jesus walks by and says to them, "Come, follow me ... and I will make you fishers of men" (Matt. 4:19). Jesus' directions are crystal clear, and the two men leave their boat to follow Him.

> Vision is the God-given ability to imagine an attractive and exciting future for a group of people and uniting them for a common purpose.

Confident of His purpose on earth, Jesus recruited the twelve disciples who could best help Him carry out His vision. Jesus was sure of His mission, and He definitely had a strategy.

How clear are your directions to the people you lead? Are they aware of your God-given vision? Do they understand their mission? Do they have a strategy to get there? As leaders, we must always be devoting ourselves to answering these questions. This chapter and the next will focus on three critical components to effective student ministry: vision, mission, and strategy.

VISION

The distinguishing characteristic between merely maintaining a youth group and building a dynamic student ministry is the existence of a clear, compelling vision. Vision is the God-given ability to imagine an attractive and exciting future for a group of people and uniting them for a common purpose.

With a clear vision, students know where you are taking them and are able to follow you. Leading a student ministry without vision can be disastrous. Christian researcher George Barna states:

> Unless God's people have a clear understanding of where they are headed, the probability of a successful journey is severely limited. Unless you attend to His call upon your life and ministry, you and your ministry are likely to experience confusion, weariness, dissipation, impotence.[1]

Last week, I browsed in a shopping mall with my wife, Gloria, and came across Magic Eye greeting cards. Have you seen them? If you stare at them for about thirty seconds, a 3-D image is supposed to pop out at you. It took me several attempts before I could see any hidden images. I'm sure I looked pretty ridiculous standing in these stores with different cards ten inches from my nose! Once I got them, though, I was amazed at what I saw: the Empire State Building; a coyote; a baseball field; and dinosaurs. I even saw Elvis Presley!

Once I got the hang of it, I started to watch other people try to uncover the mystery, and I made a few interesting observations. Some people got it the first time they tried it. Others tried two or three times before the image became clear. Still others kept trying and trying to no avail; they couldn't see it at all.

Casting a vision in student ministry can be a lot like these Magic Eye cards. When you cast a vision for your ministry, there will be some students and leaders who will see your vision right away and start following. Others may need some time to fully understand where you are taking them, but eventually, they'll get on board. And, unfortunately, like the people who couldn't see the Magic Eye images, there will be people who cannot see your ministry vision. They may try to focus and adjust, but in the end, they just do not see it.

God has a vision for your student ministry, and He wants you to share it with others. You can communicate your vision confidently, knowing that God is in control and "able to do far more than we would ever dare to ask or even dream of—infinitely beyond our highest prayers, desires, thoughts, or hopes" (Eph. 3:20 TLB).

The challenge we face as student ministers is to create and communicate a vision that students and leaders will be able to see.

We must begin, though, by asking ourselves, "Do *I* see it? What is God asking me to see?"

What Do You See?

I like the story of the little girl who was drawing with her new set of sixty-four crayons. Her mother asked what the picture was about and the little girl answered, "I'm drawing God." The mother, questioning her daughter's artistic direction, responded, "But honey, nobody knows what God looks like." The girl continued drawing and then said confidently, "They'll know when I'm finished."

Vision starts with you and what God is revealing to you. Take time to slow down and listen to His leadings. When those leadings become clear, you can then create a vision for your ministry and communicate it to those around you. Effective student ministry will happen as students and leaders understand exactly where you are taking them and rally together to make the vision come to life.

Creating a Vision: What Do I Want the Ministry to See?

Fifteen years ago, when I was leading a student ministry in southern California and I heard Bill Hybels cast a vision for ministry, I became fired up. It was exactly in line with who God made me to be and my dreams for student ministry. I grabbed onto that vision, and the vision I have today for Student Impact is a result of God's leadings and Bill's message.

Too often, leaders feel guilty because they do not have a vision of their own. The important truth to remember is that leading high school students to Christ is God's vision. We may devise various methods to accomplish this vision, but ultimately all our visions come from God. The Great Commission in Matthew 28:19–20 applies to all of us in student ministry:

> Therefore go and make disciples of all nations, baptizing them in the name of the Father and of the Son and of the Holy Spirit, and teaching them to obey everything I have commanded you.

It is difficult to give "how tos" in creating a vision statement, because it starts in quietness with you and God. God will give you leadings and direction and impress upon your heart the vision He has for your student ministry. What I can share with you are several values that may assist you in developing a vision statement:

1. Vision must come from God. You can't manufacture a vision; you need to be quiet and listen to God to recognize the role you play in His vision to redeem the world.
2. Vision must answer the "where" question—"Where are you going?" and "Where do you ultimately want to be?"
3. Vision can be exclusive; it may not always be shared by everyone.
4. Vision inspires.
5. Vision attracts leaders and students to a cause.

We must give our students and leaders an exciting vision to which they can rally around and participate in. Creating a vision that is concise and easy to understand is a lofty task, but crucial to your effectiveness in student ministry. Once your vision has been determined, it's time to share it with others.

Communicating the Vision: How Will the Ministry See It?

After you have created a ministry vision statement, you must prepare to share it. Many students will begin to wonder, "If I am going to follow you, where are we going? Please tell me where you are taking me." It is important to answer this question clearly, confidently, and with excitement. Students want to follow; they need to know how to do so.

> Students want to follow; they need to know how to do so.

I want our students to see the vision God has given us as a ministry and the important role each of them play in making the vision become reality. Part of Student Impact's effectiveness is that our vision is communicated to students and leaders on a regular basis. I know our students and leaders receive frequent reminders of why we do what we do and where we are going as a ministry so that, together, we can stay on track and head in the same direction. I have also found it effective to paint the vision on an individual basis as well as corporately.

Throughout the year, I look for opportunities to communicate vision with students and leaders. On several occasions, I have sat with different leaders in the empty balcony of our church auditorium. Looking down over the empty auditorium, which has a seating capacity of 4,500, I like to ask each leader, "What do you see?" Their response is indicative of whether or not they have seen our vision and truly understood it. Some leaders do really see it and understand, but others say, "All I see is empty seats" or "Wow, this auditorium is so big."

No matter the response, I use this moment to cast the vision to each leader and say, "There are a lot of empty seats in here. Wouldn't it be great to see the auditorium filled with high school students eager to learn more about God? Wouldn't it be great to see car after car coming onto our campus with core students and their unchurched friends? Wouldn't it be great to see students building the church? Wouldn't it be great to see students impacting the world for Christ?" Painting the vision for these leaders in this way fires them up! They become excited and motivated to do the ministry God is asking them to do.

I often catch leaders on Tuesday nights when there are hundreds of high school students all around and ask them, "What do you see tonight?" I hope they are able to see that lives are being changed by God's grace and because people care.

On Sunday nights, I'll pull a leader aside and ask, "Tell me what you see." Again, I want them to see the church in action—to see high school students worshiping the Lord and allowing Him to change their lives. I want them to see the sense of community that is deepening among students and leaders. I want them to see the church being built right before their eyes.

Student Impact's Vision for Ministry

The vision statement for Student Impact is:

a unique community of students and leaders committed to letting God:
   change their lives;
   change their friends' lives;
   build the church; and
   impact the world.

I love being a part of this vision and sharing it with others! The Student Impact vision statement is played out in the lives of students and leaders in four seasonal "waves" of ministry programming.

Wave One The focus in the first wave is on God changing individual lives. It runs from September through December. In all four waves, the ministry's desire is to enable students and leaders to grow in their personal relationship with Jesus Christ, but during the first wave, special emphasis is placed on allowing God to change lives through small group relationships, understanding God's Word, and prayer. The teaching during this wave may center on such topics as identity in Christ, developing Christlike character, forgiveness, and God's love.

Wave Two In the second wave, students and leaders concentrate on how God can also change their friends' lives. This wave begins in January and ends in March. Once change has happened in a student's life, his or her compassion to bring about change in a friend's life is heightened. During the second wave, students begin to better understand that their unsaved friends matter to God. They are encouraged and challenged to build relationships of integrity with their unsaved friends, to share their testimonies, and to invite them to a supplemental witness such as a Student Impact program on Tuesday nights or another event designed to reach unsaved students. The highlight of this wave is Blast, a weekend retreat in February where students grow personally and then take steps to pray for and invite their unsaved friends to a target Impact night in March. On these nights, the gospel is shared and students are invited to make a decision for Christ.

Wave Three During the third wave, in April and May, students and leaders grow further in their understanding of the importance of the church. They begin to discover how God can use their gifts to build the church and to experience the joy that comes from serving in a variety of ways. Three times a year, each student has a chance to help direct traffic in the parking lot during our weekend services. This small act of service gives students a chance to see that they can play a part in building the church.

In the third wave, students are also taught how they can take ownership in the ministry. During the month of May, students put ownership into action by serving the church through Operation STRIVE (Students Turning Responsibility Into Valuable Experience), our annual workathon and fund-raiser. The completion of this wave is marked by baptism, a celebration of how God has changed lives throughout the ministry year.

Wave Four The months of June through August focus on impacting the world. Students and leaders have the unique opportunity to learn about and experience community through the Insight Summer Challenge on Sunday nights and through summer camp. As the students and leaders understand the power of true community among believers, it becomes clear that God can impact the world through community. There are several missions trips during this wave, through which students and leaders experience together the joy in sharing God's love with another culture. Throughout the year, students and leaders also serve in the inner city of Chicago and minister to needy people. Their worldview is broadened as they see what they can do to impact the world with the love of Christ.

Last year, I had the privilege of speaking at a church leadership conference in Wales and casting a vision for student ministry. While there, I called back on a Sunday night and, via speaker phone, talked live to those attending Student Insight, our worship and teaching time for believers. I used this opportunity to paint the vision to the students and leaders that they were impacting the world from South Barrington, Illinois.

On the night I called, there were four banners around the back of the auditorium, each with a portion of our vision statement: my life; my friend's life; the church; and the world. I told the students and leaders to turn around and read these banners and then said, "Students and leaders of Student Insight, this vision is happening. I'm in Wales representing you, sharing stories about you, to the student leaders of Wales. God and you have helped to make this vision reality. You are impacting the world!"

After I got home, several students told me they were excited more than ever about Student Impact and committed to its vision. My vision-casting stirred something in the hearts of these students as they realized the role they could play in impacting the world.

The fourth part of our vision statement, "impact the world," has played out in exciting ways through our internship program. For the past several years, we have trained like-minded men and women from all around the country and then sent them back out to fulfill their God-given vision for student ministry. It has been incredible to see God's vision spread around the country. We hope some day to be able to train interns from all over the world.

Proverbs 29:18 (KJV) reminds us that "where there is no vision, the people perish." Don't underestimate the importance of a vision statement. It can make the difference between maintaining a youth group and building a student ministry.

MISSION

Without a mission, a vision can create an atmosphere of overzealous entrepreneurs who see only the product and not the process. Mission is what happens along the way toward the vision and answers the "what" question. George Barna defines a mission statement as "a broad, general statement about who you wish to reach and what the church [your ministry] hopes to accomplish."[2]

A mission statement provides a set of general ministry objectives and communicates the philosophical value of the vision. The business world has long recognized the importance of articulating mission:

> A mission statement is a broad, general statement about who you wish to reach and what your ministry hopes to accomplish.

> Only a clear definition of the mission and purpose of the business makes possible clear and realistic business objectives. It is the foundation for priorities, strategies, plans, and work assignments. It is the starting point for the design of managerial jobs, and above all, for the design of managerial structures.[3]

When an organization determines what it will be about, each decision and action will revolve around the pursuit of that mission.

Did you ever have a pet rock? Can you believe that so many people actually paid money for a rock? Who thought of such a gimmick, and why didn't it last? The company that distributed pet rocks lasted for a short time, but when the fad wore off and people no longer wanted their product, the company had to invent a new gadget.

Have your ever studied or observed companies with strong, charismatic leaders? People in such companies are willing to work hard and do just about anything that leader says. But what happens when the leader leaves the company? Morale seems to quickly sink. Perhaps you have not seen this happen in a company, but in a church. When a dynamic pastor leaves a church, many congregations are soon paralyzed.

Companies or churches that revolve around the personality of a leader fail to realize that, eventually, that leader will die or leave. When a company or church has no mission, their life span has proven to be short. How do companies and churches last over the long haul?

In their book *Built to Last*, authors James Collins and Jerry Porras studied eighteen exceptional and long-lasting visionary companies to determine the factors that had made them the best in their industry. One of the constants they discovered among the eighteen companies was the following:

> A visionary company almost religiously preserves its core ideology—changing it seldom, if ever. Core values [or mission] in a visionary company form a rock-solid foundation and do not drift with the trends and fashions of the day; in some cases, the core values have remained intact for well over one hundred years. And the basic purpose of a visionary company—its reason for being—can serve as a guiding beacon for centuries, like an enduring star on the horizon.[4]

The mission of the companies these authors studied had "remained intact for well over one hundred years." Do you realize that our mission in student ministry has endured for over *two thousand* years? Christ started with a vision to redeem the world. His mission was to be a "fisher of men." This is still our mission today. The church has served as a "guiding beacon for centuries" and will continue to do so, because our mission is eternal.

Defining Your Mission

Because God has given each of us different visions, the way we go about accomplishing those visions will vary. Our mission statements and what we are trying to do will be diverse. Here are a few values to assist you in articulating your mission statement:

1. Mission statements should be philosophical, not how-to guides.
2. Mission answers the "what" questions—"What are the targets?" and "What are we trying to do?"
3. Mission is clear and targeted.
4. Mission isn't about motivation; it's about focus.
5. Mission clarifies objectives.

Student Impact's Mission for Ministry

The Student Impact mission statement is:

> to turn irreligious high school students into fully devoted followers of Christ.

This is what we are all about. Every activity, program, and event revolves around accomplishing this mission. We desire for high school students to become fully devoted followers of Christ. For years, this has proven a challenge to measure. What exactly does a fully devoted follower of Christ look like? How do you know if your ministry is fulfilling its mission? What are some of the signs to look for?

The senior leaders of Willow Creek decided to define what a fully devoted adult follower of Jesus Christ should look like. They came up what is called the Five G's. Student Impact also uses these Five G's with a few adjustments to define a fully devoted student follower of Jesus Christ. A fully devoted student follower of Christ is someone who:

1. personally understands the *grace* of God and has trusted Christ as Savior (Eph. 2:8–9);
2. is committed to spiritual *growth* and demonstrates a pattern of life change (2 Peter 3:18);
3. is committed to a small *group* of fellow believers to pursue maturity and community (Acts 2:46);
4. is learning to express his or her God-given *gifts* as a servant of Christ (Rom. 12:6–8); and
5. is *giving* to the church by taking responsibility to own part of God's work in the church (Phil. 4:11–19).

The Five G's are a tool that have helped us measure the spiritual health of our students. We also want students to know the signs to look for in monitoring their own spiritual growth. Every time we celebrate communion at Student Insight (our program for believers), we put up a slide showing the Five G's. During worship, we offer students time to reflect on the Five G's so that they can determine the areas that need growth. We ask, "In which area do you need to take a growth step or in which area do you just need a reminder?" We are encouraged to see students growing in the Five G's and maturing in their faith, but when we notice students stuck in any of the areas, we can make the needed adjustments and help them regain their focus. The Five G's give us a way to measure the effectiveness of our mission.

God is still calling men and women to be fishers of men. He wants us to be about the Father's business and to fulfill His vision and mission. Because we are His beloved, His vision is in our hearts.

Perhaps, though, you are frustrated because you don't yet see that vision. Like looking at those Magic Eye cards, seeing the vision God has given you may take some time. Be quiet and wait for God to share His vision, just as He did with Simon Peter and

Andrew. In time, you will see His plan for your ministry. Keep trusting Him!

REWIND

What Did You Learn?

Vision and mission are critical components to effective student ministry because they answer where you are going (vision) and what you are trying to do (mission).

VISION/"WHERE"	MISSION/"WHAT"
What vision has God given you, and where will this vision take your students?	What are you trying to do? What are your targets?

PAUSE

What Action Will You Take?

Vision:

1. What is your vision statement?

2. Questions to ask yourself:
   • Is my vision clear enough that I can articulate it to others from memory?
   • Is my vision compelling enough that it encourages others to make a commitment to be a part of it?
   • Is my vision inspired by God and His Word speaking to me, or does it simply fulfill the wishes of parents and committees?
   • Is my vision worth the time and energy investment of my life to fulfill it?
   • Do my students know where I am taking them?
   • When was the last time I communicated vision to my students?

Mission:

1. What is your mission statement?

2. Questions to ask yourself:
   • Do I have a thought-out reason for everything that I do?

- Do my programs clearly target the audience I am trying to reach?
- What am I trying to do?
- Do my students and leaders know what I am trying to do?

What's Next?

*You've established a vision
and determined your mission.
How will you accomplish them?*

CREATING A STRATEGY

The 1996 summer Olympics in Atlanta were exciting to watch. I especially enjoyed hearing the different stories of the athletes and their training strategies. Yet despite their varied training strategies, every athlete was committed to one purpose: to win the gold.

Training to win a gold medal is a great goal, but it doesn't compare with our purpose in student ministry: to lead students into a personal relationship with Jesus Christ. This goal is eternal! How unfortunate that athletes and coaches put more thought into developing a strategy to win a gold medal than many youth leaders spend on creating a strategy to win students for Christ.

Whenever I talk with other student pastors, I ask, "What do you want to do in student ministry?" They easily answer "to change high school students' lives for Christ." I then ask them how they plan on doing this. Many times, they admit that it's not completely clear to them or that they haven't thought that far.

> Strategy answers the question of how to accomplish the vision and mission.

DEVELOPING A STRATEGY

We often get so excited about developing the vision and mission that we sometimes overlook the need for a strategy. Strategy answers the "how" question, and is the energy you spend toward reaching the vision and mission. Strategies cannot stand alone; they act only as conduits for vision to flow. They are the plan of action that will support the missions' values. Every purpose-driven ministry must have a clear strategy to funnel its energies in the proper direction toward the vision.

Here are some values to assist you in developing your strategy:

1. Strategy is driven by vision and mission.
2. Strategy must be detailed and clear.
3. Strategy answers the "how" question.
4. Strategy must be effective.
5. Strategy must be continually refined. Ask yourself, "Does this work?" and "Will this get us there?"

STUDENT IMPACT'S STRATEGY FOR MINISTRY

The Student Impact strategy is a seven-step process for students to evangelize their campus, become fully devoted followers of Jesus Christ, and build the church. We call this strategy full-cycle evangelism. We do not believe that the most effective method to reach people for Christ is by leaving a tract on a windshield or wearing a Christian T-shirt. Instead, we see God working in and through people over time. People win people to Christ; programs are simply tools in the hands of God's people. Thus, the first step in our seven-step strategy involves relationships.

Step One: Integrity Friendship

The first step begins as Christian students build a "relational bridge" with their non-Christian friends and demonstrate integrity in that relationship. So often, the only people who have friendships with non-Christians are other non-Christians. A Christian student must identify a non-Christian friend with whom he or she wants to share Christ and be willing to establish a credible friendship with that person.

Building friendships of integrity can be accomplished when Christian students "walk their talk" at school, on the athletic fields, and at home. We challenge our students to let their lives show what they believe. A senior girl in our ministry said about this first step, "It's so important to invest in integrity friendships and show my non-Christian friends my beliefs through my actions. My friend Mike is an atheist and skeptical towards church and God. I've started to let him see my life and what I do and don't do. When I'm at a party and he sees me, I'm the same as when I'm at church. I'm authentic. He has started to trust me, and he knows I'm not perfect. He also knows that what I believe is very important to me. He's even come to Impact with me. It's awesome to see God work this way."

Integrity friendships are not about students trying to stick out by carrying a big Bible, leaving tracts on all the cars in the parking lot, or wearing T-shirts that say, "Ask me about Jesus." Integrity friendships are all about students being real and honest and allowing trust to build with their unsaved friends. In time, these non-Christians will notice a difference in the way Christians live their lives, and they will begin to ask questions like, "You're kind of normal. Why don't you party?" A senior guy said about this first step, "Integrity friendships are the building block of the entire strategy. In order to share Christ or bring someone to Christ, the person has to trust you." Once this step is taken, the doors open up for step two.

Step Two: Verbal Witness

As friendship and trust grow between the Christian student and his or her non-Christian friend, the Christian student looks for opportunities to explain and discuss what a relationship with Christ has meant to them. A senior girl in our ministry suggested beginning step two like this: "I like to tell my friends how God has changed my life and personalize things. I share what my life was like before God and how it has changed since God came into my life." Sharing a verbal witness is not necessarily going through the four spiritual laws and giving the gospel message in full. It could be about certain life circumstances and how God has proven faithful or changed a human heart.

We train our students in this step by giving them tools to use like the "Roman Road" explanation of salvation or by helping them write out their testimony. This gives them confidence to share their faith and teaches them about lifestyle evangelism. Once students are trained, many of them are eager to share Christ with their friends. Ryan, a senior, said he likes to be prepared to give his story and talk from his heart. The best way for students to succeed at giving a verbal witness is by actually doing it. Through repetition, sharing a verbal witness becomes natural and genuine.

Many students, though, are fearful to share a verbal witness. They are afraid of rejection or of turning their friend off. They need to pray for God to give them boldness. Taking this second step requires courage.

John, a senior, knew what it meant to live life in God's kingdom. He understood both the fear and also the urgency of sharing Christ; he wanted so badly for his friends to experience the incredible joy and peace he had found in Christ. He wrote this poem last summer about sharing Christ with a friend:

What am I afraid of? Why do I wait?
If the world ends tomorrow, it will all be too late.
Talk to her today, yet still I'm scared,
We don't have to convince,
Only speak the truth.
But I do neither.
I pray for strength day and night.
I want to help everyone to the Lord
If this be His will.
Strengthen me Lord, help me gain my fill.
Fill me with the Spirit
That I may face the world.
Let my life shine through your Son's name. Amen.

Tragically, John never got a chance to share Christ with this friend. A few hours after he wrote this poem, he and a friend went for a walk. A drunk driver veered onto the sidewalk, striking John and ending his all-too-brief life. John's life was a source of inspiration to the students in our ministry. Those who came to the funeral were amazed when this poem was read and realized that John was concerned about the spiritual condition of his friend right until the day he died. The girl whom he wrote this poem about came to the funeral and was deeply moved by John's compassion for her. God continues to use John's life to affect others.

Step Three: Supplemental Witness/Seeker Service (Impact)

The Impact program on Tuesday nights is designed to nurture a non-Christian student's interest in spiritual things by introducing him or her to the message of Christ in a contemporary and relevant way. This program is a tool for the Christian student to point his or her friend toward a spiritual challenge and to supplement an ongoing witness. Our seeker service gives our core students a safe place to bring their non-Christian friends that is specifically targeted to reach them.

It's great to have a place for my friends to learn the basics about Christianity and not be overwhelmed. I had two friends who started asking me a lot of questions about spiritual things. After taking steps one and two with them, I brought them to Impact and it was just what they needed. One of the girls received Christ last Christmas. It's cool to see life change happening.

A junior girl

Impact is a place for seekers to investigate Christianity at their own pace and in their own way. Our core students know that Tuesday nights are geared for their friends and that Sunday nights (Insight) is where they themselves can grow spiritually. By separating the needs of believers and seekers, our purpose is clear. If we tried to meet the needs of believers and seekers at the same program, there would be constant pressure to feed the Christian and reach the seeker, not to mention the confusion if an altar call was needed each week.

"I'm not afraid that my friends will come and be turned off," says Mike, a senior. "I'm proud of my church. I've brought friends out and some have said they're not ready to make any spiritual decisions yet, but they keep coming with me. I had one friend who said to me, 'I'm not really getting into this spiritual stuff so far, but I like it here. It's cool.' He comes with me most weeks."

At Student Impact, we understand that conversion is a process. Our Christian students realize this too, and are grateful to have a strategy for reaching their friends for Christ. They are willing to be patient and let God work.

Step Four: Spiritual Challenge

During our Impact program, we leave students with a spiritual challenge in the form of a question based on the theme of that night's particular message. It is bold, but not offensive. For example, in the first week of our series called "Under Pressure," the message focused on the different kinds of pressure students face—the pressure to perform, conform, and reform—and what God's Word says about how to deal with pressure. Students were left with this challenge to talk about on the way home: *What pressures hit your life the most and how do you deal with them?*

In week three of our "Formulas for Excitement" series, the message was about how unfulfilling "outer" things are because they are temporal and do not satisfy; true fulfillment can only be found in God who can satisfy the "inside." The spiritual challenge that night was: *What is preventing you from checking out God?*

Our core students are told this question at the previous Student Insight on Sunday night so that they can be prepared with follow-up conversations after the Impact program with their non-Christian friends. This also gives them the opportunity to ask pointed questions and intentionally challenge their friends to consider the claims of Christ. One student leader said, "I don't just let my friends hear the message of Christ and not do anything about it. I take this step of boldness and challenge them."

The program opens the door to talk about spiritual things, usually outside the building and on the way home or at a booth in McDonald's. One student told me about the way his leader consistently asked questions each week on the drive home and throughout the week. He said, "He kept me on my toes! There was no way I could get away with not paying attention to the message or letting Christ work in my life." This leader's persistence paid off as this student trusted Christ and began to grow in his understanding of the Christian life.

We believe that once a seeker has spent time listening to God's Word and observing fully devoted Christian students, he or she will discover, through the conviction of the Holy Spirit, the need for a personal relationship with Jesus Christ. At some point, conversion takes place and the student trusts Christ.

Step Five: Integration into the Church (Insight)

After conversion takes place, the new Christian is invited to attend Insight on Sunday nights. It is here that a spiritual

> The relationships I've made through Insight are so different than my friendships at school; they're much deeper.
>
> Katie, a senior

foundation can be built as a new Christian learns from God's Word, participates in prayer, engages in worship, celebrates communion, and experiences the church. The believer's faith also matures as he or she begins to better understand what it means to be a fully devoted follower of Christ. Insight is the place where students can become a part of the body of Christ. It's so exciting to see new Christians worship or take communion for the first time.

When I randomly asked a few students why they come to Student Insight, here is what they said:

"I come to learn more about God."

"I love the worship. Insight has taught me how to worship."

"Insight is where I learn how to live life correctly."

"I can see Jesus in everyone here."

"I want to learn more about God so I can teach Him to my friends."

"I desire to grow in my knowledge of God."

A program targeted specifically to Christian students allows them to grow in their walk with God and develop a spiritual foundation.

Step Six: Discipleship/Small Groups (D-Teams)

We call our small groups "D-Teams." *D* stands for the Greek letter Delta, which means change. We want our small groups to help bring about the life change that develops students into fully devoted followers of Christ. In a small group, a student can further learn what the Christian life is all about and have a safe place to feel connected and ask questions. We value open groups, and new students are always invited to join a small group.

Small groups provide accountability, encouragement, biblical teaching, and support. Recently, one small group studied the parable of the soils and the parable of the mustard seed. They learned that even a small mustard seed can grow and spread out. Two of the guys in the group could really relate to this parable.

Brad's mom had originally made him go to Student Impact. In fact, she had even paid him ten dollars to try it out just once. Brad liked it and kept coming, with no further payments from his mom! Over time, he committed his life to Jesus Christ and took steps to grow and mature. His new-found faith was so exciting to him that he wanted to share it with his friend Jeff. He began building an integrity friendship with Jeff and shared a verbal witness with him. Brad started bringing Jeff to Student Impact and Jeff, too, made a decision to trust Christ. They are now in a small group together and marvel at how the love represented by one mom's ten dollars has grown and spread, just like a mustard seed. Their lives continue to minister to others.

In small groups, students learn from the Bible and also from each other. A senior told me, "D-Teams help me keep the faith and give me accountability. It's easy for me to fall into the routine of Christianity instead of being refreshed by the amazing things God is doing."

Every small group is composed of up to eight students with a leader and an apprentice leader. (We will discuss small groups in depth in chapter 11.) By keeping the student-to-leader ratio low, we are able to maximize life change and deepen discipleship.

Step Seven: Ownership

At this stage of the Christian student's spiritual development, he or she begins to take an active role in the church by serving and using spiritual gifts and tithing.

> Serving is a way to give back to the ministry and take responsibility. I've had incredible leaders all through high school and now I have a chance to be a leader and lead some freshmen girls.
>
> Rachel, a Student Impact leader

Katie has been in small groups since her freshman year. Now, as a senior, she leads a small group and also gives back to the ministry. She has realized the joy that comes from serving and says, "Being in the life of my girls is really fun." T.J. uses the talent God has given him as an actor and is on our drama team. "It's a way for me to give back to the church," he explains.

Students also start to own the responsibility to make a difference on the campus by repeating the cycle with someone in their circle of influence. The process really does come full-cycle as the new Christian gains the maturity to reach out to a non-Christian friend.

Last year, I asked each team leader to identify two student leaders to represent their campus team on a student board we called Inside Out. Inside Out gives students an inside voice on making decisions that affect the entire ministry. These students also provide me with helpful feedback on programs, events, and how they feel the ministry is going. Inside Out gives students a chance to feel ownership and responsibility by showing them their input is needed and welcomed.

GOING FULL-CYCLE

All the seniors at Beth's high school were required to take a class called Senior Survey. Jody sat behind Beth in this class. They had been acquaintances since junior high, but sharing Senior Survey helped them to become better friends. Beth had grown up in the Catholic Church and believed in God, but she had never known that God desired to have a personal relationship with her. Over the course of the semester, Beth discovered that Jody was a Christian and attended something called Student Impact.

Jody worked hard to build an integrity friendship with Beth. She also began praying for an opportunity to share her testimony with Beth. When that happened, Jody boldly invited Beth to come to a Student Impact program.

Beth was amazed at what she experienced: music she had heard before; a well-executed drama with a powerful message; a sports competition; and a challenging, relevant message. She felt as if the whole night were made just for her! The message and spiritual challenge answered many of Beth's questions about God. Beth liked the evening so much that she continued to go with Jody. The third time she attended, Beth says, "God used the message to challenge me to take a stand for Him and accept Christ into my life. And that is exactly what I did. My life was different from that point on. I had found my foundation in life: Jesus Christ."

Beth began to grow in Christ by plugging into the church (Insight) and deepening her knowledge of God's Word. She experienced further growth by joining a small group and allowing others to encourage her and hold her accountable. Over time, Beth began to show ownership in the ministry by identifying and using her spiritual gifts in many different ways.

With a core of literally eleven high schoolers, we took the principles we learned from Student Impact and developed a strategy: we started a midweek outreach program called Inside Out that targets unbelieving high schoolers, and we turned our Sunday school into a high school worship service for believers. Five years later, we now have seven paid staff for high school ministry, over 250 students attending our weekly outreach, and almost 150 high schoolers in small groups. We have seen many, many high schoolers come to know Christ, and the student core has an incredible heart to see their friends know the God they worship. In fact, it is the students who do a large bulk of the ministry, and their faith is energized by being in ministry teams and by their seeing their schools as a mission field. Last school year, we saw over seven hundred high schoolers come to Inside Out, which is eight percent of the entire student population of the county. We are now also taking Student Impact's lead and focusing a vast amount of energy into our relationally-based discipleship small groups (we call them Insiders) as the heartbeat of the current ministry.

This all evolved out of the philosophy of having a strategy and vision for the full process of reaching the non-Christian to seeing them fully disciples and involved in the ministry.

Dan Kimball, Santa Cruz Bible Church, Santa Cruz, CA

After high school, Beth continued to serve in the ministry while attending a local college, and eventually became a small group leader. She is currently one of our interns and is pursuing a degree in youth ministry.

God used Jody to build a bridge with Beth and help her along in her spiritual journey. This story is just one of hundreds of students whose lives have been changed by the love of God. Please understand that full-cycle evangelism is a process, not a program. As the Christian student invests his or her life in a non-Christian friend and then sees the converted friend invest his or her life in another, together they use God's most effective method—multiplication—to accomplish the Great Commission.

This seven-step strategy permeates our church. My daughter, Tiffany, is in junior high. She regularly practices steps one and two with her non-Christian friends. She then brings her friends to Sonlight Express, our church's junior high ministry, where Christianity is explained in a way that twelve- and thirteen-year-olds can understand. Full-cycle evangelism is effective because of relationships. It takes a substantial investment of time, prayer, and energy to go full-cycle with someone, but if properly done, it can yield eternal returns.

REWIND

What Did You Learn?

Strategy is important because it answers the question of how to accomplish the vision and mission.

STRATEGY STEPS	CARRYING OUT THE STRATEGY
1. Integrity friendship	How can you motivate your Christian students to build relationsihp with non-Christians?
2. Verbal witness	How can you equip your core students to verbalize their testimony?
3. Supplemental witness	Does your program assist your Christian students in their evangelism efforts?
4. Spiritual challenge	Do you challenge seekers to learn more about God?
5. Integration into the church	How do you help students grow in their faith?
6. Discipleship/small groups	Where do your students find accountability?
7. Ownership	How can your students give back to the Lord and use their gifts in ministry?

PAUSE

What Action Will You Take?

1. What is your strategy?

2. Questions to ask yourself:
   - Is the current plan working?
   - Does my strategy help accomplish the vision and mission?
   - Do my students and leaders understand the strategy?

FAST FORWARD

What's Next?

You are now set with a strategy.
Who will help you implement it?

STRUCTURE WITH PURPOSE

7

MOTIVATING A HIGH SCHOOL CORE

Maybe you've seen *Sandlot*, a movie about a group of young boys who love to play baseball. The best player on the team and leader of the group, Benny, has assembled a team of eight guys, but they are short one player. One day Benny sees Smalls, a new kid who has just moved into the neighborhood, sitting outside with a plastic, ripped baseball mitt. Smalls hadn't had much luck throwing or catching a baseball; in fact he didn't even know how to play the game. I'll never forget what happens next. Benny asks Smalls if he wants to play baseball on his team, but Smalls, lacking confidence, declines by holding up his broken mitt. "I don't have a mitt," he explains. Benny quickly pulls an extra mitt from his back pocket and throws it to Smalls. "Well, now you do," Benny says. "Let's play ball."

We need to see the Smalls around our ministries—students waiting for someone to throw them the mitt. We need to see students not just for what they are, but as what they can become. We need to be like Benny. God has called us to be the leaders of our teams. We must constantly be looking for those students with a heart to be players. Then we need to throw them the mitt.

When student ministers ask me, "Where do I even start in building a core?" I like to describe seven different steps that must be taken so students who are ready have an opportunity to grow in their faith. These seven steps challenge students who have played the Christian game or become complacent about growing spiritually. The seven steps are:

1. Identify the players
2. Draw the line of commitment

3. Give them something to believe in
4. Invest in the hitters
5. Build confidence
6. Play the starters
7. Become their biggest fan

Let's take a closer look at each of these steps.

IDENTIFY THE PLAYERS

When I coached football, the first day of practice was always interesting. Many players would show up. Some of them were there because their parents had forced them; others just wanted to be on a team; and then there were the kids who really wanted to play the game. As a coach, I had to determine who the real players were.

In ministry, we need to identify the students who really want to be a part of building a core and are ready to play. I'm not implying that we should make cuts like a football coach, but we do need to realize that not every student is ready to take steps of growth. We must look at each student in our ministry and evaluate where he or she is spiritually. Is this student simply a "fun seeker" looking for a good time at ministry events, or is he a spiritually sensitive student looking for answers about God, or is he a committed, fully devoted follower? Just as Christ in Matthew 4 chose His team, we too need to know who is on our ministry team. A chart at the end of this chapter gives you a chance to write down the names of students in various categories as you begin the identification process. The first step in building a core involves identifying the players God has entrusted to us.

When I was just beginning to build a core of students at the ministry I led in southern California, I did things that some might call "on the edge." I remember talking one morning during Sunday school to my students about the reason they were there. Most of them wanted to grow and make a difference. I talked to them about integrity and not being afraid to say they were Christians. I told them that when I was a non-Christian, I was not afraid to say that I was not a Christian. My purpose in telling my students about this was to challenge my students to have the courage to take a stand for Christ and to get off any spiritual fences.

I asked each of them to stand and indicate where they were in their spiritual journey. I gave them three choices by placing three chairs in front of them: the first chair represented seekers; the second chair represented casual Christians; and the third chair represented fully devoted followers of Christ. I told them to not be ashamed of being in any of these chairs. One by one, each stood and gave an answer. I applauded the students who stood and said, "I'm really not sure if I'm a

> Students are making decisions daily. It is appropriate to challenge them to identify where they are spiritually.

Christian. I think I'm in chair number one" or "I know I'm not where I should be—I'm in chair number two."

That Sunday school became a safe place for students to be who they were and to take off any masks. And another benefit was that I now knew where my students stood spiritually, which helped me know how and what to teach.

Students are making decisions daily: *Should I get high? Should I go to that party? Should I sleep with that person?* They are faced with huge decisions and required to take stands. I believe students respect leaders who are not afraid to challenge them to make decisions about their faith and identify where they are spiritually.

Another way I identify the players in my ministry is by holding up a mirror in front of my students and saying, "We need to look at ourselves and identify who we are in our relationship with Christ. We're all at different places, and that's okay. All of us have areas where we really need to improve and grow. We each need to evaluate ourselves honestly as we look in the mirror."

I explain that, as we draw closer to Christ and look in the mirror, we will see Him. And that, ultimately, one day, we will see Him face to face! First Corinthians 13:12 says, "Now we see a dim reflection, as if we were looking into a mirror, but then we shall see clearly. Now I know only a part, but then I will know fully, as God has known me" (NCV).

I also teach my students what Christ said about hypocrites and how He feels about those who are lost. By this time, I am starting to see how committed my students are and how willing each of them are to take steps of growth. I challenge them to think how they could apply this teaching practically to their lives. I begin to share with them what it means to be a difference-maker and how they can be heroes for Christ. I ask them the same question Christ asked His disciples: "Are you willing to follow?"

At this point, students are faced with a choice requiring a decision. Do they want to be part of the core of your ministry? If the answer is yes, you will know who your players are. Realize that not every student will or should choose to be a player at the start. Only those students who are willing are ready for the next step.

DRAW THE LINE OF COMMITMENT

Once you've identified the players in your core, those players need to understand what is at stake and what kind of commitment you expect. It's difficult these days for students to be fully committed to anything. They are pulled in different directions by family, friends, activities, sports, work, and other factors that demand their time and energy and force them to make choices. It's no wonder students have a hard time being committed, especially to growing in their walks with God. Students need to see that you expect at least as much out of them as they give to their other commitments. Growing closer to Christ should be their top priority. Students will respect you for challenging them to do so.

In drawing the line of commitment, I explain to students that God has called me to build a student ministry, not a nursery. The purpose of this ministry is to develop fully devoted followers of Christ. One time, I made this point by setting some baby rattles on a table and telling students, "See these rattles? These rattles are good for babies; they help keep babies entertained. I'm not here to entertain you." On another occasion, I walked students into our church's nursery and said, "This class is appropriate for babies. It's a good place for one- and two-year-olds to be. They enjoy it in here." The point I emphasized was this: I'm not interested in babysitting; my purpose is different. I *am* interested in helping young men and women become difference-makers for Christ. Students were given the opportunity to put down the "baby rattles" and cross the line of commitment.

As I mentioned earlier, in California I started out in student ministry with a Sunday school composed mostly of comfortable, casual Christian students. Many of them had their arms crossed with "How long are you going to last" looks and a "been there, done that" attitude. Thankfully, I was prepared with a vision, mission, and strategy, and also had my support teams in place. I knew I did not want to maintain a youth group; I wanted to build a student ministry by building a core.

I'll never forget the student who sat in the back row week after week. It was obvious by Dave's body language and lack of interest that he did not want to be in the group; his parents forced him to come each week.

One Sunday morning, I walked to the back of the room and asked Dave, "Are you mad at me?"

He shook his head.

I asked, "Are you having a bad day?"

Again, he shook his head.

Finally, I asked, "Then what is the problem? Do you want to be here?"

Dave answered, "No!"

I continued. "Dave, how can I help you not be here? I don't want you to be here either. Can I call your parents or what can I do?" He was shocked! My response surprised him.

For the first time, a youth leader cared about Dave. It was also the first time someone had ever challenged him and really heard what he had to say. Dave could see I wasn't begging students to come hear about Jesus. I had given him the chance to make a choice. I talked with Dave's father and together we decided

Challenge students; don't baby-sit them!

which meetings Dave should attend. I cared for Dave and wanted him to be there, but only if he wanted to make the commitment for himself.

I learned from this example the importance of challenging students. We cannot force students to step across the line of commitment, but we can make challenges and see who will respond. Drawing a commitment line forces students out of their comfort zone and gives them a choice to make. I also learned how important it is to target programs for students like Dave and give them a safe place to learn about God.

It is imperative to tell seekers or new believers that you will continue to care for them and minister to them and that you are glad they came. But with the line of commitment drawn, you need to take those who have crossed the line and encourage and disciple them in their walks with God. I believe this means meeting with those who want to grow at a different time apart from the rest of the group.

In my ministry in California, I told a group of students, "If you want to learn more about Jesus, come on Wednesday nights at 7:00." I wanted to see who would show up. Six students came the following week. We opened our Bibles and studied passages in Matthew; began to build trust and community; and showed care for one another. I also set down the rules: (1) Don't be late, and (2) bring your Bible each week. Week after week, these six faithful and teachable students attended my Bible study. Our sense of community continued to grow. When someone missed the Bible study, that person would receive a phone call expressing how much we had missed the person in our group.

After several weeks, one of the students said, "You know, Mary Jo should be here. Maybe I could bring her next week." Each of the members began bringing friends to Bible study. They started to build a small group without even knowing it! Before long we had a team of twenty.

We started to worship together—truly worship. We had created a safe place where students felt comfortable singing out loud; we trusted each other. This was no "turn and scratch your neighbor's back" worship. Our desire and hunger to enter into God's presence was rich. We grew to love our times of worship.

You need to figure out what will work for you. Where and how do your students need to grow? I make it clear exactly what it is my students are crossing into. Students who cross the line of commitment are saying, "I'm ready to grow and serious about my walk with Christ." When I draw this line, I need to make sure that the environment I had promised is what I had said it would be and that I teach these students from God's Word. Once a student has made this commitment, it's up to you to take him or her the next step.

GIVE THEM SOMETHING TO BELIEVE IN

Students want to believe in something and are waiting to follow you. This is why painting a vision is imperative in leading a student ministry. Years ago in California, my student ministry met for Sunday school in a room that was not optimal for effective ministry. I decided to paint a vision for the students to see what the room could like if we started an outreach. I asked them to imagine this room filled with their friends in an environment where everyone felt accepted, welcomed, and wanted to come. I asked them, "Can you see it?"

I took the group downstairs to a larger room and asked them to imagine what this room would look like with a stage on which we could design outreach programs. I continued on my walking vision tour by taking the group outside and talking to them about the values of physical competition and why it would be an important component of our outreaches. The vision walk concluded in the chapel where I challenged students to see their friends sitting next to them, eager to learn more about the Lord.

Several years ago, at the start of a new ministry season, I and a few other staff members took a group of students and leaders to a college football field to communicate vision and motivate them. Earlier, we had received permission to turn on the field lights and also use the locker room. In the locker room, each student went and sat by a

> **Students want to believe in something and are waiting to follow you.**

locker with a player's name on it. They were told that they were now players, too. Drawing on my experience as a football coach, I gave them a pep talk and talked to them about game preparation and what it takes to be on the field. I compared the game of football to what it was going to be like to be in the game spiritually during this next ministry year. We discussed our opponent (the Enemy) and what our line of defense and offense would be against him. I also described the end zone and what it would take for us to get there and "win the game."

When my pep talk was over, we ran onto the field. As each person stepped onto the field and ran to the ten-yard line, his or her name was announced over the loudspeaker. Imagine what they must have been thinking and feeling! Perhaps it was the first time they felt part of a team or the first time they had made the starting lineup. It was exciting for me to watch these students and leaders come onto the field.

We met the students at the ten-yard line and told them we needed to commit to one another to stay between the lines because so much is at stake. I reminded them that our ministry was much more important than scoring touchdowns; our goal was to make a difference for Christ in the lives of high school students. I warned them that times would get tough in the coming months, and it might seem that no one was applauding for them.

I also challenged the students to confront certain areas of their lives. Earlier we had placed hurdles every ten yards down the football field. Each hurdle represented a different obstacle to overcome, like fear, anger, lust, temptation, and others. I asked each student and leader to stand behind the barriers they thought would pose the biggest challenge and to pray for God's protection and strength. I was encouraged to see the students and leaders responding to the challenge and lining up behind the hurdles. I encouraged them to jump over that hurdle and to defeat the Enemy. It was exciting to see all of us win together as we walked down the field.

Students need answers to the question, "Why am I in this ministry?" In chapter 7, I talked about ways you can own the vision God has given you. Students want to be assured that you see something and that you will lead them. For some students, you will have to regularly paint the vision until they are able to see it. Once students see where you are taking them, they will desire to be a part of making that vision come to life. When they really understand what it means to build the roller coaster, so to speak, and how they can be difference-makers, many of them will be ready and willing for you to take them the next step.

> Pour your life into those students who are willing, teachable, and ready to be difference-makers for Christ on their campus.

INVEST IN HITTERS

I think it is a common tendency among student ministers to occasionally fall into the trap of using students to accomplish various purposes instead of building Christ into them. That is why this next step in building a core is so important. We must invest in, not use, the hitters and pour our lives into them.

Second Timothy 2:2 says, "And the things you have heard me say in the presence of many witnesses entrust to reliable men who will also be qualified to teach others." The greatest rewards for me in ministry have resulted from living out this verse and investing myself into others.

I have had the privilege to disciple a number of students and leaders over the years. Over fifteen years ago, I went through these steps with Troy Murphy, one of the roller-coaster builders from my ministry in southern California. I saw tremendous potential in Troy to become a difference-maker for Christ, and I wanted him to be on my ministry team. I began giving him something to believe in and painting a vision for him. Every line of commitment I drew for Troy, he crossed over, eager for the next step of growth. I then began investing in him by just "doing life" with him, using what I call the "be with" factor. Troy matured from a wild, uncommitted Christian student to a committed core member to my disciple.

Now, I am learning from him as we continue to "do life" together. His friendship is a blessing in my life.

I will never apologize for selecting a few hitters in which to invest. To me, it makes sense to use your best time to invest in your best people. Some people may say to me, "Bo, it seems you have favorites in the ministry." My answer is always, "Yes, I do. They are the ones who want to grow in Christ." I desire to pour my life into those to which God is calling me, and I intentionally invest in those students and leaders who are willing, teachable, and ready to be difference-makers for Christ.

Besides discipleship and using the "be with" factor, I also invest in hitters by motivating them to grow in various ways. One such way is to make the truths of God's Word come alive. Too many students think God and His Word are outdated and not applicable to their daily lives. How wrong they are! Our God is a creative God, and He has given us the gift of creativity to use so that our students can see Christianity is relevant today.

To motivate the students in your ministry, remember these four realities:

1. Effective learning often takes place outside the classroom.
2. Students learn by seeing, hearing, and doing.
3. A message often hits home when it is practical.
4. A picture or a visual, tangible object makes it easier for students to remember what is being taught.

Using these four realities can help build your core. Be intentional and strategic as you take the next step with students on their way to becoming fully devoted followers.

BUILD CONFIDENCE

Think back to the person who saw potential in you and threw you the mitt. Who told you you could become a player in God's kingdom? How did you feel? You probably felt like Smalls, amazed that someone believed in you. One of the key steps in building a core is instilling confidence in the lives of the students from our ministry by empowering and encouraging them and giving them opportunities to lead.

Empower and Encourage

Students want to be assured that, with God's strength, they can continue to grow in their faith, honor the steps of commitment to Christ they have made, and make a difference. Over the years, our team has come up with some great ideas I have used to empower and encourage. For example, it is difficult for students to stay "BTL" (between the lines) when it comes to purity. A few years ago, I was teaching on the issue of sexual purity and what God has to say about it in His Word. I knew every student wanted to stay sexually pure. I gave each person a penny that had been painted white to symbolize purity. I encouraged the students to keep their pennies in their pockets as a reminder to stay faithful.

Another way I have encouraged students to grow is in the area of unity. Ecclesiastes 4:12 says, "A cord of three strands is not quickly broken." Students learned about the power of friendship when Christ is in the middle and how much they need to support and encourage one other. This requires a commitment to live in unity as brothers and sisters in Christ. We gave each student three cords that they wore on their wrists or ankles as a reminder of this verse. Over the following weeks we noticed that students were still wearing these cords and talking about the encouragement they felt in not being alone. They began to see the unique community of difference-makers we were trying to build.

I also tried to build the students' confidence in their faith by teaching on Matthew 17:20, which says, "If you have faith as small as a mustard seed, you can say to this mountain, 'Move from here to there' and it will move. Nothing will be impossible for you." We distributed a mustard seed to each student so they could learn that faith requires the commitment to believe, even if it is as small as a mustard seed.

One fall day, I took a group of leaders to a ropes course. Working together to accomplish some of the missions built team unity. Several of the leaders were hesitant to go on the high ropes, but the instructor showed them how the carabiners would assure their safety. At the end of the day I gave each leader a carabiner, and we hooked our carabiners together as a reminder of what we had accomplished working together. Each leader kept a carabiner as an encouragement to work as a team and to help one another throughout the year.

Provide Opportunities

Building confidence into students also means providing enriching opportunities for them so that they realize the tremendous difference they can make in the lives of others. At Christmastime every year, each campus team adopts a needy family in our community. Most of these families are served by our church's food pantry and are struggling financially, emotionally, even spiritually. It is a rewarding opportunity for students and leaders to learn in a new way the true meaning of Christmas and to reach out to those in need. Students and leaders pool their money together and buy

> Students want to know they are needed in our ministries to use their God-given gifts to minister to those around them.

special gifts and food for their adopted family. They spend an afternoon experiencing the joy in giving as gifts, smiles, and tears are shared. One year, a student had a baseball card collection worth several hundred dollars. He decided to brighten a little boy's Christmas and gave him his collection with great joy.

Three of our female campus directors took their core girls to the baseball field in Dyersville, Iowa, where the movie *Field of Dreams* was filmed. They used that setting to dream and to commit to being a player during the year. They showed the famous vision clip from *Field of Dreams* when Kevin Costner hears in the cornfield, "If you build it, he will come." When they arrived at the field, the leaders encouraged students to walk in the corn and around the bases in the field. They challenged the students to dream about the ministry year ahead and to ask God to give them vision. Each girl was given an opportunity to cross the line and commit to "playing ball" and being on the ministry team. Then she received a baseball, which each player signed, as a symbol of their commitment to the Lord and to one another as players on the same team.

Students desperately need to be empowered and encouraged and given opportunities so that their confidence in themselves and God can grow. They want to know they are needed in our ministries to use their God-given gifts to minister to those around them. Once their confidence has increased, they can take the next step of growth.

PLAY THE STARTERS

With added confidence, students are now eager for game day. Like athletes, students want to be on the field and in the game; they want to be players and can't wait to be "BTL" for Christ and not go out-of-bounds and get disqualified from the game of ministry.

One of the best ways I play the starters is by giving them ownership in the ministry. Their presence can be seen throughout the ministry: from making phone calls to first-timers to speaking on stage to participating in STRIVE, our one-day workathon that raises the entire operating budget of the student ministries at our church. Ownership strengthens the ministry and gives the starters opportunities to play.

BECOME THEIR BIGGEST FAN

I'm always on the lookout for stories. I ask all my leaders to tell me stories about their students so that I can personally encourage these students and become their biggest fan. I'll look a student in the eye and say, "I heard this about you, and I just wanted to say I'm proud of you."

Every week, I make it a point to encourage a student. Recently I heard a story about one of our core Christian students who had been praying for his non-Christian friend to come out to Student Impact. One night, the friend finally came. I found this core student and told him how proud I was of him for reaching out to his friend. I said to him, "Your commitment to lost people is really making a difference. The steps you've taken may possibly help change your friend's eternity. Great job!" As students mature in their faith and really become players in ministry, they need a steady dose of encouragement to keep going. Our role is to give them that encouragement.

> Let your students see what they can become and how God can use them in the lives of others.

We support and encourage when we celebrate with our students. One year, for our end-of-the-year celebration, we hung a large banner with the names of students who had come to our outreach program that year. Many of them came to know the Lord, many didn't; but the banner showed the influence we had had. It was a tremendous time of celebration as students realized what they had done in reaching out to their friends was truly significant. Students felt encouraged not only for the ministry year, but to commit to being players for a lifetime.

We can let our students see what they can become and how God can use them in the lives of others. When we look a high school student in the eye and say, "Tom, I see a lot of potential in you. God has given you some amazing gifts. He is going to do great things in and through your life. Believe Him!" we encourage that student to live up to his potential.

THROW THE MITT

Building a core starts with one life at a time—and I do mean *one*. Even if you only have one student, you can throw the mitt to him or her and begin to take these steps. We can be like Benny to our students. Take time to identify the Smalls in your ministry. Pray that God will give you eyes to see what students can become.

Programs and outreaches can wait until you have built a core. I think one of the biggest mistakes student ministers make is to become program-driven instead of taking the time to build relationships with students. It takes at least six months to build a core. If your ministry has become program-driven or activity-driven, I urge you to stop and begin back with step one: identifying the players. When you start throwing the mitt to students in your ministry, I assure you great things will happen. Before you know it, you'll have a whole team.

REWIND

What Did You Learn?

Students are waiting to be led. Building a core gives students a chance to take steps of spiritual growth.

BUILD A CORE BY ...	SO THAT STUDENTS CAN ...
Identifying the players	Examine their spiritual life
Drawing the line of commitment	Make a choice
Giving them something to believe in	See the vision
Investing in hitters	Experience discipleship
Building confidence	Feel empowered
Playing the starters	Demonstrate ownership
Becoming their biggest fan	Be encouraged

Pause

What Action Will You Take?

I have found it helpful to evaluate the students in my ministry by using the chart below to identify which students fall into the following categories. This way, I know how to challenge them to grow.

Take some time to think through the students in your ministry:

UNKNOWN (not sure where this student stands spiritually)	FUN SEEKER (attends church socially)	SPIRITUALLY SENSITIVE (open to God's Word)	UNFOLDED CHRISTIAN (no commitment to the body)	FOLDED CHRISTIAN (in the ministry but not yet core)	SMALL GROUP MEMBER (committed to a small group)	FULLY DEVOTED FOLLOWER (mature core student ready to serve)

Fast Forward

What's Next?

Your core is growing.
Who's going to lead these students?

RECRUITING A LEADERSHIP TEAM

How many ministry hats do you wear in a typical week? Have you ever found yourself calling and meeting with leaders (shepherd); organizing and running competition (sports leader); listening to students' troubles (counselor); preparing and giving inspiring messages (teacher); negotiating parents' complaints (firefighter); hanging out with students (discipler); and planning the ministry calendar (administrator)? Sometimes those involved in youth ministry find themselves wearing too many hats, unable to do any one of them with much excellence. This is why building and recruiting a leadership team is critical. No one can do ministry alone. You may think you can, but eventually you will wear out.

Just look at Moses.

Moses thought he could do it all. He tried to meet his peoples' needs, but then he learned from his father-in-law, Jethro, a crucial leadership lesson that altered the way he did ministry. Here's what happened to Moses:

> The next day Moses took his seat to serve as judge for the people, and they stood around him from morning till evening. When his father-in-law saw all that Moses was doing for the people, he said, "What is this you are doing for the people? Why do you alone sit as judge, while all these people stand around you from morning till evening?"
>
> Moses answered him, "Because the people come to me to seek God's will. Whenever they have a dispute, it is brought to me, and I decide between the parties and inform them of God's decrees and laws."
>
> Moses' father-in-law replied, "What you are doing is not good. You and these people who come to you will only wear

151

yourselves out. The work is too heavy for you; you cannot handle it alone. Listen now to me and I will give you some advice, and may God be with you. You must be the people's representative before God and bring their disputes to him. Teach them the decrees and laws, and show them the way to live and the duties they are to perform. But select capable men from all the people—men who fear God, trustworthy men who hate dishonest gain—and appoint them as officials over thousands, hundreds, fifties and tens. Have them serve as judges for the people at all times, but have them bring every difficult case to you; the simple cases they can decide themselves. That will make your load lighter, because they will share it with you. If you do this and God so commands, you will be able to stand the strain, and all these people will go home satisfied" (Ex. 18:13–23).

Can you imagine hearing the phrase, "What you are doing is not good," from your father-in-law? Jethro knew what he was talking about when he spoke those words to Moses. For too long, Moses had tried to bear all the burdens of his people, continuing to take each matter into his own hands without once considering the potential of the people surrounding him. When Moses acted upon the wise counsel of Jethro and incorporated a leadership team by selecting "capable men who fear God, trustworthy men who hate dishonest gain," he learned to work smarter, not harder.

Lessons Moses Learned

1. Whoever attempts to take all leadership responsibility upon himself will surely wear out (v. 18).

2. Select people to be leaders who are able, God-fearing, and full of truth (v. 21).

3. God promises leaders the ability to endure if they follow the prescribed path (v. 23).

4. Make clear to your leaders the way in which they should walk and the work they are to do (v. 20).

5. Teach the leaders the ways of the Lord (v. 20).

6. The load will be lighter and the leaders unified when they bear the burden together (v. 22).

7. All that is required is obedience, and the people will go to their places in peace (v. 23).

Applying the truths of this passage will enable you to build effective leadership teams—teams that will "make your load lighter, because they will share it with you." We should make every effort to avoid falling into the same trap as Moses of doing the job on our own. There is no place for a Lone Ranger mentality in student ministry.

I hope you will take some time to study this passage and others in order to further understand the importance of a leadership team when ministering to high school students. The rest of this chapter will focus on how we can begin to build a team by practicing three leadership disciplines: leading from quietness; being prepared; and investing in key leaders.

LEADERSHIP DISCIPLINE #1: LEADING FROM QUIETNESS

It's a struggle to lead from quietness. The pace of ministry can be overwhelming, and sometimes ministry feels like a black hole. With so many needs, it is easy to get so busy "doing" the work of God that the work of God is hardly present in our daily lives. Our role in youth ministry should never negate God's work in us.

I have a tendency to live my life extremely fast, and sometimes the discipline of quietness is difficult for me. Many times when I try to be quiet, I'm thinking about my agenda: What needs to happen today? Which leaders do I need to meet with this morning? Trying to quiet down in my office and pray is nearly impossible. If I'm praying for leaders, I find myself thinking of what I have to tell them. It's also easy to shoot up quick "Lord, help me" prayers and then get to business. Staying quiet for long periods of time is a real stretch for me.

On the other hand, I also experience many quiet moments with the Lord when He tells me the direction to take or the things I need to do. It is when I am quiet that I hear the whispers of the Holy Spirit and am filled up to serve.

God desires for us to be men and women who draw close to Him through the discipline of quietness and look to Him as our source for strength, wisdom, and direction. Practicing quietness in our daily lives may look different for each of us. There is no "rule" that says it must be done a certain way. Richard Foster warns, "Spiritual disciplines are intended for our good. They are meant to bring the abundance of God into our lives. It is possible, however, to turn them into another set of soul-killing laws. Law-bound disciplines breathe death."[1]

Spending time in prayer and in God's Word are two excellent methods, but not the only means to quieting our hearts before the Lord. You may experience God's presence by taking a walk and marveling at His creation. Others may be drawn into His presence through worship. All of us need to discover the method that best allows us to focus on our Lord. Quietness gives us the opportunity to hear the leadings of the Holy Spirit from a heart that is fully submitted.

Leading from quietness keeps us full. Imagine you're holding a full cup of coffee in your hand and someone bumps into you. What is going to spill out? Obviously, coffee! Now if you take that same cup of coffee with just a few drips of coffee in there and someone bumps into you, what happens? Chances are, the coffee is not going to spill out.

I believe we have to lead out of quietness so that our cup is full with the leadings and directions of the Holy Spirit. God has given us the Holy Spirit as a gift. Being quiet before the Lord will allow us to stay "filled" with the Holy Spirit. Then, when we get "bumped" by the call of ministry or the frustrations of leadership, we're so full that what comes out is the Holy Spirit. Because we're full, the gratitude of serving spills out. When my cup becomes full, my focus for the day becomes clear, and I can operate through the work of the Holy Spirit rather than the flesh.

When I neglect quietness and start seeing only the agenda, my cup starts to empty out. If I get bumped during this time, watch out! I react out of the flesh instead of the Spirit. I can hurt the people around me with careless words or selfish actions. I need to regularly check the gauges mentioned in chapter 1 so that my spiritual tank does not reach empty.

As you think about building a leadership team, how full is your cup? Are you able to fully trust the Lord to provide leaders and trust Him for wisdom to make the proper selection? God has already selected the leaders who are ready to serve in your ministry. *He* has chosen them. The discipline of quietness gives you the confidence to speak the truth He has told you to say to the leaders who are all around you. Being quiet to hear the Holy Spirit's leadings allows you to approach the right people and ask the right questions.

Perhaps you are facing a season where you need to ask the Lord to refill your cup. We all encounter these times in our ministries. Take a minute right now to assess the discipline of quietness in your life. Place yourself on the following continuum: If you had the range of 0–100 percent, what percentage of your ministry is led from quietness versus quick, impulsive decision-making? Chances are, your answer was not 100 percent. If it was, I'd like to talk to you!

When we honestly look at the discipline of quietness, we begin to see the areas of our lives that need to change in order for the percentage to increase. Submitting our hearts to God and leading out of quietness is a necessary discipline that allows God to work in and through our lives. John 15:5 sums it up best: "I am the Vine; you are the branches. Whoever lives in me and I in him shall produce a large crop of fruit. For apart from me you can't do a thing" (TLB). Trying to lead a student ministry on our own strength and self-sufficiency produces little lasting fruit, but a yielded and quiet heart before the Lord harvests fruit that is eternal.

Benefits of quietness:
- It prepares you to hear God's leading.
- Your cup becomes full and your focus clear.
- You are able to face ministry pressures calmly.
- You gain confidence to lead.

LEADERSHIP DISCIPLINE #2: BEING PREPARED

It's a "normal" Wednesday. You're in your office writing a message when suddenly your phone begins to ring off the hook—and continues to ring for the next three hours. Each of the calls you receive is from a spiritually mature Christian leader looking to serve in your student ministry. How would you respond? What would you do?

I'm sure you'd be ecstatic and thanking the Lord! No one would argue that adding ten qualified leaders to your team could increase your ministry's effectiveness and really make a difference in students' lives.

It could also provide the means to take your ministry the next step. I believe that building an effective leadership team is the key to how far your ministry can go or grow, transitioning from maintaining a youth group to building a youth ministry, moving from simply baby-sitting to being difference-makers.

But the real question is: Would you be prepared? In what ministry role would you place these new leaders? Effectiveness in building a leadership team requires a second discipline: preparation.

Football coaching legend Woody Hayes once said, "Even the best team, without a sound plan, can't score." This is true in student ministry as well. You need to prepare by defining the playing field, organizing your recruiting efforts, and placing the leaders God brings your way.

Defining the Playing Field

Before an athlete steps onto the field, he or she wants to know the boundaries and rules with which to play the game. Youth leaders, too, desire to know what will be expected of them and how they can win. Leaders vary from one another in time commitment, gifts and passion, skills and experience, and spiritual maturity. How can a new leader be positioned to win in your ministry? One way you can prepare the playing field in order to properly place a new leader is by writing out ministry descriptions.

We write out ministry descriptions for every available service role in our ministry. These descriptions clearly define the boundaries so that a leader can understand the responsibilities of the role and the goals that need to be met. When a leader comes into my office, it is so helpful to show him or her on paper exactly what I am asking and what the playing field will be. Leaders want to know how success is defined and what is expected of them. You must be specific in defining the ways leaders can serve.

To be useful, a ministry description should define time commitment, spiritual gifts and passions, skills and experience, and spiritual maturity.

Time Commitment Estimate the time commitment required for each ministry position. Calculate the hours necessary for the various roles and assign realistic weekly figures. When a leader comes into your office, you can say, "This role requires a commitment on Monday nights from seven to nine." If the time commitment is not defined, a leader may become nervous and hesitant to sign up. Wouldn't you be?

Have you ever been told, "Oh, this will only require two hours"? And then a few hours turns into ten, twenty, thirty hours a week plus extra meetings, and after a few months you are crawling for the door! We need to be prepared for those leaders who come to us willing to serve one hour a week or twenty hours a week. Poorly-defined time commitments leads to leadership burnout or frustration.

Spiritual Gifts and Passions Have you ever seen a play in which the actors could not act, or attended a musical concert in which the musicians were not gifted? Sometimes it is frustrating for me to visit student ministries around the country because I observe people placed in leadership roles who should not be leading; singers who cannot sing; shepherds who need care before they can care for others; and so on. Ministry should be different than that. God has gifted each of us in different ways, and we need to be clear on recognizing the spiritual gift(s) each leader holds.

Many of us have been tempted to look for people who are available and have a pulse. I have done this and, believe me, it does not work. We must trust God to bring people with the right spiritual gifts to fill our ministry positions.

A spiritual gift is usually related to a particular passion. Sometimes passion comes from a situation God has brought you through, like a time of crisis or season of life. I know this has been true in my life. My passion for high school students runs deep because I look back on my high school days and regret the poor choices I made in several areas of my life. I desire to show the high school students God brings into my life that living God's way is the only way. If a person's passion does not relate to the ministry positions you have available, be careful! God uses passion to motivate people to serve. A person without the needed passion probably won't last very long in your ministry.

One of the ways I determine passion and gifts is by talking individually with leaders after an event or small group meeting. I ask them how they felt it went and if they enjoyed the experience. I listen carefully to their responses and try to discern if their area of service lines up with what makes their hearts beat fast (passion) and who God has made them to be (spiritual gifts).

Skills and Experience Assess what skills and experience are needed for the ministry roles you have available. For example, if you place a person in an administrative position and ask him or her to organize your summer camp, this person better be organized and able to attend to details. Work experience, education, current job, and hobbies will all give you an idea of a person's skills and experience. In our sports ministry, people who are athletic or have participated on sports teams make the best competition directors. Skills and experience are additional pieces of the puzzle that assist you in determining the proper placement of volunteers.

Spiritual Maturity Determining the spiritual maturity level needed for each service position is critical. God has given us the tremendous responsibility and privilege to shepherd and lead the students He has entrusted to our care. We must protect our students by connecting them with men and women who will influence them for Christ and teach them how to live the Christian life. High school students need positive Christian examples in their lives, and it is our task to identify spiritually mature men and women who desire to make a difference.

You can learn much about a person's spiritual maturity by asking questions like:

- How did you become a Christian?
- How did your life change after you trusted Christ?
- What do you do on a consistent basis to keep yourself spiritually authentic?
- Have you ever had a time of serious spiritual stumbling?
- If the Enemy were to tempt today, where would he take you?
- What are your spiritual gifts? How have these been affirmed?

We all are at different stages in our spiritual journeys as we strive to become fully devoted followers of Christ. Committed, spiritually mature Christians are necessary for positions that require discipling students and teaching them from God's Word, but there should also be opportunities within your ministry for young believers to serve and continue growing spiritually—for example, helping set up rooms for programs, assisting with administrative tasks, or working alongside team leaders to help plan events. Don't overlook young believers! Serving in appropriate ways is a valuable part of their spiritual growth.

Organizing Your Recruiting Efforts

Once you have written out ministry descriptions, your playing field will be ready. When a leader comes to you and expresses interest in serving, your advance preparation will prove beneficial. You will know your ministry well enough to properly place this leader in the right position. But before you place leaders, you have to find them.

Prepare to Recruit I have never seen myself as a recruiter, but as someone who gives others an opportunity to serve. I am not a salesman. When we view recruiting as providing opportunities, it changes the heart of what we do in locating and placing leaders.

It is exciting to meet potential leaders and clearly share with them the vision, mission, and strategy of Student Impact. This fires me up! Because all of us want to introduce our students to the love of Jesus Christ, we need to offer strong challenges and a clear vision to the leaders who can help make this happen. If we lack vision, we will be, as Pat McMillan warns, "tentative and hesitant to express boldly the needs of our ministry and the demands we must make to meet them. Without such conviction we issue small demands. Such demands lack challenge and perceived relevance and are seldom grasped by those looking to make a significant difference."[2]

A mistake some of us make in recruiting leaders involves confusing the line between using people and providing opportunities. It's a fine line. Each time I have violated this principle, I have deeply regretted it. We need to provide opportunities to people, but sometimes we feel the need to become like used car salespeople and beg people to join our leadership team. This perception couldn't be further from the truth! Gifted leaders want their lives to count and desire opportunities to be difference-makers. We can give them the opportunity to experience the greatest joy ever: serving the Lord and building His kingdom.

Recruiting gives us the chance to "inspire [our] followers to high levels of achievement by showing them how their work contributes to worthwhile ends. It is an emotional appeal to some of the most fundamental of human needs—the need to be important, to make a difference, to feel useful, to be a part of a worthwhile, successful enterprise."[3]

It is important for you to be excited and authentic as you talk and meet with potential leaders. Be enthusiastic! You need to communicate that serving God is a privilege and that God wants men and women to use their gifts for His glory.

When I became the pastor of student ministries at Christ Community Church, the very first step I took was to clarify my philosophy and objectives, and then to develop a leadership team around that. For starters, I needed a team leader and small group leaders. The ministry is now in its third year and we have campus directors, small group leaders, retreat/event coordinators, two bands, a video team, competition directors, a stage crew, etc. . . .

In the process of building a team of leaders, the value of two principles was verified for me. First, recruit to a need and a vision, not a job. If you need someone to set up stages and props, don't just say, "Can you be available to set up stages?" but rather, "We have a high-impact ministry that is effectively bringing students to Christ. We could not have this program without a crew of people who set up. I believe you could be a vital part in this. Would you consider?" No one really wants to set up and take down stages and chairs. But they *would* want to be part of something for a higher cause. Let them see the overall picture.

Second, recruit to personal development. Be known as one who develops people, not uses them. Give each leader a significant area of responsibility and let them own it. Never be afraid to give them feedback in order to refine what they are doing, or encourage their walk with Christ. But also, never neglect praise and encouragement for a job well done. Genuinely love your leaders. As much as possible, treat them like royalty. Serve them. Care for them. If you do all these things, you will find a loyal, hard-working group of people excited about doing a work for Christ. My leadership team is invaluable as friends and fellow workers.

Billy Burch, Pastor of Student Ministries,
Christ Community Church, West Chester, PA,
former Student Impact intern

A friend of mine once told me that many potential leaders are concerned about the WIIFM principle: What's In It For Me? Address this concern with each person investigating leadership. It is your chance to share the benefits of serving and making a difference in the kingdom. Serving is an opportunity to grow and use spiritual gifts.

Maybe communicating the vision and the difference between serving and using leaders is not a problem for you, but you struggle with where to find leaders with whom you can communicate. I've found several "fishing ponds" for leaders.

First, check your area for any Christian colleges. I am fortunate to be in the Chicago area, where we have several colleges that provide many quality leaders. To find students at a Christian college in your area, put up a flyer on the campus bulletin board or call the college's ministry office.

Second, look for leaders right in your own church. Advertise in your church's bulletin, and invite interested people to one of your programs. Ask your pastor if your ministry could do a portion of a weekend service to let the congregation know more about your vision and mission.

Third, challenge mature, upperclass high school students to accept leadership positions. There is nothing more effective than students ministering to students.

Fourth, investigate your local high schools for Christian teachers or coaches. Even if these people do not become involved in the leadership of your ministry, you'll have made valuable contacts. Perhaps they could support your ministry in prayer. You could form a prayer team (see chapter 3) and supply them with specific prayer requests each week.

Recruiting leaders needs to be a priority in our schedule. We cannot passively sit around and wait for leaders to stumble through our door. First Corinthians 14:8 issues this challenge: "And if the army bugler doesn't play the right notes, how will the soldiers know that they are being called to battle?" (TLB) As "army buglers," we have been called to sound the trumpet and make our ministry needs known. God has entrusted us with the tremendous responsibility to seek out leaders who are ready to answer the call. Have you called any soldiers to battle lately?

Prepare to Interview Once you have located a leader who is interested in student ministry, you can then begin the interview process. This is a step you should not overlook or compromise in any way. Get to know every leader before you place him or her in a leadership role. Be sure to check references. You may think this sounds too formal or threatening, but think of the marketplace.

If you were looking for a job and walked into an office, you would be told to fill out an application. The company would ask you some questions and explain the job description. If the company was not organized or did not bother to interview you, would you take the job? You probably would not, especially if you are a qualified person.

In student ministry, the stakes are even higher because all of eternity is hanging in the balance. How much greater our screening process should be! In Student Impact, we have every leader fill out an application. The application asks for references and spiritual background and offers a glimpse of the character of the leadership candidate.

When I sit down with a potential leader, I share our mission, vision, and strategy, and how he or she can play a part. This is one of the most exciting parts of my job! It does not drain me, because I am not begging people to serve; I am communicating the awesome privilege it is to serve the God of the universe. My compassion for student ministry runs deep, and I pray the leaders I interview can see my heart.

Next, I ask some direct and challenging questions. This is not meant to scare anyone away, but simply to help me discern a potential ministry fit. Some of the questions I like to ask are:

- Why do you want to serve in Student Impact?
- What is/are your fatal flaw(s)?
- Have you ever had a time of serious spiritual stumbling?
- Who are two people who have influenced you the most in your desire to serve the Lord?
- Are you in a small group?
- Have you ever had to recruit and lead a team of people to accomplish a goal?
- How do you feel about being on a team?
- Do you understand and resonate with the values of Student Impact?
- How do you plan to maintain balance in your life?
- What are your expectations from Student Impact and your director?
- Is there anything that may come up in the future about you that could compromise your character?
- Are there any other questions I should ask you?

I try to pay close attention to any yellow flags that come up during the interview. For example, when a person is not very transparent or honest with his or her weaknesses and appears to have it all together, I pause and try to dig a little deeper. Another yellow flag I look for is motivation for service. Are they stepping into this position to get their own needs met? The key during this time is to follow the Holy Spirit's promptings. When something doesn't seem right, probe and ask the person for further clarification. The Holy Spirit will make it all clear to you and help you make the right decisions.

Placing a Leader

Once you have defined the playing field, recruited a leader, and gone through the interview process, you will now be ready to place any leader that comes into your office. When I am interviewing a person for a ministry position, I have found it helpful to use the ministry entry levels placement chart below, which describes a few positions we have in Student Impact, to decide which entry level is appropriate based on the above-mentioned variables. I can then place a leader in a ministry position with confidence because all the variables have been factored. Using a similar chart tailored to your ministry will equip you as you recruit, interview, and place leaders in your ministry positions. God will honor you as you prepare yourself to make the proper leadership selections.

MINISTRY ENTRY LEVELS PLACEMENT CHART

MINISTRY LEVEL	TIME COMMITMENT	SPIRITUAL MATURITY	SPIRITUAL GIFTS	MINISTRY POSITIONS
SI 1	Light, flexible commitment	Stable, growing believer	Helps, Administration	Data entry; Frontline team (security, crowd control)
SI 2	Moderate commitment	Stable, growing believer	Leadership, Shepherding	Impact sports leader (directing sports competitions)
SI 3	Strong commitment	Spiritually mature	Leadership, Counseling, Shepherding	D-Team (small group) leader or apprentice leader
SI 4	Major commitment	Spiritually mature	Leadership, Teaching, Shepherding	Campus director

LEADERSHIP DISCIPLINE #3: INVESTING IN KEY LEADERS

Once you have placed leaders in a position of service, you must now lead and cheer them on. Vince Lombardi's greatest ability as a football coach was to get each of his players to perform optimally. Great leaders inspire great performances from those they lead by casting vision and harnessing people's energy to accomplish the mission. After Jack Welch was named CEO of General Electric, a group of Harvard Business School students asked him about his future plans for the company. One student asked him what he thought his most important task as CEO would be. Welch answered, "Choosing and developing good people."[4]

Developing the leaders on our team is vital so that effective ministry can happen. Jesus chose and developed His own team. He even prayed all night before He selected the twelve disciples to whom and with whom He wanted to minister (Luke 6:12–13). He trained, encouraged, disciplined, and inspired His chosen twelve. Jesus' example is one we should follow as we invest in our key leaders. There are four values I always keep in mind as I invest in my key leaders.

Train

Leadership training can take on many forms. In this section, I'll share a few methods that I have found effective.

Discipleship When Jesus called His disciples, He told them: "Come along with me and I will show you how to fish for the souls of men" (Matt. 4:19 TLB). Jesus was and is in the training and transforming business. He trained His disciples to catch the souls of men by using the "be with" principle. He allowed His disciples to live with, watch, and follow Him so that they would become more like Him and do as He did.

When I train leaders in the area of discipleship, I encourage them to also use the "be with" principle. When they go to the store or run errands, I urge leaders to take a student with them. If they go to the park or play volleyball on the beach, I tell them to take someone with them. It's important to create "be with" time.

Mentoring In student ministry, we also need to train our leaders to know the targets; to make sure they understand the vision, mission, and strategy; and to help them draw closer to Christ. This can be done through meetings and materials, but the greatest means I have found is through mentoring.

Mentoring starts with being an example yourself. I know that I must be a leader worth following and an example to those around me. This is a challenge! I regularly train leaders in how to follow up with students who did not attend a ministry event. When a leader calls the student, he or she should not say, "Hey, where were you? How come you didn't make it?" Instead, I advise leaders to ask, "How are you? We missed you tonight." This shows care and concern. I know that when I call a leader, I too must model this.

Evaluation Another way I train leaders is to evaluate their performance. Strong leaders want to know if they are hitting the mark and ways they need to improve performance. We need to let our leaders know if they are doing well, fair, or poorly.

I evaluate my staff team, who in turn evaluate the campus directors they lead, who in turn evaluate the small group leaders they lead. This is all done in one-on-one meetings in which specific, measurable, and realistic goals are set for each ministry wave.

Recently, our campus directors completed their quarterly goals. I went into a leadership meeting with them. It was exciting to have the opportunity to support the goals they had set using the guidelines of our vision, mission, and strategy. It is important for goals to be in line with the ministry values and the direction the ministry is heading.

Each week, I evaluate our teachers. They value feedback and want to know what they are doing right and what needs improvement. One of our teachers, Jeff, told me that when I do not give him a weekly evaluation on his teaching, he feels alone. On the day before he teaches, he puts his entire message on tape and I listen to it. The next day, the programming team sits down with him and we review his points and tweak anything that needs refining. After he has given the message, the team watches a video of his message and we evaluate him on his delivery, clarity, and how he communicated the message of Christ. Jeff sees these times as a way for us to show that we care about him and his leadership development.

Ownership I also train leaders in ownership by giving them responsibility and challenging them to rise to the occasion. One of the best examples of this in the Bible is Nehemiah. He motivated and led a team of people to rebuild Jerusalem's wall. He taught his team of wall builders to take ownership on the section of the wall closest to their homes. As a result, they took pride in their work and finished the wall in record time.

When I have identified a gifted leader and seen him or her lead faithfully and effectively, I am ready to give him or her opportunities and additional responsibility. Added responsibility, such as planning camps and retreats, organizing and leading core events, or leading competitions, gives a leader a deeper sense of ownership in the ministry. He or she can then lead students by example and encourage them also to own the ministry.

Encourage

Remember the time one of the disciples felt weary and beaten up by ministry? He timidly asked Jesus if his commitment was really worth all the pain and heartache. Jesus replied that each of them could expect a hundredfold payoff in this life and more in eternity. Jesus was encouraging that disciple to hang on, stay faithful, and stay true. It will all be worth it!

Student ministry can bring tremendous fulfillment as well as tremendous discouragement. Every leader will most likely experience a bit of both. There are definite seasons in ministry; the role of a student pastor is to know which season his or her leaders are in.

Every person receives and responds differently to encouragement. Some leaders may need to hear face-to-face the great job they are doing, while some prefer a card or short note. Others feel enriched if you send them to a seminar or give them a book. Some leaders may feel encouraged when the vision is reiterated on a regular basis to remind them that their sacrifice is worth it. Still others may feel encouraged when you take them to breakfast or lunch and spend time with them. People have diverse needs, so study your leaders and determine how you can best encourage them.

We wildly underestimate the power of the tiniest personal touch. And of all personal touches, I find the short, handwritten "nice job" note to have the highest impact. It even seems to beat a call—something about the tangibility.

A former boss (who's gone on to a highly successful career) religiously took about fifteen minutes at the end of each workday to jot a half dozen paragraph-long notes to people who'd given him time during the day or who'd made a provocative remark at some meeting. I remember him saying that he was dumbfounded by the number of recipients who subsequently thanked him for thanking them.

Tom Peters, "Management Excellence,"
Business Journal, September 9, 1991, 24.

Discipline

On several occasions, Jesus disciplined the apostles and corrected their words and behaviors. When John and James asked Jesus if they could sit on the throne next to His (Mark 10:37), Jesus rebuked them. They had not yet learned about life in the kingdom. Jesus also recognized this instance as an opportunity to teach the rest of the disciples about servanthood.

Disciplining leaders is a part of leadership development that many of us dread. The reasoning goes like this: "I can't afford to lose any of my leaders. I need every one of them!" As a result, youth pastors shy away from correcting, exhorting, and rebuking those leaders who have stepped out-of-bounds. They also miss many teachable moments in which a leader can grow and learn from mistakes.

In our weekly BTL leadership meeting, we discuss how our leaders need to stay within the boundaries that have been defined so that they can be players in the kingdom and make a difference in the lives of students. We need to stay together so that the Enemy does not push us out-of-bounds.

Unfortunately, however, the Enemy does push some leaders out-of-bounds. What do you do when that happens?

A few years ago, I noticed a change in attitude of one of our campus directors. I called him into my office to talk. I asked him about how his relationship was going with his girlfriend. He replied that everything was fine. I was very straightforward with him and encouraged him to keep honoring God in the relationship. He left my office, only to return a few hours later. "Bo, I wasn't truthful with you, " he said. "I'm having some problems with my relationship I think you should know about." He sat down again and he explained the situation; he had crossed lines he hadn't wanted to cross.

Each situation and circumstance is different, but I believe we serve a God of second chances. I decided to use this as an opportunity to encourage this young man and to redefine the playing field for him. I asked him if he was willing to be under stronger accountability and serve under a different set of guidelines. He agreed. Discipline had been applied.

The next month, though, I found out that the set plan was not working. The problem persisted. What was I to do now? I sat down with him again and asked him to step out of leadership and work on his walk with Christ. When I felt the appropriate amount of time had passed and I discerned that he had indeed taken steps to get his life back in order, he was placed back into leadership. He is still using his leadership gifts in our ministry today.

In leadership, we have to apply discipline. We must learn the appropriate times to apply grace as well as the times to draw lines. It requires quietness and discernment to follow the leadings of the Holy Spirit so we can make wise decisions.

Inspire

Leaders are inspired when they realize the contribution they are making to fulfilling the vision and the potential they possess to do great things. No one saw the potential for greatness in people the way Jesus did. Jesus changed Simon's name to Peter, meaning "the Rock." He told Peter, "On this rock I will build my church" (Matt. 16:18). Jesus inspired Peter to become the first great leader in the church.

In student ministry, we have the privilege to work with young men and women as they are maturing into fully devoted followers of Christ. We have an opportunity to inspire them and to tell them how much we believe in them.

Inspiration is a valuable tool. You know what if feels like when someone sends you a note or says that they believe in you. Most likely, it encourages you to step up to the plate and swing hard.

I love to inspire leaders to step out on faith by giving them encouragement from Scripture. James 3:5 says that "the tongue is a small part of the body, but it makes great boasts." The tongue is powerful; we can use it for good or, as it says later in the passage, for evil. Wouldn't it be great if we could always "make great boasts" about the students and leaders in our ministry? They need to hear the encouragement from us; we can be a source of inspiration for many of them.

I have experienced the rewards of inspiring others. When I see a young leader come into our ministry, I make it a priority to try to inspire that leader all along the way. I encourage, draw lines, and if necessary, discipline that leader. It is so fulfilling to see each leader grow and develop in leadership ability and love for the Lord.

Last year I met a student who was having a hard time at school and at home. He started to head down the wrong path and joined a gang. Each week, I would see him at Student Impact, usually sitting in the back row of the auditorium. I started to talk with him and encouraged him as best I could. He kept coming, and I sensed that he was spiritually sensitive, looking for God's love to fill his empty heart. I started to call him regularly to let him know I cared about him. Pretty soon, he was knocking on my office door just to talk and hang out. During these times, I would tell him, "I see great potential in you and I know you will be a difference-maker. Keep searching for Christ."

Over time, I had earned his trust, and he started to open up more to me. He revealed to me that he had a problem with drugs, and I was able to get him some professional help. I saw this young man start to change the path he was on as he began to make better choices. One day, I approached his campus director and asked him to give this student a chance to lead in some way on the team, with the proper lines drawn and boundaries set.

Over time, the young man's life slowly turned around. He began to understand Christ's love and God changed his life. He is now serving as an apprentice leader in the ministry. His story reminds me that God can use us to inspire leaders and students at a time when no one else believes in them.

THEY WILL COME

In the movie *Field of Dreams*, actor Kevin Costner was determined to make his dream baseball field come to life. He spent many hours preparing for game day by developing a plan and building the field. Likewise, in ministry, if we focus on leading from quietness, being prepared, and investing in key leaders to build a leadership team, I can assure you, like in the movie, "they will come!"

When leaders serve in positions that they love and are gifted by God to do, the church achieves its God-directed vision and leaders are fulfilled. This is how God intended the body of Christ to operate! God, in His infinite wisdom, knew we would function best in community with a team of people around us. Like Moses, we will be able to minister over the long haul if we build a leadership team and share the ministry load with like-minded men and women. Only then can we impact the kingdom.

Rewind

What Did You Learn?

We cannot effectively minister to high school students alone. We need to build a leadership team by leading from quietness, being prepared, and investing in key leaders.

BUILDING A LEADERSHIP TEAM GOD'S WAY	BUILDING A LEADERSHIP TEAM THE WORLD'S WAY
Lead from quietness—a submitted heart and a yielded spirit	Lead from impulsiveness— "if it feels good, do it" mentality
Recruit leaders by trusting God and offering opportunities for service	Recruit leaders by begging and using people to fill positions
Interview leaders without apology to discern the Holy Spirit's promptings	Interview leaders without asking tough questions and ignore the role of the Holy Spirit
Place leaders according to ministry description and ministry structure	Place leaders wherever there are holes and fill with nearest warm body

PAUSE

What Action Will You Take?

Questions to ask yourself:

1. What must change in my life to increase my quietness?

2. Do I have leaders in service slots who are wrongly matched or ill-suited to their positions? If so, what do I need to do about it?

3. Whom have I chosen or who do I plan to choose to invest in and develop?

4. Of the three disciplines mentioned in this chapter, which one do I need to focus on this week?

FAST FORWARD

What's Next?

Your leaders are in place and understand the playing fields. What can they lead?

Building Balanced Small Groups

The world has become a scary place for high school students. Faced with peer pressure and a morally deteriorating culture, students battle daily to make wise choices. As the influence of the family and church continues to weaken, students are often left searching for safe places where they can share their struggles, ask questions, and be accepted. They seem to be looking for answers in all the wrong places.

Jenny thought sex really was "safe." She didn't think she'd get pregnant. Nine months later, she had a baby girl.

Drinking beer at a party didn't seem like a risky deal to fifteen-year-old Jeremy. That is, until the police showed up. He was arrested and charged with underage drinking.

Curtis joined the Gangster Disciples in order to feel accepted. He has taken part in a dozen drive-by shootings, his first at the age of thirteen.

Temptations and distractions surround high school students today, and many students walk down dangerous paths. They wonder if there is anyone or anything they can turn to for guidance and encouragement. Our changing culture is also causing more and more students to feel disconnected. Because of such challenging times, many students find themselves feeling all alone economically, emotionally, socially, and spiritually.

But there is hope. Throughout the Bible, God refers to people as His sheep. Jeremiah 23:3–4 reminds us that God is faithful:

> "I myself will gather the remnant of my flock out of all the countries where I have driven them and will bring them back to their pasture, where they will be fruitful and increase in number. I will place shepherds over them who will tend

them, and they will no longer be afraid or terrified, nor will any be missing," declares the LORD.

BALANCING THE SCALES

Evangelism   Discipleship

THROUGH SMALL GROUPS

I believe God designed small groups so that every student could have a shepherd here on earth. Small groups provide an opportunity for students to become more like Christ and to experience care, acceptance, and true community. One of the principle functions of a small group is discipleship. However, teaching students how to grow in Christlikeness must be balanced with evangelism. Striking this balance proves to be a challenge. I hope this chapter will help you to balance the scales of discipleship and evangelism in your small groups ministry.

THE BENEFITS OF SMALL GROUPS

Students are talked to quite a bit in an average week. They come to school and their teachers lecture about the Civil War, protons and neutrons, compound sentence structures, and isosceles triangles. Then they come home from school, and most of them turn on the TV and listen to more "talking heads." When they come to church, they once again are given a message by someone talking to them. Obviously, students need to go to school, and we definitely need biblical teaching in our ministries. I believe, though, that students need a place where they are not only talked to, but given an opportunity to talk. They need not only to hear a voice, but also to be a voice. A small groups ministry can meet that need as well as others.

At Student Impact, we believe that small groups

- maximize life change;
- stop program-driven ministry;
- keep the ministry small in bigness;
- disciple leaders and students; and
- build community.

Let's take a closer look at each of these benefits.

Maximize Life Change

Life change happens best in small groups. As we mentioned in chapter 8, the small groups in Student Impact are called D-Teams—with the letter *D* standing for Delta, which is Greek for change. Small groups are opportunities for students' lives to change as they grow in their walk with God and understand their purpose in life.

Think about the important truths you have learned in the last few years. In what setting did that learning take place? Most likely, it was not in a classroom setting or even a church sanctuary. It was probably outside the four walls of a building, in the context of a relationship. Perhaps someone said something to you that the Holy Spirit used to sharpen your character. Or maybe a friend modeled to you what it means to be a servant.

One senior told me, "I know for me, if it weren't for a small group, I wouldn't have become a Christian when I did. At Blast freshman year, our group was all together and my leader shared the gospel. She told us her testimony and challenged each of us spiritually. Later that night, I became a Christian. If it weren't for that small group, my life would not be the same!"

There is no doubt that life change can happen within a large setting, but small groups and the relationships formed within them are a powerful conduit for life change. Often the problems students face can be adequately addressed not from the platform, but by students reaching out to one another.

Stop Program-Driven Ministry

Our weekly outreach program, Student Impact, is filled with excitement, energy, talented singers and actors, and relevant messages. I have found that some students jump on the program train and just ride this buzz. They are like groupies you see at concerts! They come week after week and go through every series all year long. I'm glad these students attend, but at some point each of them needs to be challenged to cross lines and take steps on the way to becoming fully devoted followers by joining a small group. It is vital that each student has a chance to be a participant, not just a spectator. When a student takes this step, we need to be ready to assimilate them into a small group as soon as possible.

I often run into students when they come back from their first year of college on Christmas or spring break. Sometimes it is disconcerting to hear from the ones who are not walking with the Lord as strongly as they did in high school. More often than not, though, the students who crossed the line and joined a small group are the ones still walking with the Lord. They also desire to give back to the Lord, and I often see these students return as leaders in our ministry. Small groups give students a spiritual foundation for life stronger than any program or series of activities ever could. It is connecting people relationally that makes the difference.

Keep the Ministry Small in Bigness

Large churches are often viewed as impersonal. Student Impact is a large ministry. We average over eight hundred students each week. I would love to see our 4,500 capacity auditorium filled with high school students. But Student Impact is not about numbers; it's all about reaching the unsaved students in our community. There are approximately eighty thousand students within forty-five minutes of our church, and I want to reach each one with the love of Jesus Christ!

If God would bless us with more students, how could we best care for them? Through small groups, our ministry can grow and yet stay small. As more and more students and leaders are connected relationally, the ministry can continue to assimilate any newcomers.

Disciple Leaders and Students

One of my favorite verses in the Bible is 2 Timothy 2:2: "And the things which you have heard from me in the presence of many witnesses, these entrust to faithful men, who will be able to teach others also" (NASB). This verse calls leaders and students to continually invest in the lives of others. Small groups are not the finish line in the discipleship process; rather the process must begin again with others so the gospel can reach the next generation.

Leaders and students are discipled differently in our ministry, yet the goal is the same: to produce fully devoted followers of Jesus Christ. We desire this goal for our leaders and students so that they can also impact those around them for Christ. As we discussed more thoroughly in chapter 8, we call this full-cycle evangelism.

Build Community

The church described in Acts 2 is a model for us to follow. They lived together in true community. Our students and leaders can build this kind of community by praying for one another, being open and honest about their struggles, encouraging each other, and teaching others about God's love.

In a small group, you can blend with different people and you are accepted for who you are. Being in a small group makes Christianity fun and the community is awesome.

Rachel, a D-Team member

A small group of students experiences authentic community by loving one another; encouraging one another; reaching out to one another; confronting one another; praying for one another; teaching one another; laughing and crying with one another; accepting one another; and forgiving one another. Members of the group form meaningful and caring relationships that help them grow in their devotion to Christ.

Obviously, there are many other benefits students experience through small groups. Once you recognize the benefits of small groups, your next step is to identify the values that might best suit your ministry.

BUILDING A SMALL GROUPS MINISTRY ON VALUES

Structures, programs, and organizational charts can change each week, but ministry values should stay consistent. You cannot build your ministry on a program, but you can build it on a set of core values. I found the following five key nonnegotiable values to be necessary in building a small groups ministry:

1. Accountability
2. Decentralization
3. Care
4. Community
5. Multiplication

Accountability

As your leadership team grows, how can you best evaluate and check the way small groups are being led? We are entrusting the most precious commodity, our students, to a group of leaders. Therefore, we should choose leaders wisely and set up a way to keep them accountable.

I believe you cannot expect what you don't inspect. I cannot expect small groups to run smoothly without inspecting them and giving some direction. All of our small groups, though, meet at the same time (Sunday nights), and I can't be at every small group each meeting. So how can I keep leaders accountable and provide them with appropriate direction? To address this issue, we developed a tool we call the CLEAR method. We use it for shepherding and planning as well as a way to hold our leaders accountable. The CLEAR method is:

C = Teaching about Christ
L = Listening to students; meeting their need to be heard
E = Placing value and praying for a friend to fill the empty chair (you'll read more about the empty chair later in the chapter)
A = Affirming students, both in what they learn and how Christ is changing their lives
R = Reading the Bible and praying

We give our leaders freedom to be creative and lead in different ways, but all our leaders use the CLEAR method. In this way we are able to monitor what the leaders are teaching our students by inspection. After every meeting, our small group leaders fill out a Shepherding Summary Form, in which they are asked to describe how each element of the CLEAR method was accomplished and who attended their group.

Not only does this accountability sharpen the leader and help with preparation, it also helps us to more effectively shepherd the students God has entrusted to our care. We have what we call a "net" of over four hundred students who have crossed over the line and joined a small group. Our goal is to tighten that net so we don't lose even one student.

Using the Shepherding Summary Form allows us to know exactly what is going on in every small group and how to celebrate victories or deal with issues. It gives us the heartbeat of the life change happening throughout the ministry. We can then better control the "net."

Decentralization

In student ministry, leadership turnover tends to be high. Some college students are able to serve for a year or two before they graduate. And many leaders are in their twenties, which is usually a very transient stage of life. The race to find new leaders seems to happen every spring. This is why the value of decentralization is so critical to your small group ministry strategy. Let me explain.

I vividly remember what the months of April, May, and June used to feel like. They were my recruiting season! I spent these months figuring out which leaders were coming back in the fall and how many holes there were going to be on each campus team. I would then begin to seek out potential leaders and challenge them to serve in student ministry.

I still feel the pressure of recruiting leaders, but to a lesser degree than in the past. I have learned how to decentralize the recruitment process by challenging existing small group leaders to identify what Carl George calls apprentice leaders. These are leaders in training, the next wave of the leadership team. Training up the next generation of leaders ensures that the gospel of Jesus Christ will continue to be shared.

The concept of apprentice leadership has proven valuable to our ministry. Instead of my running around looking for leaders, small group leaders are responsible to find their own apprentices—either upperclassmen or adults. (When the apprentices are students, we have found it best to place them in a group leading underclassmen. Peers leading same-age peers can be difficult.)

■ Shepherding Summary Form ■

Complete this form immediately after every meeting and give a copy to your ministry director or small groups coordinator.

ATTENDANCE

Leader:

Apprentice leader:

Members present: Guests filling the empty chair:

Members absent: Starting core number:

ACTIVITY SUMMARY

Briefly describe how you incorporated the CLEAR values listed below.

Christ—How was Christ made the central focus of your time together?

Listen—Were you able to meet the students' needs to be heard? What concerns arose?

Empty chair—Are students praying for specific friends they could invite to join the small group? How are you fostering an openness toward new members?

Affirm—In what ways were you able to affirm your students?

Read and pray—How effective was your time in the Word and in prayer together?

CELEBRATION

What's happening in your small group that you'd like to celebrate or note? Are there any problems or questions with which you need help?

These new apprentices are brought into the leadership structure by the small group leader and challenged to help lead the small group. They learn leadership skills by observing and also assisting in leading the small group. Apprentices are taught one-on-one by their small group leaders about leadership and shepherding students. They are receiving on-the-job training and will, at some point, be ready to lead their own group. They also receive monthly ministry-wide training at our leadership meetings.

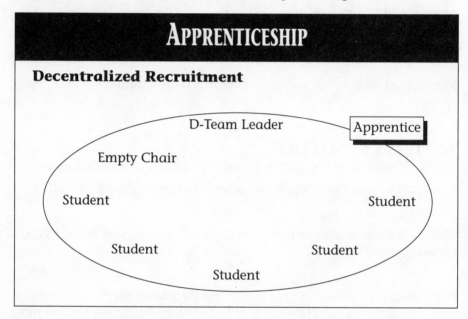

Apprentice leadership also allows groups to grow numerically. When a group has a leader, apprentice leader, and eight students, it is ready for the next step. We call this next step "creating": the leader and the apprentice leader decide how to divide the group, and the apprentice becomes the primary leader of one of the groups formed. Now the whole process can begin again.

Care

In ministry, there is the danger of using people up and not showing them care and value. We can prevent burnout and enable leaders to serve over the long haul by writing ministry descriptions, allowing for appropriate span of care, providing training and development, and incorporating leaders into small groups where they can be members instead of leaders.

CREATING D-TEAMS

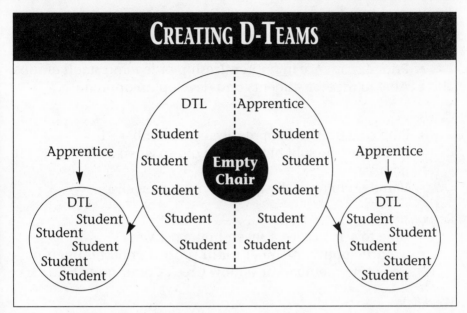

Ministry Descriptions Writing out ministry descriptions is a simple yet often overlooked way to care for leaders. We reflected on the importance of ministry descriptions in the last chapter, but I believe so strongly in their importance that I want to remind you again! If I were a part of your ministry, would I know what I was trying to do? Would I know my playing field? Would I know what I was trying to accomplish outside of just loving students?

Because our ministry descriptions include time commitments, spiritual profile, qualifications, and responsibilities, our leaders feel cared for; they have direction and they understand what they are doing. If you are having a problem finding leaders or keeping strong leaders, consider the reality that strong leaders won't stay around people who are unorganized. Take time to write out ministry descriptions.

Sample Ministry Description for a Small Group Leader

A small group leader is to lead and shepherd a small group of high school students through the small group structure to become fully devoted followers of Jesus Christ.

Spiritual Profile:
- Practices disciplines of daily prayer, quietness, and study of God's Word
- Committed to intercessory prayer for students and leaders

* Gifts include shepherding

Skills:
* Prior experience in apprenticeship or leading small groups
* Able to mentor students and develop an apprentice

Goals:
* Find and train an apprentice by December 31
* Negotiate the split of the small group when it reaches eight members
* Value and model discipleship and evangelism

Responsibilities:
* Able to serve at least seven hours per week
* A participating member (or in process of becoming a participating member) of Willow Creek Community Church

Weekly
* Attend core nights
* Attend target nights
* Contact apprentice by phone or appointment
* Contact students by phone or appointment
* Attend Insight on Sundays
* Lead a small group every other week (materials provided)
* Attend a small group led by the Campus Director on Sundays from 3:30–5:00 p.m.

Monthly
* Plan one small group event per month

Annually
* Complete small group orientation

Events to attend:
* Summer camp
* All-church small group leaders' retreat in September
* Blast (weekend retreat in February)
* Operation STRIVE & STRIVE Bash (one-day fund-raiser in late April)
* Monthly leadership training

Appropriate Span of Care It's no wonder that some leaders burn out trying to care for too many people. In Student Impact, we strive to keep our ratio five students to one leader. Each small group has five to ten students. Practically speaking, this means no leader makes more than five phone calls a week and is responsible for only five people. This span of care makes it possible for leaders to last over the long haul. If the ratio increases, ministry can get overwhelming and wear leaders out. As mentioned above, when the group grows to over five students, the apprentice leader takes responsibility for the additional students.

Training and Development Leaders need to learn how they can most effectively minister to high school students. This requires ongoing training. We meet regularly with our leaders, both individually and as a whole leadership team. We have all-leadership meetings every month. The agenda usually consists of thirty minutes for me to cast vision and remind leaders why they do what they do, and what's ahead in the ministry; thirty minutes for leaders to huddle together around a table and share concerns, ideas, and prayer requests; and twenty to thirty minutes of worship. These meetings are invaluable because they help to keep us all moving in the same direction.

Not only do leaders need training and direction, they also need feedback and encouragement so that they can grow in their leadership ability. Leaders need to be treated as indispensable heroes. Our job is to give them as much care, encouragement, and training for success as possible.

Small Group Membership In addition to ministry descriptions, appropriate spans of care, and training and development, leaders themselves are cared for through small groups. Every leader is in a small group that meets twice a month for the purpose of care. Here's how it trickles down: division directors care for the campus directors in their division; campus directors care for the small group leaders on their team (up to five); small group leaders care for high school students. This way, the ratio is kept five to one throughout the ministry.

Community

As our student ministry grew, it became more and more complex to organize and administer small groups. How do you factor in so many variables like age, school, spiritual level, or interests? It became like a Rubik's cube of mixing and matching students in order to fit them into the right group.

I have found that students do not like to be forced into small groups; they like to choose their groups. Students will gravitate to those with whom they feel affinity and share a common interest. For example, very often football players hang out with football players, freshmen feel most comfortable with other freshmen, and so on. Groups seem to form naturally.

Ryan, a senior, checked out Student Impact his sophomore year. He wasn't sure he wanted to join a small group because, as he said, "I was afraid I'd get stuck with a bunch of geeks." He wanted the freedom to choose a group of guys who had similar interests and a desire to learn and grow in Christ. After Ryan joined a small group, he had this to say: "I ended up being in a group with guys who I actually looked up to at my school and who were popular, fun guys. At Blast my sophomore year, I saw things I had never seen before—I had never seen a group of guys hug and cry! I was a part of that and my life was changed!"

A few years ago, we decided that there would be no rules for students to form groups except that group members need to be all the same gender. We gave some additional guidelines and boundaries, such as: choose people you trust to be consistent and committed to a small group; find people whom you respect spiritually; and identify people who desire to grow in their walks with God and are at the same spiritual maturity level. Then we let students form their own groups.

Every twelve weeks, we have what we call "the starting line" at Student Insight. On these nights, students decide if they want to commit to six small group meetings (groups meet every other week) and regularly attend Student Insight. If so, they sign a personal commitment, called "I Will Cross the Line," indicating their agreement in serveral different areas (see following page). After the twelve weeks, students and leaders have a chance to evaluate their small group experience and decide if they want to commit to another twelve weeks. If a student is unconnected and not sure of which small group to join, we help to place him or her based on campus, grade level, etc.

Giving students a choice in forming their small group has proved beneficial to both students and leaders: leaders end up leading groups of students who actually want to be together.

Multiplication

How's your math? Do you remember learning the difference between addition and multiplication? Here's a chance to brush up on your math skills. Ready for the quiz?

▌ I WILL CROSS THE LINE . . . ▌

. . . and lead a life of personal commitment to Jesus Christ, because I believe that my D-Team will only be as strong as each member's personal commitment to Christ.

. . . and lead a life of integrity, because I believe that the way I live my life shows people my commitment to Jesus Christ.

. . . and lead a life that makes a difference in the lives of other people, because I believe that each of us needs to offer a hand back to someone else.

. . . and lead a life that is committed to attending Student Insight and Student Impact, because I believe that my participation in my church shows my commitment.

. . . and lead a life that is committed to attending and participating in my D-Team, because I believe that my participation in my D-Team shows my commitment.

. . . and lead a life that is committed to prayer, because I believe my prayer for Student Impact, the Impact staff and leadership team, my team, my campus, my D-Team Leader, the empty chair, and other people in my D-Team makes a difference.

. . . and lead a life that is committed to my D-Team leader, because I believe that I need to have a hand up and God has given me my D-Team leader for this purpose.

. . . and pray that one day I may be a D-Team leader, because I believe that I can give back to other people what God has given to me through D-Teams.

Signed: Date:

2	2	3	3
+3	x3	+4	x4

10	10	100	100
+12	x12	+256	x256

I hope, from the above examples, you were able to figure out that multiplication produced the larger numbers. If you were stuck on any of the problems, it might be time to dust off the old math book!

If we want to expand the kingdom of God, we can most effectively do this through relational multiplication. God has commanded us in John 15 to "go and bear fruit." As the branches, our role is to reproduce fruit lest we get cut off. Small groups that do not reproduce seem at odds with this analogy of a branch bearing fruit. We can best "bear fruit" through the value of multiplication.

At Student Impact, we decided that if growth through multiplication is a value, then all small groups should be open, not closed. Students understand from the very beginning of the twelve-week commitment that their group is open and that other students will be joining it. There is no "us four, no more" mentality. Open groups stop cliques from forming and also keep groups alive. Only when a group is open can it fulfill the mission of the ministry. Newcomers breathe life into small groups.

Small group ministry is by far one of the strongest aspects of our ministry because our students have grown best being together. Our small groups turned from being just another get together for Christians to an account-ability and learning time, and have created a deep thirst to know and love God. Our students have used their small groups evangelistically, too. Once a student has invited a friend to our outreach program, they usually will invite them to their small group next. In this way we have seen several students' lives change for

Christ. Growing and expanding our small groups is one of our top priorities this year.

Mary Armas, Women's Director of Student Ministries,
Central Christian Church, Las Vegas, NV,
former Student Impact campus director

One of our student leaders became a Christian her sophomore year. After attending Student Insight for a short time and growing in her new faith, she was invited to join a small group. Here's what her first experience was like:

In the movie *Wayne's World*, there's a scene where Wayne and Garth go to the airport and lie on top of their car and talk to each other. My leader, Gloria, took our small group to O'Hare Airport. We lay on top of a few cars and talked about spiritual things with one another. I loved the connection with the other girls and a chance to learn more about God. I became a part of the group that night. It really tied me into the Body.

Open groups also help keep the focus outward. Every group in Student Impact has what we call the "empty chair." An empty chair is used as a tool to remind students to invite their Christian or spiritually sensitive friends. Each week the group prays about who will come into the group to occupy the empty chair. Every small group member is asked every week, "Who is in your empty chair? Who are you praying for?" Students are challenged to build an integrity friendship with a friend, then share a verbal witness, and eventually bring that friend to an Impact program.

Maybe after a target night, that friend becomes a Christian and needs a place to go to ask questions and grow. The group can then start praying specifically for that friend to fill the empty chair. The value of evangelism has been raised, and our students have learned about compassion for the lost. In time, he or she can then bring that friend to the group.

The concept of the empty chair results in concern for the unconnected and the creation of new groups. What makes the student not feel like a stranger when he or she comes to a small group? There's been a relationship built; he or she is not totally unconnected because the group has prayed for him or her for months. We have also found the balance between evangelism and discipleship through small groups. New small groups will continue to be created as the empty chair is filled in many groups.

Last year, a small group met one night in the waiting room of a maternity ward. (Sometimes our leaders choose unusual places to lead their small group!) Mary Beth was friends with one of the girls in the small group and was filling the empty chair for the first time. She had come with a lot of questions about God and felt comfortable sharing her doubts and concerns with the other girls in the group. The group, excited to answer her questions, shared the gospel with her. That night, in the waiting room of the hospital, Mary Beth trusted Christ. In many ways, the maternity ward was symbolic of Mary Beth's new birth in Christ.

The principle of multiplication also applies to apprentice leadership. For example, an effective evangelist who reaches one thousand people a day for Christ will win the world to Christ in 13,515 years. Wow! But a very effective discipler who trains two people a year to reach others for Christ will win the world to Christ in thirty-three years. As 2 Timothy 2:2 is lived out in our lives and the lives of our leaders, we will multiply our ministry as well.

Multiplication is not about numbers; it's about connecting students to one another and to a shepherd. It is also not about getting bigger; it's about getting smaller. Growth is positive because there is a structure to support it.

A LOOK INSIDE STUDENT IMPACT'S SMALL GROUPS MINISTRY

Our small group D-Teams meet every other week after Insight on Sunday nights from 7:30 to 8:30 P.M. We use curriculum that we've developed to incorporate the values of small groups. This curriculum has been recently published by and is available through Zondervan (see back of book). Leaders receive material for six D-Team meetings at our monthly all-leadership meetings. Since all D-Teams use the same curriculum, students can talk with friends in different D-Teams about what they're learning and encourage one another. We try to connect the D-Team curriculum with what students are learning from the Bible during the teaching time at Student Insight.

Every twelve weeks, we have the D-Team "starting line" I referred to earlier in this chapter. On these nights, students who want to join a D-Team sign a personal commitment that helps students realize being in a D-Team requires an effort on their part.

On D-Team nights, the program ends a bit earlier than normal so students can still get home by 9:00 P.M. Most D-Teams meet in the church, but sometimes D-Team leaders make arrangements to meet off-campus. Much of the D-Team curriculum is written to give students practical, experiential learning about God and His Word. For example, let's say the topic for a D-Team is how to be "hot" for God and fully live your life for Him. The leader may elect to hold the D-Team in a sauna or hot tub or drive students around in his or her car with the heat on high. Students like to learn through experiences and hands-on teaching. By providing this kind of experiential teaching, biblical concepts come alive in a fresh, new way.

One D-Team leader held her small group in a Chuck E. Cheese pizza parlor and had each person play a race-car video game. They were told to drive with their knees to illustrate how challenging it is to control where you are going and avoid crashing. She told the girls that life, too, can be full of challenges and that they would "crash" if they tried to direct their own path in life. She then had each girl play the game with her hands on the wheel to illustrate the point that when God steers life is more fun and exciting. He knows the roads and how to take the corners. The girls just needed to give him control of their lives. They then studied several verses from the book of Psalms.

Another D-Team leader taught her girls about how Christ takes away burdens. She asked each girl to write on a note card a burden or struggle she was facing. The girls then took their cards and attached them to balloons. Together they let the balloons go, symbolizing how Christ takes away burdens. The D-Team leader showed the girls verses in the Bible that taught about how to give burdens to the Lord.

Are you starting to get a feel for the power of small groups? Do you see that small groups is where life change can happen most effectively? Imagine you have a leader who is passionate and willing to love, teach, and shepherd high school students. When this leader finds an apprentice to help lead the group, the D-Team is ready for students. Imagine that five sophomore guys form a D-Team and sign personal commitments at the starting line. The leaders are connected with these students and a D-Team begins. They study God's Word together, care for one another, and over time, mature in their walks with God. Compassion for their non-Christian friends starts to increase.

Imagine the leader then saying to the group, "Who can we pray for to fill the empty chair?" As these students begin praying in their D-Team for their lost friends, they also learn how to build integrity friendships and give a verbal witness. When steps one and two occur, these students then have a place to bring their friends to supplement their witness: the outreach program on Tuesday nights. When one of the friends they have been praying for comes to Student Impact, the rest of the D-Team can lend support by making this new student feel welcomed. Imagine that over the course of several weeks this non-Christian student decides to trust Christ. He or she is invited to the next Insight and then fills the empty chair at the next D-Team meeting. D-Teams stop program-driven ministry as students like this get connected with a small group and experience community with a few friends.

Do you also see how multiplication can happen in ministry? Open groups allow for new students to join D-Teams and prevent cliques from forming. Students want their friends to experience the care, community, and acceptance they have found through D-Teams. Filling the empty chair is valued by student and leaders as they work together to keep the ministry small in bigness. Life change is maximized through small groups.

THE SHEPHERD'S CHALLENGE

When they had finished eating, Jesus said to Simon Peter, "Simon, son of John, do you truly love me more than these?"

"Yes, Lord," he said, "you know that I love you."

Jesus said, "Feed my lambs."

Again Jesus said, "Simon son of John, do you truly love me?"

He answered, "Yes, Lord, you know that I love you."

Jesus said, "Take care of my sheep."

The third time he said to him, "Simon son of John, do you love me?"

Peter was hurt because Jesus asked him the third time, "Do you love me?" He said, "Lord, you know all things; you know that I love you."

Jesus said, "Feed my sheep" (John 21:15–17).

The Lord's directive to Peter challenges those of us involved in small groups ministry. Our Shepherd has asked us to feed and care for His sheep. This command is not to be taken lightly. Jesus told it to Peter three times! There is a sense of urgency in what we do as more and more of God's sheep run astray or are scattered by the storms of life. And yet God cares for every one of His sheep; He wants each of them to be safe and under the caring watch of a shepherd. Luke 15 tells the parable of one lost sheep and how God searches for it until it is found. God rejoices when one of His sheep is found. Will you be the one God uses to find His sheep? Make it a priority to balance the scales of discipleship and evangelism in your small groups ministry. You *can* be the one.

Rewind

What Did You Learn?

A small group ministry helps to balance the scales of discipleship and evangelism.

SMALL GROUP BENEFITS	SMALL GROUP VALUES
• maximizes life change	• monitor leaders' integrity through strong accountability
• stops program-driven ministry	• end centralized recruitment by practicing decentralized recruitment
• keeps ministry small in bigness	• prevent leadership burnout by caring for leaders
• disciples leaders and students	• promote real community instead of forcing students into groups
• builds community	• grow through multiplication instead of by addition

Pause

What Action Will You Take?

1. Questions to ask yourself:
   • How is my small group structure working?
   • In what ways am I balancing the scales of discipleship and evangelism?
   • What values permeate the small groups ministry?

- Do my leaders have appropriate spans of care and are they equipped to lead?
- How effective is the small group curriculum we are using?

2. Read Ezekiel 34 to see how God would shepherd.

3. Read Psalm 23 and John 10 and learn from the Great Shepherd.

Fast Forward

What's Next?

*You've developed a small group ministry.
How can you mobilize these groups
to penetrate high school campuses?*

won. I can legally get on campus now and hand out my tracts to students. Isn't that great?" I heard a youth minister say to the group of youth leaders with whom I was standing. Great? In my mind, I was wondering what it was he had actually won. He was so determined to get on campus that he took his case to court and fought with the high school principal to make his point, losing integrity in the process. Was this the right battle to fight? Is that what student ministry is all about?

Your Christian students are the "tract"; their lives are the "paper" for non-Christians to read. They are the ones on campus five days a week living the Christian life for all to see. The most effective ambassadors for Christ are your Christian students—and they are already on campus.

When you have built a core of committed students (chapter 9), identified and positioned qualified leaders (chapter 10), and developed a small groups ministry in which students are growing (chapter 11), you will then be prepared to penetrate the high school campuses in your area through your Christian students. I have not seen optimal effective ministry happen by fighting to put up posters or hand out flyers. Effective student ministry happens when a Christian student feels compassion for his or her lost friend and owns the responsibility to share Christ. The best platform our Christian students can stand on is the integrity they have built with their unchuched friends. This gives them the opportunity to give a verbal witness in a meaningful way.

If students are the best means through which to reach a campus for Christ, the question you are probably thinking is: How do I mobilize and equip these students for ministry? I think the answer is found in campus ministry. In this chapter, we will look at three components of campus ministry: structure, leadership, and campus momentum. Campus ministry begins with a structure.

STRUCTURE

Imagine that five of the freshmen guys in your student ministry are from the same high school. What would you do with them? You would probably like to stick those squirrelly freshmen in a corner somewhere until they are juniors or seniors, but for the sake of this example, that is not an option! How would you organize and train them for ministry on their campus?

One way to organize these five guys is by placing them in a small group where they can learn more about God and begin praying for their unchurched friends to fill the empty chair. We can then train these guys for campus ministry.

Because students are on their campuses every day, they can bring your ministry to their fellow classmates. This is why we value campus ministry. Providing opportunities for Christian students to gather together on campus for Bible study can be a good thing. But community without a cause goes nowhere. I believe if you took the hand of Jesus and followed Him, you would end up in a crowd face-to-face with unsaved people.

We need to help our students, once they're in small groups and praying for their friends, to take it one step further. They need to feel a part of a bigger cause. This is where campus ministry fits in. We have freshmen, sophomores, juniors, and seniors all together on a team for the purpose of penetrating their campus for Christ. Campus ministry builds excitement as the students start to see that it's more than just them—it's a whole team.

A student is placed on a team according to the high school he or she attends. In our ministry, thirty high schools are represented; some of these schools are forty-five minutes away. These thirty high schools are organized into campus teams, with some campus teams representing multiple high schools and other campus teams representing just one high school. In Student Impact, a student who attends either Barrington High School or Lake Zurich High School is placed on the Rug Rats team; a Fremd High School student on The Storm; and a Jacobs High School student on Unleaded. (The students and leaders name the teams.)

The number of students from each high school involved in ministry and the number of leaders available determines the number of teams. Each year, we make adjustments on the number of teams we will have based on these two criteria.

You can use the same criteria to figure out what works for your geographical area and the students in your ministry. Some high schools have a stronger core because of proximity to church, parental church involvement, or the size of the high school. If you have twenty core students on a single campus, you'll probably want to form a team with students from that campus alone. You can combine students from smaller campuses into a single team until the number of core students grows. Or you may want to put two campuses on the same team if the students from those high schools went to the same middle school and have already developed relationships. The two main constants are to keep students from the

> Structure campus teams to keep students from the same high school on the same campus team and to limit the span of care to five students per leader.

same high school on the same campus team, and to try to limit the span of care to five students per leader.

Breaking into campus teams is beneficial for several reasons. First, students from the same high school can build friendships and team unity. This helps foster great team spirit as students encourage one another on their campuses. Second, during the adolescent stages of social development, students are looking to belong to something and to feel accepted. Being a part of a team gives a student identity and a way to fit in socially. Third, as a student ministry grows, it becomes impossible for the youth pastor to meet students' needs on a deep, personal level. The team structure involves capable, adult leaders who can more effectively meet these needs. And fourth, Christian students from the same high school can permeate their campus with the love of Christ and be an example to the non-Christians around them.

LEADERSHIP

You've organized the teams. Now the question is: who will lead these teams? Identifying and placing leaders in the right positions is a challenge. I hope the material in chapter 10 helped you think through how to recruit and build a leadership team.

Leaders, too, can help students penetrate the campus for Christ. We encourage our leaders to get on campus as often as they can. Some of them are able to coach a sport, and a few substitute teach. We encourage our leaders to attend football or basketball games and other school events with the students on their team. Leaders need to interact with students outside of the church walls and be a part of campus life.

Over the years, we have adjusted our leadership structure and revised our ministry descriptions. One value that we work hard to keep is span of care of one leader to no more than five students. You can use the criterion of a limited span of care to determine how many leaders you need. Start at the bottom of the organizational chart pictured on the following page and work up, adding new leaders and leadership positions as the number of students involved warrants it. If you're just starting, perhaps you'll need only a few D-Team leaders (enough to try to keep the span of care no more than five students per leader) and an upperclass student to serve as Campus Director. As your ministry grows, you can refine and expand the leadership positions.

The following are descriptions of the leadership positions we have put in place for our campus teams. You will have to determine which leadership positions you need in your ministry.

D-Team Leader

The first leadership position needed for campus ministry is the D-Team small group leader. It is essential to start with the shepherd. A D-Team leader is to lead and shepherd a small group of high school students through the D-Team structure to become fully devoted followers of Jesus Christ.

Each D-Team leader commits to:

- Attend Insight programs
- Attend target nights at Impact
- Contact (by phone or appointment) D-Team students
- Lead a D-Team every other week
- Identify an apprentice D-Team leader
- Plan one D-Team event per month
- Attend a D-Team led by the campus director

If you are just starting a campus ministry, or if your core group of students is under about fifteen per campus, this may be the only level of leadership you need right now.

■ IMPACT OVERVIEW ■

West Division

North Division

Division Director

Male and Female Campus Director

10 D-Team Leaders

Male and Female Campus Director

10 D-Team Leaders

Male and Female Campus Director

10 D-Team Leaders

Division Director

Male and Female Campus Director

10 D-Team Leaders

Male and Female Campus Director

10 D-Team Leaders

**Student Impact
Student Insight
D-Teams**

South Division

East Division

Division Director

Male and Female Campus Director

10 D-Team Leaders

Male and Female Campus Director

10 D-Team Leaders

Male and Female Campus Director

10 D-Team Leaders

Division Director

Male and Female Campus Director

10 D-Team Leaders

Male and Female Campus Director

10 D-Team Leaders

Campus Director

Each campus team is led by a male and a female campus director. In Student Impact, most of these leaders are in college or recent college graduates; a few work full-time and are in their mid- to late-twenties. The gift of leadership is essential as a campus director leads and motivates a campus team of twenty to one hundred high school students and up to five D-Team leaders. Each campus director is expected to:

- Disciple one student
- Recruit D-Team leaders
- Recruit an apprentice campus director
- Lead a small group for D-Team leaders
- Observe a D-Team every other week
- Attend a D-Team led by the division director once a week
- Plan one team event per month
- Visit campus once a month and attend campus activities

When I led a ministry in California, my campus directors were upperclass high school students and the ministry description was not quite as extensive as it is now. Because my ministry in California was smaller, using students in this role was effective and I was able to work closely with them. Evaluate your particular situation and the leaders around you. Perhaps high school students could serve as campus directors in your ministry.

Imagine you have two campus teams with twenty students per team. You are now ready to identify campus directors. You could choose four high school students—two guys and two girls— who have strong leadership gifts and high integrity to oversee the two teams. At this point you should have two small groups, led perhaps by upperclass students. You could now take all the leadership and place them in your small group to disciple and care for them. You need to be in the lives of your top leaders, whether they are students or adults. With this accomplished, you are off to a great start with your campus ministry structure.

Division Director

As your teams grow, another level of leadership is needed to maintain appropriate spans of care. We call the people at this level division directors. A division director oversees four high school campus teams and provides leadership and direction to the campus directors leading those campus teams. He or she must demonstrate the kind of spiritual maturity that allows him or her to be a "leader of leaders." Some of the responsibilities of a division director include:

- Meeting weekly with campus director team leaders to give them direction and training
- Leading a Between The Lines care group with campus directors
- Leading a Student Impact division teamroom
- Observing D-Teams every other week
- Visiting the high school campuses in the division

In addition, a division director is directly involved with the leadership of his or her division. The director recruits and trains an apprentice and recruits the campus directors and D-Team leaders for the division.

We added this leadership role just a few years ago to cope with the growth in our campus ministry. It was becoming difficult, if not impossible, for me to oversee all the campus directors. We added the role of division director to help care for and lead the campus directors. In our ministry, a division director is a full- or part-time paid position.

Student Leaders

There is one more level of leadership that we should never overlook. It is the most important role in campus ministry. I'm referring to student leadership. I believe students need and want to lead and are able to demonstrate responsibility and ownership. It is vital to determine appropriate levels and boundaries in which students can lead and serve in ministry.

In Student Impact, qualified juniors and seniors can apprentice and lead D-Teams. Committed core students also serve as grade-level directors, which means they are the point persons for a particular grade. Grade-level directors make it a priority to meet and follow up on students from the grade they lead who attend Student Impact for the first time. These students exhibit leadership and integrity to others and are respected on their campuses for their faith. Grade-level directors pray regularly for the students in their grade. They also assist the campus director in generating campus momentum by planning events and outreaches. Peer leadership has proven effective as these leaders relate to others and model Christlike character.

It is so important for students to understand that they own the ministry. We encourage our campus directors to involve students in various areas of leadership so that students can see they are making a difference. We want students to know they are needed and that their gifts are valuable.

As you build a campus structure of teams and leaders, remember that the purpose is to penetrate the high school campus for Christ. This is only effective if the core is strong and onboard with the vision. Otherwise, you will just have a Christian club. We need to be communities with a cause. Only then will momentum build.

CAMPUS MOMENTUM

Since students practically live on campus, it only makes sense to understand campus life and the kinds of events happening at the schools. We call every high school represented in our area and ask for a school calendar. This information is invaluable because it helps us strategically plan the ministry year. It gives us an opportunity to familiarize ourselves with our students' worlds and to know when they are busy or on

> Think about the fall season in your area. What is happening in the lives of your students during this time? How will that influence which topics you choose to teach?

breaks. We can then make the necessary adjustments and plan accordingly.

Building campus momentum is a challenge. You really have to think through the flow of a school year. We work with the natural momentum of the school year by structuring our calendar around the four seasonal waves of ministry programming discussed in chapter 7. These waves reflect Student Impact's vision to change student's lives, their friends' lives, build the church, and impact the world.

At the start of the ministry year, in September, most students are excited to be back in school with new classes, new teachers, and a chance to make a few new friends. There are football games and the Homecoming dance to attend; energy levels are high. When November and December roll around, though, the momentum always seems to change in our ministry. Students get caught up in the holiday season and, in Chicago, winter starts its long, cold, reign of terror. (I'm a native southern Californian, you know!) Some schools plan their final exams before Christmas break. Some leaders, too, feel the pressure of college finals and may not be able to serve as much during this time.

> Evaluate the months of January, February, and March in your geographical area. What are your students thinking and feeling during these months? How will that influence your ministry?

During the first wave of momentum (September through December) Student Impact's focus is on God's changing individual lives. We challenge students to grow in their understanding of God and to deepen their love for Him. Over time, when students realize what Christ has done for them and the ways He has changed their lives, they desire to share Christ with their friends. This is why we created "The Gift," a special Christmas program given during this time that gives students an opportunity to share the gift of Jesus Christ with their friends.

We build on the energy created from "The Gift" as we head into the second season of momentum, from January through March, and help our students focus on how God can also change their friends' lives. We emphasize steps one, two, and three of our seven-step strategy: build an integrity friendship with an unchurched friend; share a verbal witness with that friend; and then bring that friend to Student Impact as a supplemental witness.

By this time winter has fully kicked in and, unless you like to build snowmen or ice skate, there is not a lot for people to do in our area of the country. Students and leaders get cabin fever and become bored from being cooped up inside. We try to break their boredom with our February weekend winter retreat, Blast. This retreat builds new momentum for the ministry as students are challenged during the weekend to begin praying for one to three non-Christian friends to come to a target night in March. The entire ministry core rallies together around this vision, and the excitement level is high. For the last several years, God has honored the prayers and efforts of these core students as hundreds of their friends have made decisions to trust Christ on these target nights.

These new Christians are encouraged to take steps five and six in the full-cycle evangelism process and integrate into the church by attending Student Insight and joining a D-Team. In the third wave (April and May), we emphasize building the church: new Christians are folded in and begin to grow in their walk with Christ, and core students begin to understand spiritual gifts and the unique role they play in building God's church.

> Assess the months of April and May as you think through campus momentum in your ministry. What are students and leaders focused on? How will you maintain momentum?

During these months we deal with "spring fever" as students get excited about shedding their heavy winter jackets and counting down to summer vacation. Leaders may be tired at this point and start to drop out. To help students take ownership in building the church, we hold our annual one-day fund-raiser called Operation STRIVE and provide other service opportunities within the church.

The months of June, July, and August complete our ministry year. For some student ministries, summer is the best season to build momentum. That's not the case for us, because so much of our strategy revolves around campus teams and the charge for Christian students to own their campuses. When students are not on campus and interacting with their non-Christian friends daily, it is difficult for them to take a friend through steps one, two, and three. We do encourage our core students, though, to continue building integrity friendships during the summer.

Although Student Impact does not meet during the summer, Student Insight continues to build up the believers so they can impact the world. Interested students have an opportunity to participate in various mission trips and inner-city ministry. Some of our college leaders have gone home for the summer, and most of our leadership takes time to replenish themselves. We encourage them to stay connected with the students in their D-Team as best they can, but their responsibilities are much looser. D-Teams in the summer are student-led discussion groups that help identify future student leaders. The new senior class leaders, as well as the graduates who decide to step into leadership, are trained, and by summer's end they are ready to lead incoming freshmen.

Every summer, we hold a weekend retreat for all the eighth graders who are transitioning into our ministry. It's a great time for these incoming freshmen to feel welcomed and informed. It's also the time these new senior leaders meet the members of their small group for the upcoming ministry year. The freshmen appreciate being connected with a senior, and the discipleship process begins.

Our summer camp comes at just the right time to bring the members of our ministry together after a summer of family vacations and going in different directions. After drawing closer to Christ and hearing the ministry vision once again at camp, students and leaders feel motivated and enthusiastic for the new ministry season ahead. We are then ready to repeat the waves of momentum.

Every student ministry's campus momentum will be different. You need to evaluate what campus life looks like in your area of the world and how you can best penetrate high school campuses with the love of Christ. You can build campus momentum wherever you live by helping students and leaders focus on the ministry vision.

> **Summer is different for every student ministry. What do your students and leaders need during this time?**

THE POWER OF CAMPUS MINISTRY

Over the years, many different organizations have rallied students together on campuses all around the country. I'm sure God has used these efforts. I believe, though, that the best student ministry occurs when students own their campus and feel deep compassion for their unsaved friends. I feel strongly about this because I have seen the effectiveness of campus ministry. Let's take a look at what God did when the concept of campus ministry was implemented in one youth ministry over twenty years ago.

The core students involved in Son City loved God and wanted to share Him with their friends. When the ministry grew to eighty students, it was divided into four teams. As teams grew, they were split again. Eventually there were twenty teams, each averaging fifty to sixty students. Evangelism became a lifestyle for them as they reached out to their non-Christian friends at school and began the full-cycle evangelism process. A leader who witnessed this firsthand recounts the hearts of these students and the compassion they felt to reach their campus with the love of Christ:

> There was always the reality of heaven and hell hanging
> in the balance, which created an incredible sense of urgency.

Dave wrote a song called "Crossroads," in which one line asked, "Have we all forgotten there really is a hell?" These kids hadn't forgotten. And because they were young, the concept of eternity had not grown old to them. They hadn't developed sophisticated defense mechanisms to cushion the blow of truth or rationalize away their responsibility. They just said, "If this is true, my friends are not going to be in heaven with me. I better do something."

I remember prayer meetings in the church basement in which kids would literally weep for the lost. Perhaps there was a Son Company concert coming up, and their parents or their best friend had agreed to come for the first time. There would be little groups of four or five kids on their knees on a cement floor, pleading that God would draw their loved ones to Himself. The kids carried that same intensity and spirit of prayer on stage with them when they put on concerts or led team meetings or sat through Bill's messages with their unsaved friends beside them.

The kids sang a song called "Two Hands," which could have been the theme song for Son City. It said, "Accept Him with your whole heart / And use your own two hands / With one reach out to Jesus / And with the other bring a friend." That's what these kids were doing. God honored their sincerity with a steady stream of conversions.[1]

God changed many lives through the ministry of Son City. He used those students and leaders to launch a new church, Willow Creek Community Church, which in turn has touched thousands of lives around the world.

Willow Creek celebrated its twentieth anniversary last year, and I marvel when I read stories like the one I just shared with you. I'm so thankful that, twenty years later, hundreds of students in our ministry are still on their knees feeling deep compassion for their friends.

Ryan, a senior in Student Impact who serves on our production team helping set up microphones and the stage before our Tuesday night program, admitted he had taken the easy way out and neglected to build integrity friendships at his school; that is, until his leader challenged him to do just that with a friend at school. Ryan started to think about this challenge, and one day in study hall the urgency of it all hit him: he realized most of the people around him were going to hell. Many of the students at

Ryan's school are Jewish, and his compassion to share Christ with them began to deepen that day.

Ryan decided to focus on his friend Kevin. They shared a common interest in computers and technology and started hanging out together. One day as they were talking, Kevin asked Ryan, "Where do you go when you die?" He had watched the TV show *Unsolved Mysteries* the night before and was curious. Ryan was ecstatic! What an opportunity! Ryan said to Kevin, "Come over on Saturday and I'll tell you. I've got absolute proof."

When Saturday rolled around, Ryan was nervous but prepared. His leader had taught him the Romans Road explanation of salvation and he was ready to share the gospel for the first time. When Kevin came over, Ryan opened his Bible and took his friend through the Romans Road and articulated the gospel as clearly as he could. Kevin was interested, but not quite ready to make a decision to trust Christ.

The following week was Target-In at Student Impact, a night designed for students who are new Christians or spiritually sensitive to sit around a table with others from their team, discuss a few prepared questions, and ask any questions they may have. Ryan invited Kevin to come help him with the production set-up and then stay for Target-In. They sat in a group and discussed the questions projected on the screen, and many of Kevin's questions were answered.

On the car ride home, Ryan and Kevin continued to talk about spiritual things. Kevin said he had loved the evening and wanted to come back the following week. Ryan asked Kevin more about his beliefs and discovered that Kevin believed in parts of the Bible and also parts of evolution. Ryan was amazed that he could answer Kevin's questions, and he finally understood the Holy Spirit in his life as he continued to follow the Spirit's leadings.

Kevin is not a Christian as I write this, but Ryan is excited to continue reaching out to his friend. Ryan told me, "I can't wait for Kevin to become a Christian so that together we can reach our campus for Christ. It will be great to have another Christian on campus with me."

I'm excited, too, to witness Ryan's commitment to keep sharing the truth of Christ with Kevin so that Ryan's dream can come true and that together, they can reach their campus for Christ.

This is only one story of many I hear each ministry year. You too will hear stories like these if you commit to focus on student ownership and campus ministry. Campus ministry is powerful. Your core students are the ones on campus every day, rubbing shoulders with their irreligious friends. Give them opportunities to minister to their friends by developing a structure for campus ministry; providing leaders who can guide and train them in becoming fully devoted followers of Christ and having compassion for their lost friends; and planning programs and events in light of school calendars and seasons of momentum. When you have developed a structure through which students can impact their campuses, lives will change. But remember: structure itself doesn't change lives; it's simply there to assist students to take the next step with their friends. Structures may change from year to year, but the underlying values must remain the same.

Make sure that students like Ryan understand the "whys" of campus ministry and the important role they can play in making a difference on their campus. Your core students are the ones who can best reach their friends with the love of Jesus Christ. Implementing a campus structure and your own strategy will help them to do just that.

Rewind

What Did You Learn?

Campus ministry is effective because students are the best means through which to penetrate a campus for Christ.

STRUCTURE	• Start with small groups. • Organize students into campus teams. • Place teams into divisions as teams grow.
LEADERSHIP	• Add leadership positions as needed to maintain appropriate spans of care. • Don't overlook students as potential leaders. • Encourage leaders to get involved in campus life.
CAMPUS MOMENTUM	• Think through seasons in your area as you plan your teaching topics. • Get area schools' calendars. • Plan strategically.

PAUSE

What Action Will You Take?

1. Write down all the high school campuses you might have an opportunity to reach and the names of students who attend your ministry from each of them:

HIGH SCHOOL	STUDENTS

2. Call each high school on your list and ask them to send you a calendar. Better yet, visit each campus and introduce yourself to the principal.

3. Ask yourself:
   - How many of the campuses have you already visited (sporting event, play . . .)?
   - What is your current structure as it relates to campus ministry? Is it working?
   - Do your leaders understand their ministry roles?

FAST FORWARD

What's Next?

*Your students are organized
into campus teams.
Do they have a place
to bring their non-Christian friends?*

PROGRAM WITH PURPOSE

PROGRAMMING VALUES

Many people think Student Impact's draw is a cutting-edge program. When people observe one of our programs, they expect to see bells and whistles. Some say, "Oh, if I had Willow Creek's budget or facility, I could do a great program too, and have a large ministry." When I hear this k⁻ _₋.₋ of statement, I question the values that drive their student ministry. Are they simply looking for a bigger and better program?

What many people fail to understand is that Student Impact has not grown because of a great *program;* our ministry is based on values. Throughout this book, I have described a number of values, such as being purpose-driven; developing a small groups ministry by balancing the scales of discipleship and evangelism; and communicating a vision, to name just a few.

So why has Student Impact grown, if not because of its program? Student Impact thrives because of *relationships.* Our program is an important part of our strategy, but if it ended tomorrow, ministry would continue. I have found that program-driven ministries quickly die, but people-driven ministries flourish. The challenge over the years has been and will continue to be focusing on the right values and remembering that people should always be more important than programs.

In this chapter, I will explain five values that we strive to include in our programming planning process so that we stay people-driven instead of program-driven.

VALUE #1: BEING MISSION-MINDED

"Come, follow me," Jesus said, "and I will make you fishers of men" (Matt. 4:19).

211

A program should always help the mission of your ministry. Without a mission, programs lack purpose and become entertainment. Student Impact's mission, "to turn irreligious high school students into fully devoted followers of Christ," is the backbone of what we are trying to do programmatically. Anything that takes us even one degree away from our mission is not worth placing in our program. Because our program is based on our mission, we make choices by asking, "Does using this in the program help accomplish our mission?" When you cannot answer the "why" question, there could be trouble.

When we plan programs in our program development meetings, we brainstorm and come up with many different ideas. Sometimes someone will throw out an exciting idea for an upcoming program and start right in on figuring out how to make it happen. Usually another person will slow us down by saying, "Wait a minute. Why would we do this? Is this in line with our mission?" Because we function as a team, we can help each other stay focused on the mission and our targets.

We work hard to understand how the mission and our targets work together. Whether trying to reach the seeker with the message of God's love or helping the believer connect with God, we program to meet specific target needs.

We must always be about our ministry's mission. All of us may hold different values in accomplishing the mission, but ultimately we all desire to reach high school students for Christ. Stay mission-minded.

VALUE #2: TARGET-BASED

> I have become all things to all men so that by all possible means I might save some. I do all this for the sake of the gospel, that I may share in its blessings (1 Cor. 9:22b–23).

In chapter 6 we talked about the importance of knowing your target and the people you are trying to hit. In programming, we need to determine to whom we are trying to communicate and the most effective way we can do so. After a program, it's common to ask these kinds of questions: "Why did we do that? Who were we trying to reach? Did we fulfill our mission? Did the program work? Did we think through the calendar well enough and take into account students' schedules?" These are great questions. Being target-based allows you to zero in on the answers.

I remember a particular night after a Student Impact program when I was asking myself these exact questions and thankful we had thought through our targets. Our theme that night was the love of Christ, and the programming and teaching focused on this life-changing truth.

It was exciting to see the arts used to prepare students to hear the message of Christ. The opening song that night was "Hold My Hand" by Hootie and the Blowfish, a secular song that presents the world's perspective on love. After the song, four high school students from our drama team performed a sketch on how the word *love* is so casually tossed around in various real-life situations. The drama was followed by the song "You Gotta Be" by Desiree. It's a secular song that communicates how hard it is to try to be all different things the world tells us to be in order to be loved. When these three segments were over, I could clearly tell how the first song connected with the drama, and the drama with the second song. I was certain why we had chosen and performed each of these elements. We had hit the target and prepared students to be more open to the message.

When the speaker came up, the students were ready to listen. Imagine how exciting it was for the speaker to have the audience prepared and receptive. He affirmed that indeed it is difficult to be loved the world's way; people expect us to be and do certain things. The speaker then had the chance to tell students about God's unconditional love for us. After the message, another song explained more about God's love.

Being target-based allows us to focus the program each week on the audience we are trying to reach. Effective ministry can happen when we know our targets and plan programs accordingly.

VALUE #3: EXCELLENCE

> And whatever you do, whether in word or deed, do it all
> in the name of the Lord Jesus, giving thanks to God the Father
> through him (Col. 3:17).

Have you ever just stopped in the middle of your day and thanked God for the opportunity to serve in student ministry and the chance He's given you to make a difference? I have. I do this every day I drive onto our church's campus. It overwhelms me at times. I can't believe I serve the King! During these times, I get excited thinking about the privilege we, as youth pastors, have to communicate the greatest story ever told. It motivates and challenges me to do it with excellence.

As I said in chapter 2, excellence is doing the best with what you have. It does not mean perfection, but excellence demands that we put forth our best effort with the resources we have been given. To explain the value of excellence in programming, we need to look at two areas: selection and creativity.

Selection

Excellence starts with the selection process. Choosing the right programming elements and personnel are key for effective programming. Selection is sometimes more difficult than actually doing the program.

We have learned the importance of using gifted people on stage who walk authentically with Christ and desire to use their gifts to glorify God, not themselves. It's tempting to buy into talent. Some musicians, actors, and other creative performers are more concerned with themselves than with reaching students for Christ. We will not tolerate any of that; we must protect the stage and guard who is communicating from it. Poor choices can be disastrous. Unfortunately, we have made them several times, learning hard lessons in the process.

We rarely use outside bands. Recently, I clearly remembered the reason why. We placed a band on stage that we didn't really know very well. They were talented musically, but we hadn't spent enough time with them to know their hearts or listened closely enough to their music. Once they started performing, I knew right away we had made a bad decision and were one degree away from our mission. We had compromised the stage in our selection by placing musicians who were more interested in performing than communicating spiritual truth. I sat there in my chair with that "Oh, no" feeling in my gut.

What made it even worse was that the evening was Parents' Night and many parents were visiting. Bill Hybels' daughter was involved in the ministry, so he was in the audience too. The next day, I had an all-day, off-campus meeting, so I missed Bill's visit down to my office. When I returned, my staff anxiously told me Bill was looking for me. I knew exactly what it was about. When I went into his office the next day, he clearly communicated his disappointment about our musical selection. I was challenged to protect the stage and never compromise it like that again—too much is at stake.

Each musician and vocalist on our programming team must go through an audition with our programming director as well as an interview process to make sure that every person has willingly submitted his or her gifts to the Lord and desire to be used by Him. Most often, our vocalists and musicians are told what to sing or play and sometimes even what to wear on stage. They quickly learn that it is not about them; they are simply God's conduit to communicate truth.

One year we had an extremely talented vocal director who was also a humble servant. She had chosen to minister to high school students in part because she found Christ while struggling through high school; she knew how much high school students need to hear about God's love. Her prayer before she went up on stage to sing was always, "Jesus, may You be the only One seen on the stage tonight."

She once sang a song called, "What's Going On?" It's a secular song, but it asks a lot of good questions. The first time she sang this song, she admitted that she did so with a performer mind-set. The next time we chose to do the song, God had grown her up. Instead of wanting to get on stage and perform, she prayed, "God, this is a secular song, written by someone who doesn't know You. But I know You. Take what You've done in my heart and my maturity and, as I'm singing this song, be in my eyes, my gestures, and the look on my face. Give me Your heart as I sing and let them see the peace I have in You. Amen." She thought she had to be a performer, but God had turned that upside down. Who you put on the stage is so important. Make your selections carefully.

Creativity

Have you ever gazed at a summer sunset or been to the zoo and marveled at the colors of a peacock's feathers? Our God is so creative! He has given us the gift of creativity to communicate more of who He is to others. We can be creative by looking at the things around us and incorporating the arts into our programming. Using music, drama, stage design, or video can sometimes make God's truth come alive in a clearer way than words ever could.

I'm so thankful to be part of a church that values the arts and the gifts of creative people. It is so important that people with these kinds of talents have an outlet for their creativity and ways to express themselves.

Encouraging students and leaders with the gift of creativity to use it in the church is a privilege. I recently did this with my son Brandon. He has expressed his creativity in interesting ways in the last few months. One night he asked me to come into his bedroom to watch a video he had made to show at school. The video featured Brandon giving his campaign speech for student body president. In the middle of the video, he had grabbed a one-dollar bill from his wallet and creatively tried to persuade (bribe?!) his fellow classmates to vote for him. It worked. He won the election.

> Creativity is like a muscle—it has to be stretched and exercised regularly to keep it fit and functioning.
>
> Gloria Hoffman and Pauline Graivier, *Speak the Language of Success,* as quoted in *Speaker's Sourcebook II* (Englewood Cliffs, NJ: Prentice Hall, 1994), 79.

That video gave me a glimpse of Brandon's creativity. I have told him that certain people see things that others do not; creativity is a gift that can help communicate God's love. You have many Brandons in your ministry. Identify these creative students and encourage them to use this gift.

Creativity expert Roger von Oech said, "One of the major factors which differentiates creative people from lesser creative people is that creative people pay attention to their small ideas."[1] Do you have any creative people involved in programming who are excited to develop their ideas, however small?

I do. I believe creativity in programming begins with the programming director, and our programming director, Troy Murphy, is by far one of the most creative people I know. I remember going to lunch with him not too long ago. At our table were some coasters for drinks. Troy looked at them and got that faraway look in his eyes; I knew his mind was racing. "Hey, this would be awesome to do for an Impact program." He went on to explain to me his idea. Seeing the coaster had triggered a creative idea we ended up using several weeks later.

Another time we were walking down a road when Troy saw a chain-link fence. "Wouldn't that be cool to roll up and put on stage and then put some lights on it?" Later in the series, I smiled as I saw a chain-link fence rolled up on our stage and marveled at what Troy's creative touch had done.

I am often amazed at the things creative people can come up with by looking around them and seeing potential in even the smallest of things. We can encourage creative people to use their gifts to serve the King and bring excellence to our programs.

VALUE #4: PROCESS

> Be completely humble and gentle; be patient, bearing with one another in love. Make every effort to keep the unity of the Spirit through the bond of peace (Eph. 4:2–3).

One night as I walked into the auditorium before a program to watch a rehearsal, I could sense that something was wrong. The rehearsal was not going well and things seemed somewhat chaotic on stage. I saw that the vocalists and drama team were uptight. After observing this for several minutes, I realized we had lost something very important along the way. We had blurred the line between performing and serving so that the pressure for excellence had overpowered the passion for service.

I called the programming team together for prayer and also reminded them that they were on the team to serve the Lord, not themselves. After our time of prayer, I could tell that attitudes had changed and the proper focus was in full view once again. By God's grace, the program went extremely well and many students responded to the gospel that night.

Situations like this one can happen if we get so caught up in the *program* that we forget the "whys" of what we do and how important it is to value people in the *process*. We can hurt people along the way and not even realize it until the damage has been done. Process is something we are trying to get better at as we continue to increase the value of people over programs. In the past, we've done some great programs to communicate the love of God, but lost people in the process. It's definitely not the way to do ministry.

I want my ministry to be organized, purposeful, and well-staffed, but not at the expense of the personal touch. I never want this ministry to evolve into a "business." In a business ministry, students become a number in a database, leaders focus on tasks versus relationship, and I spend more time with my computer than with people. I need to make sure my leaders and I are constantly building relationships with students. Life change comes through relationships— not because of programs, structures, or activities.

Pete App, Green Bay Community Church,
Green Bay, WI, former Student Impact intern

In one of our program development meetings, four video projects were assigned to our media director, Dave Cooke, all of which had tight deadlines. Dave did not complain, but I could tell he felt overwhelmed with all he had to do in such a short time. My staff team is full of players who are committed and willing to go the extra mile. After the meeting, I went up to Dave's office and asked, "How are you doing?" He said, "Okay, but I have a lot to do." When I asked him how I could help to lighten his load, he said if one of the videos could be skipped, that would really help. I agreed. Later, Dave said to me, "Bo, thanks. It really meant a lot to me that you were concerned for me and my health and not just focused on putting the program together."

We didn't even miss the video I cut out of the program, but Dave felt honored in the process. Honoring the process also honors the Lord. Ministry doesn't just happen on the day of the program; it happens on all the days leading up to the program as well. It happens when you are planning the program to rehearsing to hanging lights to actually producing the program. Don't ever forget to honor and value people along the way.

VALUE #5: EMPOWER

> And let us consider how we may spur one another on toward love and good deeds (Heb. 10:24).

Once a creative programming team is in place, it's important to empower them to do their jobs. Programming is a team ministry, not a one-man show. The ministry director cannot do everything; he or she must empower others with the appropriate gifts to help with programming. Over the years I have been extremely fortunate to work with some very talented and gifted people. My role is to trust the programming team God has assembled together and empower them to their jobs. I can do this in several ways.

The first way I can empower my team is to show each of them that they and their ideas are valuable. At our weekly program development meeting, we brainstorm ideas for upcoming programs with one rule in mind: There is no bad idea. We use the storyboarding method to brainstorm. When someone has an idea, he or she writes it down on an index card and places it up on the board. This allows everyone to feel a part of the planning process. I value each person's input as we plan programs. Once a program begins to develop, I empower the team to make it happen. I trust each person on the team and encourage them to get the job done.

The second way I can empower those on the programming team is to remind them to fight the right battles and to stay mission-minded. Sometimes those of us in student ministry do not have the greatest reputations with the deacons, pastor, or members of our church because of edgy programming or loud music, and it is easy to start fighting the wrong battles. It is a top priority of mine to make sure that the people on my programming team stay focused on the mission and do not get sidetracked with all the different distractions that can come our way.

Third, to empower people is to inspire them. One of the best ways I can regularly inspire the programming team is by being a "good finder." After a program, I like to go up to a production volunteer, shake his or her hand, and say, "Thanks for serving. You did a great job tonight with the microphones." To a vocalist, I might say, "The song you sang ministered to students tonight. Thanks for using the gifts God's given you for His glory."

I also try to inspire people when the program didn't go well. Everyone can tell when the program just didn't work, and some get discouraged. I can say to them, "It's okay," because I knew their hearts and the hard work that went into the night.

It's amazing to see what happens to people when you show that you believe in them. Over fifteen years ago in southern California, a young high school guy in my student ministry showed an interest in programming, specifically media. He started by taking pictures each week and putting together slide shows. I worked closely with him and often stretched him out of his comfort zone. I believed in him and challenged him to take projects he didn't think he could do. Now, many years later, this young, novice media volunteer has matured into one of the best media directors in the country and he, in turn, empowers others on his team.

Empowering others is a privilege. Several years ago, a young musician became part of the Student Impact band. I could see this gifted young man's heart for excellence and the humility in the way he served. I began to give him more and more responsibility. He thrived and continued to serve joyfully and with excellence. He now oversees production for the whole church.

VALUE-BASED PROGRAMMING

What programming values permeate your student ministry? Do they help you accomplish the mission of sharing Christ with students? What values do your programming volunteers think, walk, talk, and breathe?

It is so important to build your program on key values. Take time to determine the right values for your ministry so that "God may open a door for our message, so that we may proclaim the mystery of Christ" (Col. 4:3b). That's what programming is all about.

REWIND

What Did You Learn?

Core values in programming keep the ministry people-driven instead of program-driven.

VALUES	REMEMBER TO . . .
Mission-Minded	• evaluate which programming elements help you accomplish the mission • stay on course with your mission
Target-Based	• determine how you will hit the target • ask "why" questions
Excellence	• select personnel and programming elements carefully • identify creative people
Process	• recognize that people are more important than programs • honor people along the way
Empower	• value the ideas of others • help your team fight the right battles • inspire others

PAUSE

What Action Will You Take?

Where would you place your ministry on the following continuum as it relates to the programming values we just discussed?

|———————————————————————————————————|

Mission-minded   Program-minded

|———————————————————————————————————|

Target-based   Shotgun-based

|———————————————————————————————————|

Excellence   Just getting by

|———————————————————————————————————|

Process   End product

|———————————————————————————————————|

Empower   Control

FAST FORWARD

What's Next?

You've determined your programming values.
How do they play out in the actual programs?

Preparing the Outreach Program

I vividly remember observing Son City over ten years ago when Dan Webster led the ministry. At the time, I was just starting to build a new student ministry in southern California. When I saw the program, I was fired up because I finally had found a program with a clear purpose and one targeted specifically to seekers. I knew I could not start at the level Son City was at programmatically, but I wanted to plan and produce programs that were purposeful and effective. I could hardly wait to get back home and get started.

When I began weekly outreach programs, they were far from complex. The band would usually show up twenty minutes before the program, do a quick rehearsal, and then perform one song. After the song, I came up to give the message. That was it. Our programs were quite simple, but effective in accomplishing our mission. We did the best with what we had. Students were excited to have a place to bring their non-Christian friends, and God really worked in the hearts of many of those students. As I reflect back at the simplicity of those early programs, I knew they were purposeful and that we were hitting the target.

Because we hold two different programs each week at Student Impact, we are able to target the specific needs of seekers and believers and meet each group's needs with greater effectiveness. Our Tuesday night program, Student Impact, is planned specifically with seekers in mind. We use a variety of elements like music, drama, and video, to draw students closer to Christ.

This chapter is filled with practical ideas and tools you can use to create outreach programs.

PREPARING THE OUTREACH PROGRAM

As we think about being prepared, I think back to the times when my kids needed a baby-sitter. I wouldn't let just anyone baby-sit my children. I wanted to know the baby-sitter and make sure she understood what to do and was prepared for any possible emergencies. As a father, I was concerned for the safety and well-being of my children.

Our Heavenly Father cares for us too. I believe God will open the door when He sees we are prepared to care for and shepherd His children. Like an earthly father, He too protects His children. God wants the best for His children just as I want the best for my own children. We have been entrusted to care for God's children. How much more we need to be prepared!

Preparation for the outreach programs has to start with our love for the lost children and our vision to see them come back to their Father. It begins with our hearts. Once our lives are in order, we can prepare the support teams, the students, and the program.

Support Teams

In chapter 3, I mentioned five groups of people who can lend support to your ministry. Do you remember the five teams? The teams are: prayer, elders, pastor, parents, and leaders. It is important that these teams be in place before any outreach programs begin. You need your prayer team to pray for you; your elders and pastor to support your strategy for outreach; your parents to assist on the night of the outreach program; and your leaders to be willing to follow you.

I want to caution you that neglecting to build a support team before your outreach program begins can lead, I believe, to frustration and potential conflict within your church body. The people in your congregation need to know you and your heart so that they can understand and support your desire to reach the unchurched. Then if, for example, a student is caught smoking on church grounds, these people will understand why that student is there and welcome him, rather than ask him to leave.

Take time to identify the right people for your support teams and recognize their contribution to your ministry. They can help to cover your back as you go to battle with the Enemy.

Students

There could be no outreach without Christian students who care for their non-Christian friends. People assume if you have a program, students will come. Let me assure you—they will not come. Preparing students for an outreach program begins with Christian students who understand your vision, mission, and strategy.

We help our core Christian students prepare for the Tuesday night outreach program in several ways. One of the ways is through training. We train our core students in evangelism and things they can do to increase the compassion in their hearts for their non-Christian friends. The seven-step strategy challenges our core students to build a relationship with their non-Christian friends (step one) and then share a verbal witness (step two). We teach students how to build integrity friendships at school and how to share their testimony.

> When I am sharing a verbal witness with a friend and they ask tough questions, I get so excited. It's exciting to see them truly seeking because they want to know more. This builds my faith up.
>
> Jeff, a senior

We teach our core to "be wise in the way you act toward outsiders; make the most of every opportunity. Let your conversation be always full of grace, seasoned with salt, so that you may know how to answer everyone" (Col. 4:5–6). Over time, the core students begin to see their non-Christian friends with new eyes. They realize the difference they can make as Christ's ambassadors on their high school campuses. Many of the core students pray for their campus, either individually or as a small group. After steps one and two, they now have a place to bring their non-Christian friends as a supplemental witness (step three): the Impact program.

"Impact is a tool I can use with my friends to supplement my witness," said one senior girl. "It's great to have a place designed for my friends and to see life change happen. It's pretty cool."

Another way we regularly prepare our core students is through information. Every Sunday at Insight, we share with them the message theme and the spiritual challenge for the next outreach program on Tuesday. This is a great time for me to paint the vision and remind them of our mission.

One Sunday night, in order to prepare our core for an upcoming target (gospel) night on Tuesday, I had students write down the name of the friend they were planning to bring. We taped the cards with their friends' names to every other seat throughout the auditorium and then walked the students into the auditorium. We told them to sit in the seats with no cards attached. This visual allowed students see what it would be like to have a seeker sitting next to them as they looked at the names of students on their right and left who didn't yet know Christ. We spent some time praying for the program and asking God to touch these seekers' hearts. Each student also prayed for the name of the non-Christian student on their right. This exercise also helped me to see what could happen one life at a time.

Yet another way we prepare our core students for outreach is by supporting their evangelistic efforts through a ministry-wide outreach. There are a few strategic times each year when we all band together in a heavy evangelism emphasis. During these times, we focus on these specific outreaches by praying or fasting and challenging one another to reach out to a non-Christian friend.

At Christmastime, students focus on the true meaning of Christmas by offering their seeking friends our yearly Christmas program called "The Gift." Each of them spent time a few weeks before the program wrapping gifts and placing their non-Christian friends' names on the packages, praying they would open the gift of Christ. These packages were then placed under Christmas trees all over the church and on stage. It was awesome to see gifts that represented non-Christian students all around our church. During "The Gift," the gospel was presented and those students who decided to trust Christ were given the gift of salvation and the book of John.

A senior girl had invited two friends to come to the "The Gift." The day of the program, other friends at school approached her and asked if they could go with her. She ended up bringing seven friends, filling a whole row! Here's what she was thinking that night:

> I was praying the whole program, "God, please soften their hearts so that just even one person can really hear what You are saying tonight." Five people of seven stood up to receive Christ! My heart was pounding. They went up to receive their Bibles, and then I took them to the back of the

auditorium where the two guys went and talked with a guy campus director and I sat with the three girls I had been praying for for so long. I told them it was so awesome what they had just done. They talked about it at school the next day and told other people, "It was so cool. You've got to come to Impact with us next week!" They all still come out and now attend Insight.

Can you start to see how full-cycle evangelism begins to work? Once a non-Christian student trusts Christ and matures in his or her faith, compassion for his or her lost friends begins to increase. Excitement to share Christ with others builds. That's where the outreach program comes in: Students have a place to bring their non-Christian friends. You can see how the cycle repeats itself naturally!

Our other ministry-wide focus happens on target nights. Core students know well in advance that on these particular nights, the gospel will be shared. At Blast, our winter retreat, we begin to prepare our core students for a March target night by challenging them to pray specifically for a non-Christian friend they can bring. Students witness God's power in a new way as they see the benefits of banding together in prayer, encouraging one another to participate, and striving to reach their friends on the same night with the gospel of Jesus Christ.

I can't overemphasize enough the importance of preparing students throughout the year so that they can witness what God can do through them. Once Christian students build integrity friendships and reach out to their non-Christian friends, we need to provide a place they can bring those friends. We must prepare the program.

Program

In preparing the outreach program, we cannot just hope for the best; we must strategically plan. It is important to look at everything in the outreach program through the eyes of a seeker and to understand the target. What do seekers need? Why have they come to the program? How can God's truth be communicated with power and relevance? Our core students trust that we will help them communicate Christ to their seeking friends.

In Student Impact, we prepare for the outreach program in a number of ways. As I mentioned in chapter 13, we hold a program development meeting each week, where we brainstorm using the storyboarding method to plan programs. Our meeting is a safe place where ideas fly; eventually these ideas form a program.

We choose our general series topics the summer before a ministry season begins. A series usually runs for three or four weeks and focuses on a particular topic. About three weeks before a program, we study the message-giver's outline (rationale) and begin to brainstorm specific program ideas. Songs are selected about two weeks prior to the program.

We approach our outreach programs by thinking of them as a funnel. The funnel is a process in which the different programming elements draw students closer to the message of Christ. The top of the funnel is the opening of the program, usually music and/or video, and always relates to the seekers' world. He or she starts to feel safe because there is a sense of familiarity. Often the video shown is of the previous week's competition. Students see faces of their peers, including friends from their school. The music selected helps to break down the resistance non-Christians have toward church.

We continue to move students closer to the spiritual truth of that night with what we call a "turning-the-corner block." Usually a student or a ministry staff member comes up and introduces the topic of the night. This is not a "preaching" time; it is a time to tell students that we have the answer to their spiritual questions and a source of truth to turn to (the Bible) for guidance. We try to avoid using Christian lingo and words that non-Christian students don't understand.

In the diagram, you can see a bull's-eye. The bull's-eye is when a programming element, often a song and/or drama called "the package," causes students to confront issues face-to-face and to recognize the void they have in their life and their need for God. It is what we call a "moment," a time when spiritual truth is communicated through the Holy Spirit by the use of the programming elements.

As we move through this funnel, we think through details. For example, using transitions between programming elements are important to us because they help to weave a thread through the program and keep it connected. If the program just jumped from song to video to drama to message, the time between these elements could make for some long, uncomfortable silence.

When the funnel is set for a program, the programming team needs to rehearse. This is the point when I empower others to do

■ Programming with Purpose ■

*". . . praying at the same time for us as well, that God may
open up to us a door for the Word, so that we may speak forth
the mystery of Christ. . ."*

RATIONALE:
Every one of us can program an effective purpose-driven event by
implementing ten steps of development.

1. Plan: "What's the Future?"

2. Purpose: "Don't Purposely Do Everything But Do Everything with Purpose"

3. Target: "If You Aim at Nothing, You'll Hit Every Time" (What are you aiming at?)

4. Message: "Don't Make your Message Mean Something, Teach Something Meaningful"

5. Rationale: "What Are You Trying to Communicate?"

6. Direction: "Point the Evening Toward One Goal"

7. Ideas: "One Man's Ideas Are Just Not Enough" (Where do they come from?)

8. Resources: "One Man's Trash Is Another Man's Treasure"

9. Develop: "Harmony Takes Repetition" (Does the evening have a thematic thread?)

10. Produce: "Who Sees the 'Big Picture'? "

their job. At Student Impact, the drama and music teams rehearse on the Sunday afternoon before the Tuesday night program. On Tuesday night, a few hours before the program, there is a full run-through of the program.

Concentrate on building your support teams, training your core students, and planning effective programs so that you can meet the needs of seekers and draw them closer to Christ.

Now, what does it look like once you put it all together?

STUDENT IMPACT'S OUTREACH

Many of the students who come to our Tuesday night Student Impact outreach program have not been to church in quite a while—maybe never. In most cases they are on the arm of the Christian friend who invited them. When a first-timer comes to Student Impact on Tuesday night, he or she may be thinking, "Church is boring," "They probably don't understand my world," "I don't want to hear organ music," or "Will they make me do anything weird, like wear a name tag or share my story?" In many cases, these walls have been built before seekers even set foot in the building. They have preconceived ideas of what our ministry will be like. That is why we offer teamroom, competition, and a contemporary program at our outreach.

I want to give you an inside look at our outreach program by explaining the different elements we use each week. I'll also walk you through week one of our "Walking Tall" series, which focuses on how we can walk tall God's way, not the world's way.

7:00 P.M. Teamroom

A student is placed on a team according to which high school he or she attends and spends twenty-five minutes with his or her division (three or four campus teams). In teamroom, the campus director or division director welcomes students and gives a brief introduction to the topic of the night. He or she also explains what Student Impact is all about and how to get involved, as well as highlights upcoming events and important dates. Teamroom fosters unity and spirit because students enjoy being part of a group, especially one that has purpose.

Teamroom is beneficial for several reasons. First, it gives leaders an opportunity to introduce first-timers to Student Impact and begin to dispel any fears they may have. They are given a chance to socialize with other students from their high school. Second, first-timers usually wonder if the people in the room are "normal." Teamroom provides a great chance for the core students and leadership to build bridges and prove that Christians are "normal." Third, attendance is taken in teamroom, which allows for the core students and leadership to follow up on first-timers with phone calls and notes and also determine which of the regulars did not attend. As we attempt to stay small in bigness, taking attendance is an opportunity for shepherding. Because Student Impact is a large ministry, we run the risk that a student will fall through the cracks. Teamroom is a strategic, vital means to shepherd and care for each and every student who walks through our doors. And fourth, all students want to feel like they are a part of something. Teamroom also builds team identity that fosters healthy, competitive rivalries among all the teams.

What happened during Teamroom?
- Students felt welcomed.
- Seekers saw that the leaders were serious about the ministry.
- Seekers interacted with others from their school.
- Seekers came away thinking, "I'm meeting some pretty cool people."

7:30 P.M. Competition

We use competition as a strategic component of the evening. When a seeker walks into our gym, he or she notices that there is energy and excitement and that things look organized. The volunteers on our Impact sports team work hard to plan fun, safe, and creative events that allow for high participation.

Because students are placed on a team according to the high school they attend, their fears of not knowing anyone are eliminated. They most likely are surrounded by their classmates, including the friend who invited them. Participation in competition makes them feel included and a part of the ministry.

Competitions are done in a series. Here's an example of a four-week competition called "Tube City," which used inner tubes each week in a different way:

- *Week 1: Tube Mound Madness* The object of this competition is to score the most points in a limited amount of time by sending out a set number of people to retrieve the most inner tubes from the center pile.

- *Week 2: Human Ring Toss* The object of this competition is to score the most points by throwing inner tubes onto a selected inner tube catcher in a designated scoring area.
- *Week 3: Tube Wrestling* The object of this competition is to get your opponents out of the boundary circle by "tube crashing" them out of bounds and to be the last one left in the boundary area.
- *Week 4: Human Tube Tow* The object of this competition is to score points by grabbing the cone in front of each player while attached to an opponent attempting to do the same. (This competition looks like Tug-O-War.)

Teams compete against one another for points, and each week there is a team winner. Every seeker, obviously wants to be on a winning team, so this builds strong team rivalry.

What happened during Competition?
- Students were competitive and into the games.
- Walls started to come down.
- Seekers interacted with others from their school.
- Seekers came away thinking, "Wow, I'm actually having fun!"

7:55 P.M. Program

The auditorium doors swing open and hundreds of students race to their team's assigned seating section. The walk-in music is loud and is usually music a seeker knows, which helps him or her feel comfortable. After students find their seats, they look at the stage, which has been designed to be visually appealing. At this point, a seeker may be thinking, "Wow! Not bad. Competition was pretty fun and these people aren't weird. I can't believe they're playing music I know! The band's pretty good."

Our church's programming director, Nancy Beach, believes that the thirty minutes preceding the message at our adult weekend services are a treasure and need to be guarded. Not one minute of it should ever be considered throw-away time or filler. It is no different in student ministry. As I mentioned earlier, our outreach programs have three segments: the opener block; the turning-the-corner block; and the package.

Opener Block The opener block is full of energy. It is designed to further break down the walls a seeker may have built against church. This can be done by keeping the bar of excellence high and relating to the seeker's world with the programming elements.

This part of the program is a challenge. We're on the edge sometimes, and we make mistakes. We have learned that this section of the program is *not* about entertainment; entertainment does not serve the ultimate objective of painting a picture of Jesus Christ. The opener package needs to be about building a bridge with the non-Christian student and helping him or her to be receptive to hearing the message of Christ.

Our opener block most often involves a song, and sometimes the use of video. For the opening package for the first week of the "Walking Tall" series we played "Stay" by Lisa Loeb, a secular song that challenged students to think about what they hear each day and how it influences them.

What happened during the first part of the Program?
- We related to a seeker's world.
- There was high energy and excitement.
- Walls started to come down further.
- Seekers were brought one step closer to listening to what we have to say.
- Seekers came away thinking, "This place isn't as bad as I thought."

Turning-the-Corner Block The second programming block, turning the corner, quiets students down after a high-energy song. In this segment, we shift gears and tell students where we are going by introducing the topic of the night. We help students to focus on the theme and to begin thinking how this particular issue could make a difference in their daily lives. Communication is clear and up-front, not abstract.

During week one of our "Walking Tall" series, I went on stage for the turning-the-corner block and welcomed students to Student Impact. I briefly introduced the topic of the night, saying, "Today it seems as though our generation has discovered a great emptiness that has driven many of us to search and fill it with the quickest solution." Students were challenged to think about ways they try to fill their emptiness and to reflect on the question, "Is there a God, and could it be that He cares about me?"

After the introduction, one of the vocalists sang the song "Shine" by the Newsboys. The song asks the question, "Is there any light in a dark place?" and asks heaven to let its light shine down.

What happened during the second part of the Program?
- Seekers were further prepared to hear the message.
- Seekers were given some truth to start thinking about.
- Defenses were lowered.
- Seekers moved down the funnel.
- Seekers began thinking, "They really understand and relate to me, and don't talk down to me."

The Package Every song, drama, media, or other element used in this part of the funnel serves the purpose of further painting the image of Christ. This time is precious and an opportunity to use the arts in a way that honors God and reveals more of who He is to the students who are seeking. During this moment, students are challenged to face an issue as they are confronted with spiritual truth. We try to think of creative ways we can assist the speaker before he or she gets up on stage in order to further prepare students to hear God's truth.

The package we used during week one of the "Walking Tall" series went as follows: A vocalist came up before her song and did a short monologue. She suggested that walking tall does not come from the outside, but from the inside. She held up a beer bottle and said, "I used to think that when I held this at a party, I was walking tall. But you know what? I wasn't." Then she held up a purse. "See this purse? It's really nice and lots of girls have them. We think the outside stuff is so important, but is it? Is it really? Where do you stand?" She then sang "Place in This World" by Michael W. Smith, a song about how we all want to fit in and we search for purpose in our lives. The song asks God to help us find our place in this world.

What happened during the Package?
- Spiritual truth was confronted.
- Seekers heard the message.
- Programming elements touched seekers' hearts.
- Seekers began to think, "I wonder what God is all about?"

8:40 P.M. Message

Our messages are twenty to twenty-five minutes long. We've found that after twenty-five minutes, students become restless and start to lose their concentation. Those of us who give messages try hard to avoid going over the time limit and "losing" our students.

Several years ago, a few of us on staff attended Ken Davis' seminar on being an effective communicator. We learned about the importance of using a rationale statement (goal of message) to prepare for each message, and soon after the seminar we started using rationale statements for every message. It has helped the message-giver organize thoughts and deliver clearer, sharper messages. I highly recommend picking up Ken Davis' book, *Secrets of Dynamic Communication.*

I will include all four rationales we used in the "Walking Tall" series in hopes it will help you think through message-giving:

Week 1: Every one of us can understand what it means to walk tall by taking an honest look at two necessary ingredients:

1. Knowing (being) who you really are
2. Knowing what (having) true integrity is

Week 2: Every one of us can walk tall by practicing (improving) three visible areas of your life:

1. The way you talk (speech)
2. The way you act (conduct)
3. The way you love (love)

Week 3: Every one of us can continue to walk tall with consistency by practicing three biblical disciplines:

1. Develop your faith
2. Guard your purity
3. Become an example

Week 4: Every one of us can know how to walk tall on a solid foundation by knowing and believing the simple message of Christ:

1. God
2. Man
3. Sin
4. Grace
5. Jesus Christ
6. Faith

What happened during the Message?
- Content of message was made relevant to seekers' lives.

- Speaker made applications to daily life.
- Speaker raised spiritual questions.
- Speaker used words and terms a seeker can understand.
- Seekers began thinking, "I want to investigate Christianity."

We desire that each student walk away with one new truth or insight into the claims of Christianity at the end of every message. After the message, a spiritual challenge is issued in the form of a question. This is the question our core students were informed of at the previous Insight so that they could be prepared for intentional conversations after the program with their seeking friends on the way home or later that night at a booth at McDonald's.

The spiritual challenges used during the "Walking Tall" series were:

Week 1: Where do you score with "Walking Tall"?

- Trying to "walk tall," but frustrated
- Walking my own way
- Tried to "walk tall," but failed/just quit
- Don't understand "walking tall"

Week 2: What's in your heart? What do others see?

Week 3: What kind of an example are you? What do you stand for?

Week 4: What is stopping you from "walking tall" on the solid ground of Christ?

What happened during the Spiritual Challenge?
- Seekers were challenged.
- Christian students were set up to have intentional conversations
- Seekers began thinking, "What does this mean for me?"

SPECIAL IMPACT PROGRAMS

A few times a year, we design special programs and events.

Target Nights

A target night takes place several times a year on a Tuesday night at Student Impact. On target nights the gospel is presented in a straightforward manner during the message, and students are given the opportunity to accept Christ by coming forward to receive additional information and then leaving the auditorium to pray with a leader.

We make sure our core students and leaders are informed of these nights. In anticipation, we train core students in evangelism, spend time in corporate prayer, and challenge the core students to make sure their seeking friends are at the target night. These are great nights as we rally together to see what God is going to do.

Senior Night

The last Student Impact program of the ministry season in May is created, produced, and delivered by the senior Christian students in the ministry. They are given the opportunity to share any parting words of wisdom to the underclassmen and to talk about the important role God has played during their high school years. It is their final chance as high school students to share Christ with their peers.

Parents' Nights

We hold a parents' night once or twice a year. It's a great time for parents to come and see what their students are involved in and also to meet leaders. Some of the parents who come are unchurched; their sons or daughters are involved in church, but they are not. Parents have an opportunity to walk through a night, observing competition and the program. Parents' night helps to keep parents informed and it also builds a bridge with many of them. For many parents, this night is their first exposure to a Christian community and is a catalyst for their own spiritual growth.

Other Special Nights

Periodically we offer Target-In, a program encouraging students to join a D-Team. We call it a "taste of small groups," and it gives new Christians a chance to experience a small group for the first time. They have an opportunity to not just hear a voice, but to be a voice. We meet around tables in the gym to discuss basic Christianity. Core students and leaders help answer questions the new believers may ask, and one of the core students is asked to share his or her testimony.

"My friend became a Christian at a target night and I brought her to Target-In the next week," said Aimee, a junior. "It was perfect for her because it didn't blow her away. Now she comes to Insight. Target-In helped bridge the gap."

The week after Target-In, we hold a leadership night for all the leaders of Student Impact. It is a time to come together and reflect on the past series and celebrate God's faithfulness; worship as a leadership team; talk about the next series; and receive training and information. Leaders want to feel informed and cared for, and we try to meet those needs at this meeting. Every leader is given an index card and invited to write a prayer request. They then place their cards up on a bulletin board and, before every leader leaves, they take a prayer request home and commit to pray.

Core nights take place the week after leadership nights. Each campus team meets in a separate, off-campus location. These nights are not simply activities to fill the calendar; each has a specific purpose. The goal of a core night may differ for each campus team as some teams may try to deepen team unity or build momentum while others need to focus on outreach or on painting the ministry vision.

PROVIDING A SAFE PLACE TO LEARN

Since Blast, Ryan had been praying for two of his friends, Mark and Keith. They had both come to Impact a few times, but Ryan really wanted to bring them to the upcoming target night. Ryan said, "The day of the program, Mark and Keith told me something had come up and they couldn't go. I was frustrated, but I kept praying. I decided to call each of them after school to make sure their plans hadn't changed. Mark's family dinner was canceled and for some reason Keith was also available to go. I brought them both to target night and they stood and became Christians. God is so faithful!"

Ryan was grateful that he had a place to bring his non-Christian friends and God proved Himself faithful. An outreach program can be effective if support teams are in place; students are trained and challenged to reach out; and programs are target-based and mission-minded. Preparing the students is the most important part of the outreach program because programs don't change lives, people do. God uses people to reach and care for His children. We must be prepared.

Rewind

What Did You Learn?

The needs of seekers call for programs specifically prepared for them.

PREPARE THE . . .	BY . . .
Support teams	• Identifying the right people. • Recognizing their contributions to the ministry.
Students	• Providing training in evangelism. • Sharing information about upcoming programs. • Supporting students' evangelism through ministry-wide outreach.
Program	• Holding planning meetings. • Using the funnel. • Paying attention to details. • Knowing the needs of the seeker target.

Pause

What Action Will You Take?

1. Gather a few people from your ministry and brainstorm ideas for an outreach program. Try the storyboarding method by giving everyone a stack of index cards and a marker. Use a board of some kind to tape or pin the cards. Let's say the topic is dating. Come up with ideas for songs, movie clips, drama, et cetera, that could possibly be used to address students' questions or concerns about dating.

2. Using the funnel diagram, take the ideas you brainstormed and develop them into a purposeful outreach program.

Fast Forward

What's Next?

You're reaching seekers. How will you help them grow in their new faith?

PREPARING THE BELIEVER PROGRAM

The believer program is very different from the outreach program. As we did with the seeker, now we need to think through the believer target and their particular needs. In programming for the believer, our goal is to develop fully devoted followers and to focus on the Five G's :

- personally understanding the *grace* of God;
- commitment to spiritual *growth*;
- commitment to a small *group*;
- learning to express their God-given *gifts*; and
- *giving* to the church.

Because believers have the Holy Spirit, we can now worship and teach from God's Word. Our believer program, Student Insight, meets on Sunday nights.

PREPARING THE BELIEVER PROGRAM

People are more important than programs. The first step of preparing the believer program is to prepare the people involved. We need to prepare two groups of people for the believer program.

Leaders

The first group we need to prepare are the leaders. Leaders of the ministry must be an example and show up at the believer program on time with Bibles in hand. They must show the students they are leading that worship and teaching are important for Christian growth and they must encourage students to cross lines. At Student Insight, leaders can also show care and love to their students by shepherding them in a small group every other week.

Every leader needs to be prepared to be an example, a leader, and a shepherd.

Students

The second group that needs to be prepared for the believer program are the students. Students should clearly understand what Student Insight is all about and how it can help them become fully devoted followers of Christ. It is through Student Insight that students will be spiritually challenged on a deeper level.

Program

I believe it is crucial to make sure that as much thought, prayer, and creativity goes into the planning of the believer program as into the outreach program. I think some leaders feel that, since believers are already convinced, we don't need to spend as much time on planning the believer program. This is not true. Planning the believer program is of equal significance.

Our programming team also plans for the believer program each week at the program development meeting. Values like excellence, creativity, and selection, are just as important to use in the believer program as in the outreach program. The storyboarding method is used for brainstorming ideas.

In thinking through the believer program, we try to figure out new ways to draw students into the presence of God through worship and teaching. David is described in the Bible as a man who loved to worship and had a huge heart for God. Our worship leader tries to develop a heart of worship in our core students so that they too can have a heart for God. Students love to worship, and it is especially powerful for them to see our vocalists leading worship. On Tuesday nights, these vocalists often sing secular songs, but on Sundays, students see these same vocalists leading them in praise to God.

We pray for those who teach during the believer program, that God would anoint their teaching and use it to transform lives. The teaching is usually topical or expository in nature and students are challenged to dig deeper into God's Word and grow in their love and knowledge of Him.

Details matter in the believer program. We think through what needs to be announced and what our core students need to know to stay informed about the ministry. During the program, the students learn what the spiritual challenge will be at the upcoming outreach program so that they can begin to prepare for conversation with their non-Christian friends.

D-Teams meet every other week. On the nights they meet, our believer program provides the set-up for the D-Teams. Sometimes we show a movie clip that introduces that night's theme or perform a song that prepares students for their D-Team. We use the end of the program for this purpose.

The believer program requires careful planning and attention. Christian students desire to grow in their faith and need a program designed to meet their needs. It is vital to prepare the leaders and students and remind them of the importance of the believer program. When the program is planned to meet the needs of believers, Christian students can move closer to becoming fully devoted followers of Christ. That's our mission.

In planning a believer program:

1. Don't be afraid or hesitant to teach students how to worship.
2. Teach God's Word with clarity, boldness, and power.
3. Know the believer target: Who are they and what do they need?
4. Use contemporary worship choruses with meaningful lyrics.
5. Ask yourself: What kind of spiritual foundation will my students go to college with? Am I preparing them to continue walking with Christ?

STUDENT IMPACT'S BELIEVER PROGRAM— STUDENT INSIGHT

Every Sunday night, believers gather in the auditorium for a program that is designed just for them: Student Insight. The purpose of Student Insight is to challenge, equip, and assist students in their spiritual journey to become fully devoted followers of Jesus Christ. We do this by exposing God's truth in a relevant, practical way through the use of the communicative arts (music, drama, video, and media); corporate worship; teaching from God's Word; monthly communion celebrations; and Christian fellowship. D-Teams meet every other week, so either a full teamroom or D-Teams follow our time together. On D-Team nights, the program is from 6:00–7:00 P.M.; a short teamroom occurs at 7:00 P.M.; and then D-Teams take place from 7:30–8:30 P.M. On teaching nights, the program is from 6:00–7:15 P.M., followed by teamroom from 7:30–8:30 P.M. Here's what a "typical" night might look like:

6:00 P.M. Worship

Students enter the auditorium, Bibles in hand, ready to worship and open God's Word. The first twenty to thirty minutes are pure worship. Some of the choruses are high energy, stand-to-your-feet kinds of songs, while other choruses we sing are more reflective. To hear high school students lifting their voices in praise to God and reverently worshiping Him is one of the greatest sounds in all the world. These students choose to be at church because they desire to worship and draw closer to God. Authentic worship is one of the defining characteristics that distinguish a youth group from a student ministry.

Sometimes a worship leader will ask students to gather with two or three people sitting nearby to pray for the world, their friends, or maybe an upcoming ministry event. Several times a year, we hold what we call a concert of prayer, where the whole hour is devoted to praying for specific needs. Other worship experiences may include time for silent meditation, a special song sung by one of our vocalists, a Scripture reading, or a few minutes to journal to God. Once a month, students are given the opportunity to participate in the sacrament of communion.

Another important component of our weekly worship time is offering. Students are taught what the Bible says about tithing and are challenged to give as they are led. We want our students to learn the difference between earthly treasures versus heavenly treasures and to not hold tightly to material possessions. This value is very important. It also teaches them about ownership; their giving helps the ministry function. They realize the role they play in making ministry happen.

What happened during Worship?
- Students were focused on Christ.
- Hearts were softened towards God.
- Students had an opportunity to tithe.

6:30 P.M. "Going Public"

During this time in the program, a student stands up front and shares his or her testimony or the way God is working in and through his or her life. We call this the "Going Public" slot. We use the Newsboys song "Going Public" to set up this slot. When the music starts, the audience starts to snap their fingers, and when the "Going Public" student walks on stage, everyone stands and claps. The student about to talk is often nervous, and I'm sure his or her heart is beating fast, so this ovation helps him or her feel supported. Imagine a student giving his or her testimony for perhaps the first time. It's an opportunity for students to stretch and grow and a chance to publicly proclaim their faith.

A sophomore named Eric did a recent "Going Public" slot. He shared how he took a courageous step of faith in his English class. His teacher had assigned the class to deliver a speech about a famous person of their choice. Eric chose to give his speech on Jesus Christ and who He was on earth and who He is today. He clearly articulated the gospel message and witnessed in front of his entire English class! During the speech, he also told his peers that Student Impact was a great place to investigate Christianity. After the speech, Eric said, "A lot of my friends had questions and wanted to know more. A few of them are really interested to come with me to Student Impact."

"Going Public" inspires those listening as well as challenges the students who are actually talking. It's exciting to hear about the life change happening in students' lives.

What happened during "Going Public"?
- Christian students took a stand for Christ.
- Students' comfort zones were stretched.
- Believers participated in the program.

6:40 P.M. Message (on non-D-Team nights only)

We close our worship time with a thirty- to thirty-five-minute message. Our teaching corresponds to the waves described in chapter 7. In the first wave, we focus on "you and Christ." Students learn about their personal relationship with Christ and are challenged to take steps of growth. The six weeks of teaching at Insight as well as the six weeks of D-Teams revolve around this theme.

In the second wave, the focus shifts to "you and your friends" as students are taught about personal evangelism and ways they can witness to their non-Christian friends. Again, the teaching and D-Teams connect with this topic.

"Building the church" is the emphasis in the third wave. During this wave, students study in their D-Teams and hear during the message time about serving and building the body of Christ with their spiritual gifts and through tithing.

The fourth wave is "impact the world." D-Teams do not meet during this wave, so the teaching is every week and stresses the importance of every believer making a difference in his or her personal world. Mission trips are offered throughout the summer to give students an opportunity to experience how they can impact the world.

What happened during the Message?
- Believers were challenged to grow spiritually.
- Knowledge of God's Word increased.
- Believers heard truth from God's Word.

Teamroom (start time varies based on type of program)

After the Student Insight program, Christian students have an opportunity to meet with their campus teams in order to deepen their friendships with one another and to rally behind ministry causes. During teamroom, unity is built as students care for each other. First Corinthians 12:24–25 says, "But God so composed the body ... that there should be no division in the body, but that the members should have the same care for one another" (NASB). In teamroom believers are also trained in evangelism. It is the core students who will reach their campus for Christ. Campus directors can also take a pulse of their team and address any necessary issues during teamroom.

What happened during Teamroom?
- Believers experienced community with one another.
- Believers were trained, encouraged, and challenged in their evangelistic efforts.
- Students and leaders connected relationally.

Small Groups (D-Teams) (meet every other week)

Taking a stand for Christ on a high school campus requires much courage and strength. Christian students often feel alone fighting the battles of peer pressure and the lures of the world. The ministry of small groups shows students they are not alone; there are other Christians who are facing the same pressures and experiencing victory.

Since we believe life change happens best in small groups, D-Team small groups meet every other week. A believer can grow in his or her walk with God as God's Word is studied and applied to daily life. Leaders are given the small group material six weeks in advance and have ample time to prepare. Having a leader, an apprentice, and four to eight committed Christians in a small group encourages the believer to stay on the right path and make choices that honor God. The small group structure allows for growth as the open chair is filled and new groups are created.

What happened during Small Groups?
- Believers sharpened one another to grow spiritually.
- The need for accountability, encouragement, and acceptance was met.
- Believers prayed together and studied God's Word.

SPECIAL INSIGHT PROGRAMS

We hold several special Insight programs throughout the year. Christian students are given the opportunity to serve God and the church (step seven of our strategy). This helps to put their faith into action as they experience the joy that comes from serving in the church.

Mission Impact

Last year, students and leaders from one of our campus teams regularly made trips into the inner city of Chicago to minister to the needy. They served meals in homeless shelters and assisted with several building projects. About twenty-five students and leaders spent their spring break painting and working in an inner-city day-care center. They continue to visit that day-care center once a month and help distribute food to the people in the neighborhood. About forty students recently returned from a week in the Dominican Republic where they ministered to children and adults in a poor rural community.

Building the Church

There are various ways students serve in the church throughout the year. For the past five years, each campus team has volunteered to assist our church's traffic control teams three times a year. When it is a team's turn, students and leaders show up at church early and are assigned positions around the parking lot. The teams who volunteer during the brutal Chicago winters are given bright orange, insulated jumpsuits to wear. They don't seem to mind the frigid weather; they love it! Once the service starts, these students and leaders head down to the church's nursery where they help take care of the infants. Serving the church gives believers a chance to give back to a ministry that has provided them with so much. It is seen as a privilege to serve in this way.

Concerts of Prayer

Several times a year, students bring their pillows and meet in the gym for a concert of prayer. We spend time worshiping and praying for specific requests. We try to create some kind of "moment" for students, usually communion or an experience students can share with their D-Team. We try to hold a concert of prayer before each target night to pray for the seeking friends that students will be bringing to hear the gospel.

Parents' Night

Students have the opportunity to invite their parents to an Insight Parents' Night once a year. During these programs, students can sit next to their parents and together worship God. Parents get to see and experience a part of their students' world, meet the leaders, and ask any questions they have about the ministry.

Insight Baptism

For those believers who desire to make a public profession of their faith, we offer a baptism service each spring in our church's lake. Believers are encouraged to participate in this sacrament and take a significant step in their spiritual journeys.

It's an incredible sight to see parents and friends accompany those being baptized into the water. What a powerful image that is of support and love! Throughout the service, we read the testimonies of those students being baptized. This service is always the highlight of the year for me; it's a reminder of why I do what I do.

PROVIDING A PLACE TO GROW

Believers need a place to mature in their relationship with God and an environment that challenges them to take steps of growth. Through worship, teaching, and small groups, Christian students can move closer to becoming fully devoted followers of Christ. In preparing for the believer program, make sure your leaders and students understand the vision, mission, and strategy, and why attending the believer program is so important. Don't overlook the details or neglect to carefully prepare the believer program. Christian students need a place to be continually challenged so they do not become complacent or lazy in their faith. Recognize the critical role the believer program plays in students' maturity in Christ.

Imagine your auditorium or gym filled with students whose heads are bowed in worship to God, singing praises to His name. Their needs are quite different from those of seekers, and preparing a program for them looks completely different. What would your program to believers look like?

Rewind

What Did You Learn?

The goal of programming for believers is to develop fully devoted followers of Jesus Christ.

PREPARE THE . . .	BY . . .
Leaders	• Training them to be examples, leaders, and shepherds.
Students	• Challenging them to attend the believer program regularly in order to grow.
Program	• Regularly holding planning meetings. • Paying attention to details. • Setting up small groups. • Knowing the needs of the believer target.

Pause

What Action Will You Take?

1. Brainstorm ideas for the believer program. What elements would you use to illustrate the following:
   • God's power
   • our sinfulness
   • the life of Noah
   • what the Bible says about purity
   • fruit of the Spirit
   • the Bible as our source of truth and guidance

- faith
- sharing Christ with others

2. How might you use the following to provide meaningful worship experiences for your students?
   - music
   - drama
   - video
   - other forms of media

Fast Forward

What's Next?

*Your programs are in place.
Are you ready to impact the world?*

Impacting the World

I recently read about someone in the corporate world who was given an opportunity to make a difference in the world. John Sculley had become Pepsi's youngest president at thirty-eight and created the "Pepsi Generation" campaign that put Pepsi-Cola in front of Coke for the first time. He had turned down numerous opportunities to explore top positions with other Fortune 500 companies.

That is until he met Steve Jobs, the young chairman of Apple Computer, Inc. Jobs was persistent in his pursuit of Sculley, but to no avail. In their final meeting, Jobs asked once more, "Are you going to come to Apple?"

Sculley relates the story in his book *Odyssey*:

> "Steve," I said, "I'd love to be an adviser to you, to help you in any way. Any time you're in New York, I'd love to spend time with you. But I don't think I can come to Apple."
>
> Steve's head dropped as he stared at the pavement. After a weighty, uncomfortable pause, he issued a challenge that would haunt me for days: "Do you want to spend the rest of your life selling sugared water or do you want a chance to change the world?"[1]

Do you realize that you, too, have been given a chance to impact the world? Your mission is not to produce sugared water or to sell computers like John Sculley eventually decided to do. It is far more significant. God has called you to change the world by making an impact in the lives of high school students.

Take a look at a few people God chose to make a difference:

God called Moses from a burning bush to lead the Israelites out of Egypt.

249

God called Jonah to evangelize Ninevah.
God called Nehemiah to rebuild the city wall.
God called Esther to save the Jews.
God called Mary to bear His Son.
God called Paul to launch the vision for the first church.
God called you to share His love to the next generation.

Do you feel intimidated to be associated with such a group? Don't be! It's amazing to study the lives of the Bible characters I just mentioned and realize they were ordinary men and women. They were willing, though, to surrender their lives to God so He could use them in extraordinary ways. We must be willing to do the same.

The Bible tells us that God is constantly looking for men and women to stand in the gap for Him so that He can use them to impact the world. That is what He has called you to do through student ministry. I believe we need men and women in student ministry who are willing to step up to the plate and follow the calling God has placed on their lives, and who are committed to serving for the long-term. I'm excited to see more of this happening.

Student ministry is not just a stepping stone to learn ministry skills and then become a pastor somewhere else; it's a place for many who are called to start and finish. We desperately need men and women who are in it for the long haul.

That's what this chapter is about. I want to encourage those God has called to student ministry or those who are considering God's call to student ministry and cheer you on to be faithful to what God has called you to do, whatever and wherever that may be. I want to remind you that God loves you, and He's equipped you for the job at hand.

PERSEVERE, PERSEVERE, PERSEVERE

It's easy to get discouraged in student ministry. Sometimes other people crush our dreams or tell us they're too far-fetched. I want to remind you to remember that God is powerful. At our church we sing a song called "He is Able," which communicates that God is able to do much more than we could ever imagine. Don't let your dreams fall by the wayside because someone discouraged you. Listen to God's voice and He will guide you in the direction you need to go.

We also may get discouraged when we look at the size of the task in front of us. Matthew 9:37–38 says, "Then he said to his disciples, 'The harvest is plentiful, but the workers are few. Ask the Lord of the harvest, therefore, to send out workers into his harvest field.'" There will be times in student ministry when the "harvest" looks overwhelming and you may wonder, "How can I reach these students, who seem so lost, with the gospel of Jesus Christ? My workers really are too few." God has promised to be faithful. He loves those students far more than we ever could.

Often, we do not see the fruits of our labor until years later. Sometimes we question if what we are doing is even making a difference. When these feelings come, I encourage you to persevere to the greatest calling on earth: redeeming the world through the message of Jesus Christ, and impacting the lives of high school students.

A CALL TO LEADERSHIP

At our Student Impact Leadership Conference last year, I asked Bill Hybels to speak about leadership and to share his thoughts on high school ministry. His message served as a source of encouragement for me, and I thought it may be for you, too.

Bill's words were a reminder of how significant student ministry really is. He started off by stating that the first value we must always keep in our hearts is the supremacy of love. Strategies are no doubt necessary, but the most important strategy is love. He said, "When a student feels loved by another student or a leader feels loved by another leader and all are loved by God—when all in the ministry is done in love: truth spoken in love; correction brought in love; and teaching in the spirit of love—there is something that happens to the heart and soul. The spirit of grace-giving love is what students are starved for."

How true his statement is! In this book, you've read about values, structures, and strategies, and I hope they have helped you. But all will prove useless if you don't show love to your students. Students want and need to be loved. God's love is the basis on which we can build those strategies, structures, and values.

Bill went on to say that, in the days he was involved in student ministry, his students had a "welcome-to-the-party-that-God's-throwing kind of love." There was always plenty of love to go around. Students came alive as they started to feel God's love for the first time. When students experienced God's love, it not only had huge implications for them personally, but also had the potential to impact their whole family. I've seen this happen as a student's heart is filled with God's love. He or she can't help but share it with his or her family.

I was glad Bill next mentioned that "student ministry is every bit as high a calling as anything in the adult world." We cannot let anyone look down on us because we are in student ministry. God's call is not about age. Whether you're starting off in student ministry or a veteran, you've probably heard people ask, "When are you going to get a real job?" We need to be reminded that God's call on our life doesn't end at a certain age or guarantee a few years of recognition. Student ministry is difficult; those in it don't get a lot of recognition and often face pressure from all sides: parents, finances, pastors, and more. There may be times we're ready to "throw in the towel."

As you have late-night talks out in the parking lot with students who are confused, or make phone calls each week which you're not sure are affecting anyone, press on! God sees all of this and will reward you for all of eternity. I encourage you to remember the words of Jesus: "Your Father, who sees what is done in secret, will reward you" (Matt. 6:4b).

Bill's final words to us were in the form of six immutables of student ministry. They are truths we need to keep in the forefront of our mind as we lead our student ministries. The first is this: *Whatever you do, always live a surrendered life.* We are in a spiritual battle and waging war against the Evil One and the forces of hell. Bill cautioned that we will not make "spiritual gains in human strength. Learn what spiritual disciplines you need to do so you can say that most of your life, days, decisions, and relationships flow from a surrendered spirit." Being spiritually disciplined is hard work and requires consistency. When our personal life with Christ is in order, though, we will be able to lead with authenticity.

At a meeting a few months ago, a staff member gave a short devotional and said that every morning we wake up, we should say yes—yes to God and yes to following His call on our lives. What a great challenge to start each day with our first thoughts focused on Christ and a heart surrendered to saying yes.

The second immutable truth Bill shared was to *preach an uncompromising message.* He challenged those in the audience to never "give less than the biblical truth to your students. Don't shrink back from sharing the requirements of salvation or discipleship or the gospel; it will not serve students or sustain them." Students want and need to hear about Jesus Christ.

In student ministry it is tempting to share just funny stories or to make students laugh rather than teach with boldness and confidence. God's Word is the power to influence and shape the lives of the students in our ministry. We are robbing our students of this opportunity if we water down the gospel in any way.

Next, Bill warned us to *resist the temptation to use students for our purposes.* It's easy, isn't it, to pay special attention to the students who are leaders or who are popular with their peers? But, Bill cautioned, we must "never quit caring for the life of a student and only care about what he or she brings to your program." People should always be more important than programs. If we simply want to build programs rather than build Christ in students, our focus needs to be quickly recalibrated.

Bill also stated that, "God will understand if you don't have a position filled or something falls apart. He will never understand your using a student in a way that's not conducive to his or her spiritual, emotional, or relational development." We need to regularly check ourselves on this and examine our motives in how we lead our students. Are we properly challenging students or are we putting too much pressure on them? We must treat each and every student in our ministry as an individual uniquely designed by God who possesses his or her own ability to be a player in the kingdom.

The fourth truth Bill shared comes from deep within his heart: *work toward integration with the greater church body.* Too often student pastors and senior pastors develop a "we/they" mentality. Your job is to build support with your pastor and realize he is not the enemy. Together, you and your pastor need to devise a plan to connect students with the larger church body so that when they graduate from high school they do not leave the church. What a tragedy to invest in students for four years, but not provide a place for them after graduation!

Our student ministries are starting to do a better job at this. We work hard to make sure that graduating junior high students are quickly folded into Student Impact and that graduating high school students transition smoothly into our church's college ministry. We want these young adults to know they are a part of the body of Christ and to understand the role they can play in the church through the use of their spiritual gifts on their journey of becoming fully devoted followers of Christ. Over time, students begin to see that the church is the only hope of the world, and they realize they are needed to play a part. God uses the church as a powerful tool to be a light in the midst of darkness.

I was excited about Bill's fifth challenge: *develop relationships with other like-minded youth workers around the country and the world.* As I looked around the auditorium at the faces of the men and women who had come from all over the world to learn more about student ministry, I realized this goal was indeed happening. I think God was pleased as we came together with our "hands in the middle," eager to learn from one another and share ideas and resources.

I get fired up thinking and dreaming of ways those of us in student ministry can support, encourage, help, and pray for one another. We all face common pressures that those outside student ministry just don't understand. Student Impact has formed AIM (Associated Impact Ministries), a group of like-minded men and women who desire to lead purpose-driven student ministries. If you would like more information on AIM, please don't hesitate to call the Willow Creek Association (847–765–0070).

The sixth and final truth Bill shared was to *never underestimate the value of a single student that God has given you to care for.* There are students in all of your ministries that have "more potential for kingdom building than you ever imagined. The way you love them, disciple them, teach them, and pray for them might put them on a course that will allow them to become key leaders tomorrow." What an opportunity we have as student pastors to invest in the lives of students who will be the church in the near future.

UNITED WE STAND

As I finish this last chapter, our church is in the midst of its twentieth anniversary celebration. To thank God for His incredible faithfulness and goodness to our church, the leaders decided it would be important for all twenty thousand of us to be together under one roof. It had been many years since we all could meet together at one time. The only place in the Chicago area large enough to accommodate us was the United Center, home of the Chicago Bulls basketball team and Chicago Blackhawks hockey team.

I opened this book talking about how people around the world admire the way Michael Jordan jams the basketball and how kids want to "be like Mike." I have watched him on several occasions at the United Center and seen fans get completely crazy over this amazing sports hero.

But as I sat in the United Center, not cheering for a ball to go through a hoop or for Michael to make the game-winning shot but praising God for all He has done and will continue to do through lives that are surrendered to Him, I was reminded of God's power and grace and the purpose He gives to our lives. What a contrast between cheering on someone's human ability versus God's supernatural ability to change a life!

During the program, each person received a small flashlight key chain. We were told to shine our lights if any of the following statements were true in our lives:

- If your life has been changed by God through a ministry of Willow Creek
- If you have made significant relationships here and connected with others
- If you have discovered your spiritual gifts and put them into action

I was in awe of God's power! The place lit up, one flashlight at a time. The arena became bright. This exercise demonstrated that God has indeed changed many lives through the ministry of Willow Creek. Seeing all those lights turned on reminded me that God has called us to be a light to those students who are living in darkness. Matthew 5:14–16 encourages us:

> You are the light of the world. A city on a hill cannot be hidden. Neither do people light a lamp and put it under a bowl. Instead they put it on its stand, and it gives light to everyone in the house. In the same way, let your light shine before men, that they may see your good deeds and praise your Father in heaven.

Seeing twenty thousand people turning on their lights was a significant moment for me—to think it all started with a group of high school students. As I looked across the arena, I saw high school students whose lives have been impacted for all of eternity. At that moment, I was so thankful for Bill and the early leaders of the church who were committed to the vision of seeing lost people come to know Christ.

FAITHFUL TO THE CALL

That night I also reflected about my own life and the incredible life change that happened to me. My heart was filled with gratitude that God had chosen me to be a part of full-time ministry, especially at Willow Creek. I also thought of a few men and women who had been faithful to God's calling in their lives and reached out to me and touched my life. I was thankful for Bob Hubbard, who was so patient over the years in answering my questions when I was just starting to serve in student ministry, and who encouraged me to pursue it full-time. I was also thankful for Pastor Richard Lowe who taught me to be a man of integrity and to love the church, and for Dan Webster, who challenged me to come on the student ministry staff of Willow Creek and taught me about personal authenticity and leadership.

Stop for a moment and think about the people God has used in your life. Take some time to give thanks to the men and women who cared enough for you and shared Christ with you so that you could be where you are today: a difference-maker in God's kingdom. Write a letter or make a phone call to these people and thank them for seeing who you could become in Christ and for staying faithful to God's call on their life. Thank God for the people who labored before you in ministry.

If you ever wonder how in the world God could use you to change the world, look at these people. What people? The people God used to change history. A ragbag of ne'er-do-wells and has-beens who found hope, not in their performance, but in God's proverbially open arms.

Max Lucado, *No Wonder They Call Him the Savior*,
(Portland, OR: Multnomah Press, 1986), 117.

We, too, have an opportunity to make a significant difference in other peoples' lives. It's humbling to look at the legacy left by the previous three student ministry directors: Bill Hybels, Don Cousins, and Dan Webster. They each remained steadfast and faithful to their calling and God used them to touch thousands of lives. Because of God's grace and His work through me, I pray that I too will be faithful to His calling like the godly men before me, and that I will leave an eternal mark on the lives of the high school students and leaders He has entrusted to me. What an awesome calling! And He has called you to this same purpose.

On a number of occasions, I have sat in our church's auditorium when it was empty and reflected on how the ministry of Willow Creek has changed my life. I'm truly amazed that God has chosen to use someone like me, an ordinary person. As I finish writing this book, I am overwhelmed by God's goodness. It really is true that God will use *anyone* willing to serve Him with a surrendered heart.

IMPACTING THE WORLD TOGETHER

Whenever I speak to groups of leaders, I always close with this verse: "But you, be sober in all things, endure hardship, do the work of an evangelist, fulfill your ministry" (2 Tim. 4:5, NASB). I use this verse as a reminder that all of us need to focus on the work God has called us to do. It won't always be easy, but this verse reminds us to fulfill the calling God has placed on our lives and to share the hope we have found in Jesus with others. God has called us, but He does not need us. He has graciously invited us to be a part of His work. Such an incredible invitation should motivate us to serve the King of Kings with the best we have to offer.

This verse also reminds us to do our job for the glory of God. This starts by surrendering our lives daily to Christ. We need to develop spiritual disciplines in our lives so that we keep an authentic relationship with Him.

Some day, our hope is to hear, "well done, good and faithful servant" from our Heavenly Father. What a day that will be! Until that time comes, I encourage you to do your job. Go after what God has called you to do. Together, with our hands in the middle and with God's amazing grace, we can be a light in a world filled with darkness. We will make a difference. It starts with one life at a time.

APPENDIX

Sticking Points

sticking (stik ing) 1. to fasten to a surface by or as by an adhesive substance. 2. to come to a standstill; become blocked or obstructed; stop; halt. 3. to persist; persevere, as in a task or undertaking: with *at* or *to*. (Funk & Wagnalls Encyclopedic College Dictionary, p. 1315)

Can you relate to the second definition: to come to a standstill; become blocked or obstructed; stop; halt? Have you ever reached a standstill in leading your ministry? Are there times when you just feel stuck? Relax! You are not alone. We all reach sticking points in student ministry at one time or another. The key to getting unstuck is to take time to readjust and reevaluate what you are doing.

Perhaps some of the principles and ideas in earlier chapters have caused you to reach your own sticking point. In this appendix I will try to address some common sticking points other youth pastors have asked me about involving material discussed in this book.

My hope and prayer for this book is that you would lead your student ministries based on the third definition: to persist; persevere, as in a task or undertaking: with *at* or *to*. I want so badly for each of you to be sticking *to* what God has called you to do and sticking *at* making an eternal difference in the lives of high school students. With God's help, sticking points can be overcome and you can experience victory.

Let's look at some common sticking points.

PART 1: REEVALUATE YOUR PURPOSE

Sticking Point: Sometimes student ministry feels like a twenty-four-hour-a-day job. How do you stay balanced in student ministry?

The pace of ministry is overwhelming at times. It seems there is always one more student I can talk to or one more phone call I can make before leaving for the day. Yet we as youth leaders must learn how to stay balanced in our personal lives and also balance the demands of ministry.

Several years ago, I was trying desperately to maintain balance in my life. At the time, I was a full-time football coach at a local high school, a full-time ministry director, a husband, and a father to three young children. I was running fast and being pulled in all kinds of directions. I was not living a balanced life.

Through all the distractions, I realized how the phone was affecting my family life. Brandon, Tiffany, Trevor, and my wife, Gloria, had grown accustomed to the volume of ministry calls I made and received at home. In student ministry, it sometimes feels like the phone rings and never stops. And many calls are not five-minute chats, but rather half-hour problem-solving conversations.

One Saturday morning, my son Brandon and I were getting ready to play a game of dominoes when the phone rang. Brandon looked up at me and sighed. Game delays were nothing new to him; he was used to my phone calls during our times together. Sure enough, it was a ministry call for me. I decided to communicate value to my son in a new way. I said to Gloria, "Please tell whoever it is that I cannot come to the phone right now. I'm with Brandon." I will never forget the look on my son's face. I realized at that moment that drawing boundaries in my home was of utmost importance.

Boundaries is a word that has been tossed around quite a bit in recent years, but I believe it is imperative that each of us determine what those boundaries will be in our own life. Drawing boundaries will help us learn how to say no to the things or people that cause us to live unbalanced lives. Through prayer and studying God's Word, we will know upon what God wants us to focus our attention. His agenda is much more important than our own.

Sticking Point: I'm reading God's Word on a regular basis, but it's usually to prepare for my next message or small group. How do you keep your spiritual disciplines sharp?

Practicing spiritual disciplines is vital in our Christian life so that our hearts become more like Christ's. But spiritual disciplines may look different in everyone's life. As student pastors, we run the risk of only reading God's Word as it relates to ministry preparation. Fight hard against falling into this trap. I know it is a challenge, but try to find a time or times during the week when you can open God's Word without a ministry mind-set and read for your own spiritual growth.

I also strongly encourage you to seek accountability in your life. Who is in your life right now asking you the tough questions? By tough questions I do not mean, "Are you having a quiet time?" but "What did you read in God's Word this week and what did you learn?" I have determined specific questions I need to be asked on a regular basis by my accountability partner. When my friend asks me these questions, my life is an open book and he has full permission to challenge me in the areas I need to grow. He also sharpens my spiritual disciplines and helps me determine the steps I need to take to grow closer to Christ.

Sticking Point: Lately, my pastor and I have not been seeing eye to eye on some issues. What do you do when your pastor is not supportive?

I get asked this question regularly, and I know it is a sticking point for many student pastors. Early on, in my first years of student ministry in southern California, I had several differences of agreement with my pastor. I felt God was calling me to lead the ministry a certain way, but my pastor and the rest of the church wanted me to maintain a youth group. My vision and their vision did not match up. I tried several times to communicate my vision more clearly, hoping they would see it; unfortunately, they never did. It came to the point where I knew in my heart I had to be faithful to what God had called me to do: to build a student ministry, not maintain a youth group. If I couldn't follow the leader, I felt I owed it to the Lord to follow the calling He had placed on my heart. Eventually, I knew I had to make the choice to move on. I realized that life is short, and that I wanted to do the best I could with the life I had been given. I had to follow God's leadings.

I love the church and it saddens me to hear about the sharp divisions that sometimes occur between a pastor and youth pastor. We need to be building bridges instead of tearing them down. If you find yourself feeling stuck with your pastor, I encourage you to remember to fight the right battles. What are the things worth fighting for and what things can be dropped? The Bible tells us to submit to and confront in love those in authority, even when it is difficult. I know sometimes this is tough to do, but God is honored when we do so.

Do your best to keep your pastor informed and communicate with him on a consistent basis. Let him see and know your heart for students and commit your relationship to prayer. When conflict does arise, avoid the temptation to get others on your side. The Enemy loves to stir up dissension, but we must follow Matthew 18, which tells us God's plan for conflict resolution. Work hard to resolve any differences, but if that is not possible, you may have to make a major change.

PART 2: MINISTER WITH PURPOSE

Sticking Point: I'm from a traditional church. How do I make the transition to a seeker-targeted model?

Often when youth pastors attend our leadership conference, they get fired up hearing and seeing the vision, mission, and strategy. Unfortunately, they also feel stuck because they know they will hit a wall of resistance when they return to their churches.

I know I have said this several times in the book, but again, I encourage you to fight the right battles and to ask the question why. Realize that changes can't happen overnight, but through prayer and communication with your pastor, board, and elders, change is possible. I think many church leaders are slowly recognizing that "doing church" for tradition's sake does not work any longer; many spiritually-sensitive people are looking for a church that addresses their needs in a relevant way and that can answer their spiritual questions.

Every church is unique, and we all face different situations. Recognize what works in your setting and identify your targets. Be patient and make the necessary changes over time.

Tim Homa, who served as a campus director in Student Impact a few years ago, has some great advice about the transition process. He left Student Impact to become director of student ministries at a church in Las Vegas that had been traditional for twenty-five years but was in the process of becoming seeker-targeted. Here's how Tim dealt with the transition:

> When I left Willow five years ago I was going to a church where the choir sang in robes; where the organ was a part of the service; where traditional Sunday school was still the main

way of teaching; and where spiritual gifts were something reserved only for the charismatic.

I'm not saying that all this is bad. But I had come to Las Vegas committed to leading the ministry into a seeker-targeted ministry. Knowing I was entering uncharted waters, I knew I had to move slowly. I had to trust God and His timing.

The first few months were crucial. I wanted to box up everything I had learned at Willow Creek and begin to implement it all with my youth. I wanted change to take place quickly and easily. But after analyzing my situation, it seemed to me that something else had to happen first.

This was a church full of devoted Christians. They just needed to develop a passion for the lost. As the adults were learning to love the lost, so were the youth. I spent the first six months teaching about Jesus' love for the lost.

I built small groups, taking the core students and sharing with them the mission that Jesus had for the lost. But I didn't do any programming for eight months. I had to develop the groundwork slowly, building the foundation for seeking the lost of the Vegas Valley.

My ministry is not Student Impact. Students are different wherever you go, and it would be a mistake to copy Student Impact and expect it to work at your church. I've been doing transition for five years, and the transition is not complete. Your church may move at a different pace. Trust God's timing and take things step by step.

Sticking Point: We hold our programs on Sunday nights. Why is Student Impact on a school night instead of on the weekend?

Students today are busy. Often their weekends are jam-packed with extracurricular activities and family time. Many have part-time jobs.

Because our philosophy of ministry is heavily focused on student relationships and the value of lost people, it makes it easier for our core students to invite their non-Christian friends to Impact when they see them at school on Tuesday. We also were assigned Tuesday nights because our church's believer services are held on Wednesday and Thursday nights and Tuesday turned out to be the night the church facility was most often available.

I have seen effective student ministry take place on all nights of the week. My friend Garland meets with his student ministry on Friday nights, and that has worked well for him. You need to find out which night benefits you and your students. You may even need to experiment with a couple of nights and evaluate which one could work best.

Sticking Point: I also lead a junior high ministry. Do these ideas and values apply to junior highers as well?

Throughout the ministries of Willow Creek, there are common values and ministry strategies we all embrace: lost people matter to God; seekers need a place to investigate the claims of Christ; and believers have a desire to grow in Christ, to name a few. In many ways, the junior high and high school ministries share similar values, but the strategies are very different. In chapter 5 you read about the adolescent development process and the unique needs of teenagers. The needs of a junior high student and a high school student are vastly different and because of that, the approach to ministry should be different.

Our junior high ministry, Sonlight Express, is awesome and has developed its own unique structure in which to minister to junior highers. They have studied the various dimensions of a junior high student in order to know their target and what they need.

Junior high students can be difference-makers on their campus too. Teaching them how to build integrity friendships and share Christ with their friends is important. Just because they are younger than high school students does not exclude them from impacting peoples' lives for Christ. As the father of a junior higher, I have witnessed this in my home. My daughter Tiffany already understands the value placed on caring for lost people, and she regularly reaches out to her non-Christian friends at school. Our van is full each Saturday morning with junior high students Tiffany has invited to Sonlight Express. I'm so glad that my church has a ministry designed just for her to grow in Christ and also invite friends.

Every May we hold a conference focusing on both junior high and high school ministries. If you are interested in observing Sonlight Express or Student Impact in action, you can do so at this conference. Contact the Willow Creek Association at P.O. Box 3188, Barrington, IL 60011 or call (847) 765–0070 for a conference brochure and registration form.

Sticking Point: We're just starting to target to seekers. Is it critical to hold an outreach event every week?

As we discussed in chapter 6, targeting to seekers and believers separately is the most effective way to meet their needs. Seekers need a place to go to investigate Christianity at their own pace. You need to assess the students in your ministry and their specific needs. How can seekers best take the next step in their spiritual journey?

Remember, programming is not the life-change agent; relationships are. Holding an outreach event every week may prove effective, but having it once a month or three times a year could also serve you well. The important thing to determine is what the outreach events should look like in your ministry. You can begin to do this by asking several questions like, What is our budget for the ministry season? How available is our facility? Do we have the personnel to pull off a weekly outreach event? Does my pastor support events targeted to seekers? Are my core students trained yet in evangelism and is there a definite strategy in place for them to use?

Don't commit to a weekly outreach event until your core students, leaders, and support teams understand the vision, mission, and strategy and can rally around such an effort. Get the right people prepared and pray that God will show you the plan to follow. Don't ever do a program just to do a program.

Sticking Point: Student Impact seems to have a budget that never runs out. How is it funded?

For over fifteen years, the youth ministries of Willow Creek have raised their own operational funds. This is by our choice, and the elders have given us their permission to do so. It allows the junior high and high school ministries to feel tremendous ownership and a sense of responsibility.

As I discussed in the book, each spring we organize a fundraiser called Operation STRIVE (Students Turning Responsibility Into Valuable Experience). Many student ministries hold several fund-raisers throughout the year: car washes, candy sales, raffles, et cetera. At Student Impact, we have just one each year. It is an eight-hour workathon in which students and leaders collect hourly pledges from family, friends, and neighbors, and do work in their community. The work is done at park districts, public works departments, nursing homes, fire and police departments, parks, and libraries. Past work projects have included washing fire trucks, planting flowers in parks, painting, cleaning up garbage, clearing brush, and landscaping.

Everyone wins at the end of these work days: the community is cleaner and the labor was free; students have given back to their community and owned the responsibility for their ministry; and the youth ministries have raised the money needed for the next ministry year.

Last year, over eight hundred junior high and high school students and leaders supported Willow Creek's youth ministries through their participation.

PART 3: STRUCTURE WITH PURPOSE

Sticking Point: I've just started to build a core. How long do you think it will take to build?

In my experience, it usually takes about six months to build a core. Many things need to happen in those six months: a vision must be cast; targets need to be set; the ministry mission and strategy should be determined and shared; and lines of commitment must be drawn. All this can start with one student. When that student starts to grow in his or her love for Christ, it will be natural for him or her to want to share Christ with a friend. Teaching our students to be more like Christ and to have compassion for their friends is what building a core is all about.

Take your time and don't feel rushed. Be patient. Watch and see how God works. Over time, you will see students who desire to be a part and are excited about relationships. Compassion for their lost friends will increase, and they will naturally desire to share the treasure of Christ.

Sticking Point: I can't seem to find enough leaders. Do you think students can lead their peers?

We all seem to have a never-ending need for more leaders. As ministries grow or leaders get transferred, our search for additional leaders begins. Chapter 10 was filled with ideas on how to prepare the playing field for leaders and where to recruit leaders.

I would encourage you to keep looking within your ministry or church. As I was building a ministry in California, I too experienced a shortage of leaders. When I looked at the students in my ministry, I decided some of them were mature and capable enough to be leaders. My first campus directors were high school students and a part of my small group. I cared for them, discipled them, and trained them in leadership. Because I poured into them, they then could care for others. These student campus directors proved to be effective leaders and were able to make a difference on their campuses for Christ.

I believe the right students can be tremendous leaders. In Student Impact, qualified students can serve as D-Team (small group) leaders and apprentices. They also serve as grade-level directors and help generate momentum in their grade level on campus. It's extremely positive when students demonstrate ownership in the ministry through various leadership roles.

Sticking Point: Most of the students in my ministry are from a Christian high school. How do you deal with students from Christian high schools?

This can be difficult because many students who attend a Christian high school have a "been there, done that" attitude. They have heard all the Bible stories and many have become bored. Their walk with Christ is comfortable, and often complacency has set in. Many of these students have been raised in Christian homes but have never been challenged to cross lines of commitment.

Still, believers at Christian high schools can be difference-makers on their campus because plenty of opportunities for evangelism exist. Not all students from a Christian high school are believers. Students can share Christ with the non-Christians around them and also model for others on their campus what it means to have an authentic relationship with Christ by challenging others to live on the edge for Christ.

Believers from Christian high schools can also be strong leaders. In California, one of my campus teams was from a local Christian high school. I took a few mature students from that team and positioned them as campus directors on another campus team. They ministered with great effectiveness not only as an example to the students on their campus, but also to students from the campus team they were leading.

Sticking Point: I've got several leaders in place and they're ready to go. How do you train your campus directors?

Training campus directors takes place throughout the year, primarily at BTL (Between the Lines), our weekly leadership meeting, and one-on-one with the assigned division director.

At BTL, campus directors are informed of upcoming key ministry events, series, retreats, and general ministry happenings. It is so important to all stay on the same page and be headed in the same direction. Sharing information also communicates to the leader, "We think you are a valuable part of this ministry; here's what you need to know about."

Vision-casting, problem-solving, sharing strategies, and preparing leaders are all a part of the ongoing training. Equipping a leader to "win" in ministry requires planning and proactive thinking on your part.

Campus directors are trained by their division director each week throughout the ministry year. The male and female campus directors from a campus team meet with their division director to set goals; plan events, core night, and retreats; talk about team issues; and/or celebrate God's activity in the lives of students. Campus directors are given specific training related to the team they are leading and how they can most effectively minister to that team. Whereas BTL communicates more "big picture" ministry issues, training with the division director involves individual campus team strategy.

Sticking Point: I'm trying to figure out how to organize the students in my ministry. Why do you believe in team-oriented ministry?

As a student ministry grows, it becomes virtually impossible for the student pastor to continue to care for each person individually. Relationships begin to lack depth. Utilizing the team concept allows for students' needs to be met on a personal level.

Student Impact uses the model of team ministry by placing students on a team according to the high school they attend. Each campus team is led by a male and female campus director who each oversee up to five D-Team leaders. A division director oversees three or four of these campus teams.

Students enjoy being part of a team. In their social development process, students are looking to belong and crave acceptance from their peers. Being on a team with peers from their high school help give them an identity and way to fit in socially.

PART 4: PROGRAM WITH PURPOSE

Sticking Point: These ideas and strategies all sound great, but I'm just a volunteer in the student ministry at my church. Is any of this applicable to me? Where do I start?

First of all, you are more than "just a volunteer." You are a treasured student minister who desires to help students become more like Christ. The time, energy, and prayer you invest in students is of immense value.

Whether you are a full-time or volunteer youth leader, start with building a core. Find one student and begin to draw lines of commitment. Practice the "be with" principle and invest in that student. Teach him or her about Jesus and what He felt for the lost. Help that student grow in compassion for his or her lost friends. You can pray with your one student and ask, "What friend can we start to pray for? Which friend can you share Christ with?" That student can then begin step one (build an integrity friendship) with his or her non-Christian friend. Over time, that student may trust Christ and then you will have two students and you can repeat the process. When you have a few students, you can begin a small group and teach these students from God's Word. You can model Christ to these students and play a significant role in their lives. Don't ever use the word "just!"

Sticking Point: My ministry budget is practically nonexistent. Are there any inexpensive resources out there?

Start-up ministry can be tough, especially as it relates to finances. A few years ago, I organized a group of like-minded men and women youth leaders who lead purpose-driven ministries around the world and formed Associated Impact Ministries (AIM). The purpose of AIM is to encourage and support one another in ministry. We meet every May during our Student Impact Leadership Conference, and it's a great time to come together for fellowship and prayer. One of the ways we support each another is by sharing resources. Some of the leaders have traded equipment, series ideas and rationales, and ministry strategies. Many of the leaders are in similar financial situations and by pooling their resources together, they can all benefit.

We have some resources available for purchase through Zondervan such as drama scripts, a competition resource book, a camps and retreats planner, a small group curriculum, and sample program videos. If you are interested in learning more about AIM or the resources I mentioned, please call the Willow Creek Association at (847) 765–0070.

Sticking Point: My church does not allow our student ministry to use secular music even though I wish we could. Why does Student Impact use secular music?

It seems that too many churches get stuck on the issue of secular music. I have seen it split church leaders. Again, I would challenge you to be wise in choosing which battles are worth fighting. In my opinion, the issue of secular music is not one of those battles. If we were told that we could not use secular music in our programs, it would not radically alter our programs.

We do use secular music for several reasons. Our Tuesday night programs are designed with the nonchurched high school student in mind. Every element of our program is filtered through the lens of a seeker. We want to begin to break down the walls many seekers have as they step foot into the church. Using secular music helps to build a bridge with the seekers; it communicates that we relate to their world and are current with the music they listen to.

The programming team carefully selects songs by scrutinizing them for lyrical content. If anyone on the team feels a song is questionable, it is discarded. We do not use a song just because it is in Billboard's Top 10. The song must fit into the topic of the evening and serve a specific purpose. On several occasions, we have intentionally chosen a song that conveys an issue from the world's perspective and followed it with strong teaching on God's point of view. We *can* use a secular song for the King.

If your church is set on the issue of secular music, don't get discouraged. In the past few years, the Christian music market has improved greatly, and I have heard many powerful Christian songs to which a seeker can understand and relate. Choose Christian songs carefully and filter them through the ears of a seeker.

Sticking Point: I'm excited to start planning outreach programs, but I'm short on musicians, actors, and vocalists. Where do you find talented people?

We talked about excellence in chapter 13 and how important it is to select gifted, God-honoring people for your program. Offering an outreach with a Christian drama using people who cannot act or using a vocalist who does not communicate well will prove detrimental to the effectiveness of your programming. You need to keep the bar of excellence high and start small if necessary.

Many gifted people desire to use their talents for the Lord. We have several Christian colleges in the area, and some of the music and communications majors from those colleges enjoy the opportunity to serve. One year God provided a gifted actress who had performed in theater all through college. She admitted that when she started off in theater it was not to honor the Lord, but herself. After graduation, God began to turn that mind-set around, and she decided that if she ever got back into theater, she'd do it for God. God led her to Student Impact where she served for several years as our drama director.

NOTES

Chapter 1

1. John Stott, *The Preacher's Portrait* (Grand Rapids: Eerdmans, 1961), 30.

2. Henri Nouwen, *In the Name of Jesus* (New York: The Crossroad Publishing Company, 1989), 50.

3. Henry T. Blackaby and Claude V. King, *Experiencing God* (Nashville: Broadman & Holman, 1994), 1.

4. Ibid., 19.

5. Henri Nouwen, "Moving from Solitude to Community to Ministry," *Leadership,* Spring 1995, 81.

6. Dallas Willard, *The Spirit of the Disciplines* (San Francisco: Harper & Row, 1988), ix.

7. Bill Hybels, *Honest to God* (Grand Rapids: Zondervan, 1990), 27.

8. Nouwen, *In the Name of Jesus,* 24.

Chapter 2

1. George Barna, *The Power of Vision* (Ventura, CA: Regal Books, 1992), 28, 30.

2. Ibid., 30.

3. Hans Finzel, *Top 10 Mistakes Leaders Make* (Wheaton, IL: Victor, 1994), 186.

Chapter 4

1. Josh McDowell, *Right from Wrong* (Dallas: Word, 1994), 6.

2. George Barna, *The Frog in the Kettle* (Ventura, CA: Regal Books, 1990), 205.

Chapter 5

1. William Rowley, *Equipped to Care* (Wheaton, IL: Victor Books, 1990), 48.

2. Ibid., 50.

3. American Psychiatric Association, *Depression,* 1988, 1989.

4. Walt Mueller, *Understanding Today's Youth Culture* (Wheaton, IL: Tyndale, 1994), 296.

5. Ibid., 297.

6. American Psychiatric Association, *Depression,* 1988, 1989.

7. "Suicide's Shadow," *Time,* 22 July 1996, 41.

8. Mueller, *Understanding Today's Youth Culture,* 295.

9. "Suicide's Shadow," *Time*, 22 July 1996, 41.

10. Mueller, *Understanding Today's Youth Culture*, 264.

11. "Out of the Mouths of Babes," *Time*, 21 August 1995, 33.

12. "Teens and Cigarettes: Rebels with a Cough,"*Chicago Tribune,* 13 August 1995, 12.

13. Mueller, *Understanding Today's Youth Culture*, 268.

14. Ibid., 213.

15. Josh McDowell and Bob Hostetler, *Handbook on Counseling Youth* (Dallas: Word, 1996), 293.

16. Ibid., 325.

Chapter 6

1. "American Gangs," *The Economist,* 17 December, 1994, 21.

2. Walt Mueller, *Understanding Today's Youth Culture* (Wheaton, IL: Tyndale, 1994), 222.

Chapter 7

1. George Barna, *The Power of Vision* (Ventura, CA: Regal Books, 1992), 11.

2. Ibid., 38.

3. Peter Drucker, as quoted by Glenn Van Ekeren, *Speaker's Sourcebook II* (Englewood Cliffs, NJ: Prentice Hall, 1994), 254.

4. James Collins and Jerry Porras, *Built to Last* (New York: Harper Business, 1994), 8.

Chapter 10

1. Richard Foster, *Celebration of Discipline* (San Francisco: Harper & Row, 1978), 9.

2. Pat McMillian, *Hiring for Excellence* (Colorado Springs: NavPress, 1992), 245.

3. Warren Bennis and Bert Nanus, *Leaders* (San Francisco: Harper & Row 1985), 93.

4. McMillian, *Hiring for Excellence*, 38.

Chapter 12

1. Lynne and Bill Hybels, *Rediscovering Church* (Grand Rapids: Zondervan, 1995), 35.

Chapter 13

1. Roger von Oech, *A Whack on the Side of the Head: How to Unlock Your Mind for Motivation* as quoted in *Speaker's Sourcebook II* (Englewood Cliffs, NJ: Prentice Hall, 1994), 79.

Chapter 16

1. John Sculley, *Odyssey* (San Francisco: Harper & Row, 1987), 90.

STUDENT IMPACT

Over twenty years ago, God gave a vision to a group of high school students to reach out to their non-Christian friends in a purposeful and creative way and share with them God's love. This vision to reach lost people helped build a vibrant student ministry from which Willow Creek Community Church was formed.

Today, that vision lives on in Student Impact, the high school ministry of Willow Creek, as high school students continue to reach their friends for Christ. Student Impact's mission is to turn irreligious high school students into fully devoted followers of Jesus Christ. With a student core and small group participation of five hundred, over one thousand students have attended the weekly outreach program and lives continue to be changed.

If you'd like to see this dynamic high school ministry up close and in person, plan on attending the annual Student Impact Leadership Conference held each May. You can write or call the Willow Creek Association for more information:

P.O. Box 3188
Barrington, IL 60011–3188
(847) 765-0070

Student Impact offers a two-year internship for men and women interested in hands-on student ministry experience. Call the Student Impact office for more information: (847) 765-5029.

Additional Student Impact resources are available through Zondervan.

WILLOW CREEK

RESOURCES

This resource was created to serve you

It is just one of many ministry tools that are part of the Willow Creek Resources® line, published by the Willow Creek Association together with Zondervan Publishing House. The Willow Creek Association was created in 1992 to serve a rapidly growing number of churches from all across the denominational spectrum that are committed to helping unchurched people become devoted followers of Christ.

The vision of the Willow Creek Association is to help churches better relate God's solutions to the needs of seekers and believers. Here are some of the ways it does that:

- **Church Leadership Conferences**—3-day events, generally held at Willow Creek Community Church in South Barrington, IL, that are being used by God to help church leaders find new and innovative ways to fulfill and expand their ministries.

- **The Leadership Summit**—a once-a-year event designed to increase the leadership effectiveness of pastors, ministry staff, and volunteer church leaders.

- **Willow Creek Resources®**—to provide churches with a trusted channel of ministry resources in areas of leadership, evangelism, spiritual gifts, small groups, drama, contemporary music, and more. For more information, call Willow Creek Resources® at 800/876-7335. Outside the U.S. call 610/532-1249.

- **WCA Monthly Newsletter**—to inform you of the latest trends, events, news, and resources.

- **The Exchange**—to assist churches in recruiting key staff for ministry positions.

- **The Church Associates Directory**—to keep you in touch with over 1000 other WCA member churches.

For conference and membership information please write or call:

Willow Creek Association
P.O. Box 3188
Barrington, IL 60011-3188
(847) 765-0070

ANOTHER GREAT RESOURCE FOR STUDENT MINISTRY FROM STUDENT IMPACT

Small Group Resources

*Bo Boshers
and the Student Impact Team*

Small groups create tremendous opportunities for growth, and *Small Group Resources* will help your youth ministry do that. Each of the books in the Student Impact Small Group Resources series provide a complete short-course curriculum for a quarter's worth of small group meetings.

Volume 1: *Walking with Christ: Twelve Lessons That Will Change Your Life*
Softcover: 0-310-20124-1
Volume 2: *Compassion for Lost People: Twelve Lessons That Will Change Your Friends' Lives*
Softcover: 0-310-20126-8
Volume 3: *Learning to Serve: Twelve Lessons That Will Build the Church*
Softcover: 0-310-20127-6
Volume 4: *A Lifelong Calling: Twelve Lessons That Will Impact the World*
Softcover: 0-310-20128-4

Look for Student Impact Small Group Resources
at your local Christian bookstore.

ZondervanPublishingHouse
Grand Rapids, Michigan 49530
http://www.zondervan.com

ANOTHER GREAT RESOURCE FOR STUDENT MINISTRY FROM STUDENT IMPACT

COMING SEPTEMBER 1997!

Programming with Purpose
Developing a Process for Programming
Troy Murphy with Kim Anderson

Drawn from the proven programming principles used by Student Impact, *Programming with Purpose* helps the youth worker develop more effective programs by following ten basic steps, including making a plan, realizing a purpose, identifying the target, developing the message, and so on. These principles work equally well whether the target is believers or seekers, and can be used in Sunday school programs, retreats, or other events.

Softcover: 0-310-20129-2

Look for *Programming with Purpose*
at your local Christian bookstore.

ZondervanPublishingHouse
Grand Rapids, Michigan 49530
http://www.zondervan.com

ANOTHER GREAT RESOURCE FOR STUDENT MINISTRY FROM STUDENT IMPACT

Impact Sports
Creative Competitions for Team Building
Bo Boshers and Troy Murphy

Impact Sports are fun, competitive, team-building activities with a clear-cut ministry purpose. This book contains nineteen exciting games and activities from Student Impact. There are diagrams and detailed instructions for each game, as well as a chapter with tips and hints to help youth leaders get maximum results. Plus—an eye-opening look at how and why sports play such a key role in the effectiveness of the Student Impact Ministry… and can do the same for your youth ministry.

Softcover: 0-310-20130-6

Look for *Impact Sports*
at your local Christian bookstore.

ZondervanPublishingHouse
Grand Rapids, Michigan 49530
http://www.zondervan.com

ANOTHER GREAT RESOURCE FOR STUDENT MINISTRY FROM STUDENT IMPACT

COMING SEPTEMBER 1997!

Life-Changing Camps and Retreats

Everything You Need to Lead Two Weekend Retreats, a Four-day Camp, and a Week-long Camp

The Student Impact Team

This helpful resource provides youth workers with four complete programs for camps and retreats—one week-long summer camp, one four-day weekend retreat, and two weekend retreats. Each program includes a purpose statement and suggestions on applying the material to that purpose as well as complete programming ideas, games, drama, creative learning strategies, message outlines, and more.

Softcover: 0-310-20123-3

Look for *Life-Changing Camps and Retreats*
at your local Christian bookstore.

ZondervanPublishingHouse
Grand Rapids, Michigan 49530
http://www.zondervan.com

We want to hear from you. Please send your comments about this book to us in care of the address below. Thank you.

ZondervanPublishingHouse
Grand Rapids, Michigan 49530
http://www.zondervan.com

92595

LINCOLN CHRISTIAN COLLEGE AND SEMINARY

259.23
B743
c. 1

92595

3 4711 00093 0869